THEY
ALSO
SERVED

Other Books By Bill Gilbert

This City, This Man

All These Mornings with Washington Post columnist Shirley Povich

Keep Off My Turf with All-Pro Linebacker Mike Curtis

They Call Me "The Big E" with basketball Hall of Famer Elvin Hayes

Public Relations in Local Government with contributing coauthors

From Orphans to Champions with Coach Morgan Wootten

High School Basketball: How to Be a Winner in Every Way with Coach Joe Gallagher

The Duke of Flatbush with baseball Hall of Famer Duke Snider

Now Pitching: Bob Feller with baseball Hall of Famer Bob Feller

Real Grass, Real Heroes with baseball Hall of Famer Dom DiMaggio

The Truth of the Matter with Bert Lance

5 O'Clock Lightning with baseball star Tommy Henrich

THEY ALSO SERVED

Baseball and the Home Front, 1941–1945

BILL GILBERT

CROWN PUBLISHERS, INC.
NEW YORK

TO LILLIAN AND DAVE
AND TO SHIRLEY POVICH

Grateful acknowledgment is made to the following for permission to reprint
previously published material: Warner/Chappell Music, Inc. and Polygram/
Island Music Publishing Group for an excerpt from "Johnny Zero" written by
Mack David and Vee Lawnhurst. Copyright © 1943 by Chappell & Co. & Alta
Music Corp. Copyright © 1943 Polygram International Publishing, Inc. All
rights administered by Chappell & Co. and Polygram/Island Music Publishing
Group. All rights reserved. CPP Belwin, Inc. for an excerpt from "Comin' In On
A Wing And A Prayer" by Jimmy McHugh and Harold Adamson. Copyright ©
1943 Robbins Music Corporation. Renewed 1971 Robbins Music Corporation
and Jimmy McHugh Music Inc. Rights for Robbins Music Corporation assigned
to EMI Catalog Partnership and controlled and administered by EMI Robbins
Catalog Inc. International copyright secured. Made in USA. All rights reserved.
Herman Helms and the Columbia, S.C. State for Roberto Ortiz story and
"Yellow Dog." Richard Goldstein for excerpts from SPARTAN SEASONS:
HOW BASEBALL SURVIVED THE SECOND WORLD WAR. Copyright ©
1980 by Richard Goldstein. The New York Times for excerpts from HANK
GREENBERG: THE STORY OF MY LIFE edited by Ira Berkow, 1989. Copy-
right © 1989 by The New York Times Company; and excerpts of quotes by
Arthur Daley from THE NEW YORK TIMES BOOK OF BASEBALL. ABC
News for excerpts from episode entitled "Together and Apart, 1943" broadcast
December 4, 1986. Courtesy ABC News OUR WORLD. William Mead for
excerpts from EVEN THE BROWNS. Copyright © 1978 by William Mead.
Published by Contemporary Book. Reprinted in 1985 by Farragut Publishing
Company, Washington, D.C. SNS for excerpts from ESPN's Major League
Baseball's Magazine's episode entitled "Baseball Goes to War." Courtesy Major
League Baseball Productions.

Copyright © 1992 by Bill Gilbert
Published by Crown Publishers, Inc.,
201 East 50th Street, New York, New York 10022.
Member of the Crown Publishing Group.
CROWN is a trademark of Crown Publishers, Inc.
Manufactured in the United States of America
Library of Congress Cataloging-in-Publication Data
Gilbert, Bill, 1931–
    They also served : baseball and the home front, 1941–1945 / Bill
Gilbert.
    1. Baseball—United States—History. I. Title.
GV863.A1G55 1992
796.357'0973—dc20   91-35813
                                                            CIP

ISBN 0-517-58522-7
Book Design by Shari deMiskey
10 9 8 7 6 5 4 3 2 1
FIRST EDITION

CONTENTS

v

Part Three: 1943

Part Four: 1944

Part Five: 1945

THANK-YOUS

NO BOOK ABOUT THE PEOPLE AND THE TIMES FROM HALF A century ago is possible without the assistance of many persons in different capacities. I am pleased to express my deep thanks to the following men and women.

The baseball players themselves are at the top of my list. All were gracious and generous in talking with me and providing insight, information, humor, and drama for the telling of this story. For this and the pleasure of it all, I thank:

Lou Boudreau, Phil Cavarretta, Ellis Clary, Tony Cuccinello, Dom DiMaggio, Bob Feller, Rick Ferrell, Pete Gray, Tommy Henrich, Tommy Holmes, Whitey Kurowski, Buddy Lewis, Danny Litwhiler, Walter Masterson, Hal Newhouser, Mickey Owen, Bert Shepard, Cecil Travis, Johnny Vander Meer, Charlie Wagner, and Ted Williams.

The staff of the National Baseball Library at the Baseball Hall of Fame was extremely helpful, as always—Bill Deane, the senior research associate; his intern, Sean Rooney; and

Pat Kelly, the library's photo collection manager. Fern Solomon at the Montgomery County (Maryland) Public Library and the staff at the National Archives in Washington also provided valuable assistance.

Special thanks are also due Shirley Povich, the baseball writer and columnist of the *Washington Post,* whose willingness to give me his autograph innocently led me into the world of journalism after World War II.

Other members of the media also shared wartime experiences or information with me—Billy Rowe, then a columnist for the *Pittsburgh Courier,* Willie Weinbaum and Mike Kostel of the Phoenix Communications Group, producers of "Major League Baseball Magazine." Another TV program, ABC's "Our World," was a helpful source for which I thank Walter Porges, vice president of news practices for ABC News, and hosts Linda Ellerbee and Ray Gandolf and their staff. Two fellow authors, who wrote the most informative and entertaining books on baseball during this period—Bill Meade, author of *Even the Browns* (since reprinted in a paperback edition as *Baseball Goes to War*), and Richard Goldstein, who wrote *Spartan Seasons,* deserve special mention.

Lillian Gilbert and Dave Gilbert performed their usual excellent services in aiding with research and editing. Bob Gregoire thoughtfully lent me his priceless wartime magazines and other publications from his extensive collection of baseball information and memorabilia items. Ed Liberatore—again—was a valuable communications link with many of the players listed above and a source of rich stories of his own from these years.

Joyce Engelson, my editor at Crown Publishers, proved she is as knowledgeable about baseball as she is about editing, so this book is better on both counts. An extra expression of gratitude is always due to the man who finds a publisher for me first and gets mentioned last, my agent and a vice president of the Scott Meredith Literary Agency, Russell Galen.

MAJOR LEAGUE BASEBALL AT THE START OF WORLD WAR II

American League

BOSTON RED SOX
Owner: Tom Yawkey
Manager: Joe Cronin
Home: Fenway Park

NEW YORK YANKEES
Owner: Estate of Colonel
Jacob Ruppert
Manager: Joe McCarthy
Home: Yankee Stadium

CHICAGO WHITE SOX
Owner: Grace Comiskey
Manager: Jimmy Dykes
Home: Comiskey Park

PHILADELPHIA ATHLETICS
Owner and Manager:
Connie Mack
Home: Shibe Park

CLEVELAND INDIANS
Owner: Alva Bradley
Manager: Lou Boudreau
Home: League Park

ST LOUIS BROWNS
Owner: Don Barnes
Manager: Luke Sewell
Home: Sportsman's Park

DETROIT TIGERS
Owner: Walter "Spike" Briggs
Manager: Del Baker
Home: Briggs Stadium

WASHINGTON SENATORS
Owner: Clark Griffith
Manager: Bucky Harris
Home: Griffith Stadium

National League

BOSTON BRAVES
Owner: Bob Quinn
Manager: Casey Stengel
Home: Braves Field

BROOKLYN DODGERS
Owner: Estate of Charles Ebbets
Manager: Leo Durocher
Home: Ebbets Field

CHICAGO CUBS
Owner: Phil Wrigley
Manager: Jimmie Wilson
Home: Wrigley Field

CINCINNATI REDS
Owner: Powell Crosley, Jr.
Manager: Bill McKechnie
Home: Crosley Field

NEW YORK GIANTS
Owner: Horace Stoneham
Manager: Mel Ott
Home: Polo Grounds

PHILADELPHIA PHILLIES
Owner: Gerald Nugent
Manager: Hans Lobert
Home: Shibe Park

PITTSBURGH PIRATES
Owner: Mrs. Barney Dreyfuss
Manager: Frankie Frisch
Home: Forbes Field

ST. LOUIS CARDINALS
Owner: Sam Breadon
Manager: Billy Southworth
Home: Sportsman's Park

BASEBALL'S CHAMPIONS DURING
WORLD WAR II

Pennant Winners

American League	Year	National League
New York Yankees	1942	St. Louis Cardinals
New York Yankees	1943	St. Louis Cardinals
St. Louis Browns	1944	St. Louis Cardinals
Detroit Tigers	1945	Chicago Cubs

World Series Winners

1942 St. Louis Cardinals
1943 New York Yankees
1944 St. Louis Cardinals
1945 Detroit Tigers

Batting

American League	Year	National League
Ted Williams, .356 Boston Red Sox	1942	Ernie Lombardi, .330 Boston Braves
Luke Appling, .328 Chicago White Sox	1943	Stan Musial, .357 St. Louis Cardinals
Lou Boudreau, .327 Cleveland Indians	1944	Dixie Walker, .357 Brooklyn Dodgers
George Stirnweiss, .309 New York Yankees	1945	Phil Cavarretta, .355 Chicago Cubs

Pitching (most wins)

American League	Year	National League
Tex Hughson, 22 Boston Red Sox	1942	Mort Cooper, 22 St. Louis Cardinals
Spud Chandler and Dizzy Trout, 20 New York Yankees	1943	Mort Cooper, Elmer Riddle, and Rip Sewell, 21 Cincinnati Reds
Hal Newhouser, 29 Detroit Tigers	1944	Bucky Walters, 23 Cincinnati Reds
Hal Newhouser, 25 Detroit Tigers	1945	Red Barrett, 23 Boston Braves/St. Louis Cardinals

Most Valuable Players

American League	Year	National League
Joe Gordon New York Yankees	1942	Mort Cooper St. Louis Cardinals
Spud Chandler New York Yankees	1943	Stan Musial St. Louis Cardinals
Hal Newhouser Detroit Tigers	1944	Marty Marion St. Louis Cardinals
Hal Newhouser Detroit Tigers	1945	Phil Cavarretta Chicago Cubs

Part One

1941

A BATBOY'S MEMORIES

WAS IT REALLY FIFTY YEARS AGO?

. . . Since Joe DiMaggio's fifty-six-game hitting streak produced almost as many headlines as the approach of World War II?

. . . Since Ted Williams became the last player to reach the magic level of a .400 batting average, while the Japanese prepared to attack Pearl Harbor?

Has it been half a century since Bob Feller, the winningest pitcher in baseball for the previous three years—and just turned twenty-three—put aside his draft deferment as the sole support of his dying father, his mother, and kid sister to join the Navy two days after Pearl Harbor?

. . . And since Hank Greenberg, discharged from the Army on December 5, reentered four days later?

Has it been half a century since five hundred other major-league baseball players and another four thousand minor leaguers marched off, sailed off, and flew off on journeys to faraway places with strange-sounding names like Guadalcanal and Iwo Jima, Salerno and Bastogne? Since they were

3

followed—but not really replaced—by players who were classified "4-F" in the military draft, deferred because of physical problems, including a one-armed outfielder and a one-legged war hero, plus players in their midteens and men in their late forties?

As America marks the fiftieth anniversary of that era, which is more and more being called "America's last popular war," we reopen a unique chapter in the 150-year bond between baseball and us. It is one that no future generation will be able to experience because our wars are different now, and so are the public's opinions about them.

Those years and baseball's integral role in them form a story worth remembering if you were a slightly bewildered ten-year-old at the time of Pearl Harbor, as I was. If you weren't around then, as grown-up or child, the story has even more value in its retelling because it is unique.

The adults were alternately scared and confident, discouraged and optimistic, weary and exhilarated. We kids felt the same full range of emotions in our confused, uncertain state, compounded by the tenderness of our years.

But all of us, kids and grown-ups, had one steadying element that helped to hold our lives together, giving us a badly needed sense of continuity and stability, something that even a world war couldn't take from us—baseball.

No less than the president of the United States, Franklin Roosevelt himself, said baseball was too important to us to be stopped because of the war. In fact, he said more than that. He said baseball could even help us *win* the war, because it would be a strong force in improving the morale of our men and women in uniform. FDR said baseball would give all Americans, including those of us on "the home front," something to cheer about, an interest that would take our minds off the war. He didn't say it about any other sport.

In the eventful and formative years that belong to the very young, fate gave me a double view of that parade of events that few teens or preteens were allowed to experience. I was growing up in the city where our nation's survival was being decided—Washington, D.C. The war news came from my hometown as much as from the battlefields overseas.

And in the biggest thrill any kid can feel in either war or

4

peace, I became a major-league batboy in 1945, the last year of the war, proving that by then we suffered from more than just a manpower shortage—we had a *boypower* shortage, too.

It was a rare time, but it was a hard time, too—men and women by the millions going off to war, twelve million before it was all over, and the rationing of such essential items as meat and sugar and gas (you were allowed only three gallons a week for your car). German submarines were sinking American ships so close to our East Coast that residents of beach towns from New England to Florida could see our ships go down, and Japanese "balloon bombs" landed on the West Coast.

Hope and Crosby clowned and sang with Dorothy Lamour in their first "road" picture, and Kate Smith sang "God Bless America." A hollow-cheeked kid from New Jersey named Frank Sinatra attracted a mob scene of "bobby-soxers" when he appeared at the Paramount Theater in New York, and the new comedy team of Abbott and Costello performed a baseball routine that still has Americans asking "Who's on first?"

Roosevelt and Thomas Dewey opposed each other in a wartime presidential election, and John L. Lewis pulled his coal miners off the job despite organized labor's no-strike pledge at the start of the war. Dreaded polio epidemics spread their fear and tragedy every summer. The newspapers published a casualty list every day, which you checked to see if you knew any of the dead, wounded, or missing in action. We experienced frequent air-raid drills and blackouts, and people stood on wooden observation towers, holding binoculars to their eyes trying to spot approaching enemy bombers—maybe wondering how much good it would do to spot them if the planes were already in binocular range.

In baseball, too, life was different. One of the star pitchers, who was so good he remained a star in the postwar competition, Hal Newhouser, was declared 4-F because of a heart condition, even though he tried to enlist and become a pilot. That didn't stop one fan from sending him a one-word letter—"Bastard"—on yellow paper.

The St. Louis Browns, who had never won a pennant before, won the American League flag in 1944 mainly because they escaped damage from the military draft that year better than most other teams. It was the only pennant they ever won. The next year, the Chicago Cubs won the pennant in the National League. They haven't won one since.

Major-league teams trained in the north because of wartime restrictions on unnecessary travel. Instead of the warm breezes and swaying palms of Florida and Arizona, they were training in snow and cold near Boston, Chicago, New York, and other northern cities.

Men and women in military uniform got into games free. Most of baseball's owners and players voluntarily took 10 percent of their salaries in war bonds to do their part to help pay for the war effort. Fans actually threw foul balls back onto the field so they could be shipped to military bases for "the boys" to enjoy.

The war produced some of the best of the postwar crop of big-league players—Newhouser, Stan Musial, Johnny Pesky, George Kell, Allie Reynolds, Dave "Boo" Ferriss, Eddie Lopat, "Snuffy" Stirnweiss, and Hank Sauer. Two teenagers who got a chance to play in the big leagues because of the war, Ed Yost and Joe Nuxhall, made good after the war too and became stars.

But the men who really kept the sport alive for our national morale—and for "our fighting men overseas"—were the 4-Fs, and kids like Yost and Nuxhall, plus the one-armed outfielder, Pete Gray, and Ellis Clary, "Bingo" Binks, Nap Reyes, Danny Gardella, and the draft-exempt Cubans on the Washington Senators—Gil Torres, Alejandro Carrasquel, Bobby Estalella, and Roberto Ortiz.

It was a time when one of history's greatest home-run hitters, Jimmie Foxx, became a pitcher. Another pitcher, Hod Lisenbee, born during the Spanish-American War, returned after nine years of retirement and pitched in thirty-one games for the Cincinnati Reds. Pepper Martin left four years of retirement to play in forty games for his old team, the St. Louis Cardinals, at the age of forty, hit .279, and helped the Cards win their third straight National League pennant.

Maybe the kids and the 4-Fs weren't the greatest players baseball fans ever paid to see, and maybe the old-timers were imitations of their former greatness, but for four seasons beginning in 1942, they were our favorites. They were the ones whose exploits we cheered, whose shortcomings we

6

overlooked, and whose contributions to the war effort qualified them to feel that, in a manner considered important even by the president, they also served.

Whatever they lacked in talent, the wartime teams provided four years of entertainment that other seasons have not always matched: one of the biggest upsets in World Series history in 1942, the first night All-Star Game in 1943, pennant races in the American League decided on the last day of the 1944 season and again in '45, Newhouser's fifty-four wins in two seasons and his back-to-back Most Valuable Player awards, the only pitcher to win the prize two years in a row. Wartime baseball wasn't all incompetence and pratfalls, although we had our share of that, too.

The war produced heroes and victims in baseball—like Bert Shepard of the Washington Senators, whose experiences as a fighter pilot, amputee, prisoner of war, and a big-league baseball player pitching on an artificial leg exemplify those years and this book. Two other baseball players, no better known than Shepard, were also heroes in World War II. They played a total of six games in the major leagues, but were heroes nevertheless because they never came back. They were the two major-league players who gave their last full measure of devotion, an outfielder for the Senators in five games before the war, named Elmer Gedeon, who died on a battlefield in France in 1944 five days after his twenty-seventh birthday, and Harry O'Neill, a catcher for one game with the Philadelphia A's before the war, who never came to bat and was killed on the sands of Iwo Jima in 1945.

And there's the story of Moe Berg, the veteran catcher and veteran spy, too, who played a critical cloak-and-dagger role for our intelligence agency before the war in Japan and during the war in Europe.

One of the war's most tragic victims wasn't killed or wounded. He was another Senator, Cecil Travis, a perennial all-star shortstop who was trapped with thousands of other American troops in Europe's Battle of the Bulge at Christmastime, 1944. Baseball people from that era unanimously agree that Bastogne ended his baseball career prematurely, although Travis modestly disagrees.

The wartime players weren't the only ones who were serving our nation through baseball. In New York, a one-of-a-kind campaign to sell war bonds raised well over one hundred million dollars through an "auction" of players from the city's three big-league teams. In Washington, columnist Shirley Povich of the *Post* turned promoter for a night and staged an exhibition game between the Senators and a team of ex-major-league players in the Navy, and raised enough money in war bonds to build a warship.

The Baseball Writers' Association of America cooperated with the big-league teams in a "Keep 'Em Slugging" campaign that raised enough funds to pay for 18,000 baseballs and 4,500 bats for our military bases in the early days of the war. Clark Griffith, Washington's owner, was instrumental in the effort, saying the equipment would be "the best we can get—none of that cheap stuff for the soldiers and sailors. Only the best for them."

Older people in baseball knew Mr. Griffith wasn't kidding. Exactly twenty-five years earlier, in 1917, he had done the same thing for the soldiers and sailors of World War I.

Washington, which grew into its present role as the capital of the free world during and after World War II, was also the site for many of the baseball events during these years and the operating base for many of the personalities in this story. That, plus my own presence here and my job as a spring-training batboy—one barely able to lift a major-league bat much less swing one—accounts for the many stories about Washington, its scenes and its people during the war.

Through it all, baseball changed. At the same time, its grip on us grew even stronger and more enduring, giving the sport the special place in our lives that enabled it to survive and prosper later, even through the tumult of recent years with seven-figure salaries, free agents, strikes, lockouts, and the fall from grace of the man with the most base hits in history.

This is not just a baseball story—although it is that—but a different view, in a unique context, of World War II as we lived it on the home front. That's why the story of those four years is worth telling now to those too young to have lived through them and retelling to those of us who did.

8

We're Fighting for a Lot of Things in This War, and Baseball Is One of Them.

A wounded American soldier, 1944

1

A TEN- YEAR-OLD'S WORLD

IN 1941, THE FEAR OF A SECOND WORLD WAR SEEMED TO BE the only thing most adults talked to each other about, except for Joe DiMaggio's fifty-six-game hitting streak and the .406 batting average of Ted Williams. When you're just a skinny ten-year-old kid and your parents and their friends are talking about a war coming, sometimes it worries you. Other times, you pay more attention to the really important things in life, like baseball.

That's what millions of Americans did, and not just ten-year-olds, and baseball responded magnificently by providing us with its most historic season. In addition to Joe's streak and Ted's average, there was Ted's dramatic home run with two outs in the bottom of the ninth inning in Detroit to win the All-Star Game for the American League, plus Tommy Henrich's strikeout that wasn't a strikeout in the World Series when he and Brooklyn's catcher, Mickey Owen, both missed a third-strike curve ball from Hugh Casey. Tommy reached first base, the Yankees staged a two-out, ninth-inning rally and won the game that day and the Series the next.

11

It was a season to remember at a time when we were trying to forget, forget the coming war and enjoy baseball every chance we got. And what a year to enjoy, except for men like Hugh Mulcahy.

Mulcahy was a big right-handed pitcher for the Philadelphia Phillies, six feet two inches and 190 pounds. His misfortune was to be pitching for one of the worst teams in baseball, a team that finished no higher than next-to-last, and usually last, in his six prewar seasons with them beginning in 1935.

With the Phillies losing more than one hundred games a year, Hugh led the National League in losses twice—twenty defeats in 1938 and twenty-two in 1940. Even though he achieved the impossible by winning ten games with the Phillies in '38 and thirteen in 1940, he acquired a nickname that no other player has ever wanted—"Losing Pitcher" Mulcahy.

Not long after President Roosevelt went on the radio with one of his "fireside chats" and told us, "Never before has our American civilization been in such danger as now," Mulcahy became the first major-league baseball player to be drafted. He was inducted into the Army on March 8, 1941, as one of the new members of the 101st Artillery at Camp Edwards on Cape Cod. He was twenty-seven years old, a prime age for any professional athlete.

On reporting to camp, he told reporters, "It might be a little tougher and might take a little longer for me to get into shape when I report for spring training next season, but I don't think this year of Army life will hamper my pitching any."

He even went one better, adding, "Personally I think this conscription bill is a great thing for the young men of today." He said his only regret was that he had not been able to finish making the payments on the new home he had bought for his parents in the Boston suburb of Newton.

For the first time, a caption writer composed a line that was destined to became a wartime cliché. Next to a picture of Mulcahy, the New York *Daily News* caption hailed him:

PITCHING FOR UNCLE SAM!

The expectation, or at least the hope, was that our young men would be gone for a year. That's what the law said at the time. A songwriter made the most of it with a 1939–1940 hit, "Good-bye, Dear—I'll Be Back in a Year."

As events unfolded, the length of sevice was made indefinite—the duration of the war and six months, abbreviated in conversation to "the duration and six." Mulcahy missed spring training in 1942, also 1943, '44, and '45. He returned near the end of the '45 season, and was able to pitch in only twenty-three more games before retiring in 1947.

Phil Rizzuto's hopes of making the grade with his hometown team as a rookie with the New York Yankees received a severe jolt eleven days after Mulcahy was inducted. At the Yankees' spring-training camp in St. Petersburg, Florida, Rizzuto was informed that he had been reclassified 1-A in the draft—fit for military service.

Dr. Frederick Kumm of the St. Petersburg draft board, after a preliminary exam revealed Rizzuto might have diabetes, said a second urinalysis showed the first reading was "due to excitement," according to one newspaper account. "The recheck this morning," the article said, "proved that Phil last night had become quite nervous over the examination."

There was reason for concern at the Rizzuto family home back at 7801 64th Street in Brooklyn's Glendale section. Phil was the primary support of his parents, a kid brother, and himself. Without Phil's salary as a rookie major leaguer, the family would have to get by on his father's salary as a night watchman—twenty dollars a week.

Near the end of spring training the rookie was reclassified again, this time 3-A as the main support of his family. He entered the Navy after the 1942 season and served for three years.

The Yankees weren't overly concerned, even though they said they didn't want to lose a rookie of Rizzuto's potential. President Ed Barrow told reporters, "It would be tough to lose Rizzuto, who is one of the greatest young shortstops I have seen in fifty years. However, we have a big job to do in this country and ball players cannot expect favors. . . . Personally, I refuse to get excited about ball players and the draft."

As spring training neared its end, our Washington Senators, still called the Nats by many as short for Nationals, their other nickname, beat the Detroit Tigers for the seventh straight time in a rainy spring-training game in Greenville, South Carolina.

Five days later, FDR opened the 1941 major-league season, throwing out the traditional first ball at Washington's Griffith Stadium for the eighth time as president. He even threw it out once when he wasn't president. That was back in 1917 when he was assistant secretary of the Navy and President Woodrow Wilson was preoccupied with our entry into World War I.

In '41 it was our right-handed knuckleball ace, Dutch Leonard, versus the Yankees and one of their left-handers, Marius Russo. While FDR greeted well-wishers in the presidential box next to the Washington dugout on the first-base side, Vice President Henry Wallace and the Nats' owner, Clark Griffith, led the traditional march to the flagpole in center field.

The temperature was eighty-eight degrees, and most of the fans were in shirtsleeves. The atmosphere was upbeat due to the warm April sunshine and the eagerness of the 32,000 fans to forget the war in Europe and the growing threat of America's involvement. Instead they were interested in enjoying baseball in the sunshine and the pleasing aroma of fresh bread coming down from the Bond Bakery just above the ballpark on Georgia Avenue. The headline in the *Washington Post* the next morning captured the mood:

WAR CLOUDS ARE FORGOTTEN
AS THRONG HAILS PRESIDENT

In keeping with another sacred baseball tradition, there were no other games played that day. Major-league baseball showcased itself by allowing the Nats, or the Senators, to start every season at home, with no other games in either league except those seasons when the Cincinnati Reds, as the sport's oldest professional team, might open the National League season the same day. But Washington always had the American League opener for itself, and often the entire baseball stage.

With the president always there—beginning with William Howard Taft in 1910, until the Senators were hustled out of town to Texas by Bob Short after the 1971 season the year before he sold them—baseball reaped a publicity bonanza each April, thanks to its association with the Oval Office.

It's something no other sport has accomplished even once for an opening day. No president ever threw out the first football of the season or the first basketball or the first hockey puck. In baseball, with a team in Washington, it happened every spring.

In 1941, one of Washington's rookie pitchers, Arnold (Red) Anderson, caught FDR's opening toss. That was an improvement over the year before, when Roosevelt's presidential pitch hit a *Washington Post* camera and smashed it. As the former manager of his prep school baseball team at Groton, FDR seemed to have lost a little of his control.

The outcome of the game was also traditional—3–0, Yankees. Leonard held the Yankees to only six hits, but the Nats got only three off Russo. Joe DiMaggio began his historic 1941 performance with a triple over Doc Cramer's head in center field to drive in the first run of the season.

Anne Hagner reported in the *Post* the next morning that a woman going to the opening game found herself in a dilemma. "To look feminine or be comfortable," she wrote, "is the choice she must make—and you'd be amazed at the number of them who prefer the former."

She said knowledgeable women wear "sports frocks and low heels." She said others dress in a "floppy hat, a sheer print, and expensive nylon hose."

By the time the next opening day arrived, President Roosevelt would be unavailable—and so would nylons.

2

FREIGHT TRAIN TO
A BETTER LIFE

IN THE TINY FARMING COMMUNITY OF CLINTON, INDIANA—
population 2,500—the grim future facing the world early in
1941 wasn't enough to dim the enthusiasm of a strapping
twenty-one-year-old tenant farmer's son named Bert Shepard.

He was a minor-league baseball player, and the biggest
problem facing him wasn't the war—it was how to improve
his control as a left-handed pitcher so he could make it to the
big leagues. Young Bert had no way of knowing that events
to come in 1941 would start a series of developments that
would change his life forever and would, incidentally, bring
us together four years later in a way that no Hollywood
scriptwriter could have imagined.

For young Bert, with his roots in America's heartland, life
was definitely getting better and his enthusiastic, positive
nature was easier to maintain. The hard times of the Great
Depression, which wasn't great at all to anyone who lived
through it, were felt as keenly on Clinton's Main Street as on
New York's Wall Street, but those bad old days of the 1930s
were receding for Lura and John Shepard and their six sons.

16

And Bert, their second son, was making good money as a baseball player—sixty dollars a month.

The family had moved from Dana Bert's birthplace, also the hometown of a man whose name would become a household word in the war that was on the horizon—Ernie Pyle. He became America's best-known and -loved war correspondent—yes, a correspondent who was *loved* by the public—and he was from right there in Dana, seventy miles due west of Indianapolis on Highway 36, only ten miles from the Indiana-Illinois line. The whole town wasn't any bigger than some of the crowds Bert pitched in front of—750 people.

Bert's dad had a "delivery business"—a horse and a wagon—before the Depression took it away from him. Then he became a farmhand at a salary of fifty dollars a month plus a house for Lura and their boys. It was a transient existence, and as a youngster Bert lived in thirteen different communities. And yes, they really did walk four miles one way in all kinds of weather to a one-room schoolhouse for the first eight grades.

In the first full year of the Depression, 1930, Bert was sent to live with his grandmother in her small home across the street from the train depot. She was one of the fortunate town folks who owned a radio, and through that magic box Bert learned about baseball games and their stars, especially Pepper Martin and the St. Louis Cardinals.

In the mid-1930s, Bert, now in his early teens, began hanging around the high school baseball team, watching its practices, shagging fly balls, chasing foul ones, and doing anything and everything to stay close to the sport that was becoming his lifelong love. He didn't even mind that he had to cover those four miles home after practice by running all the way because it was dark by then.

As his high school years unfolded, folks began to see that the second oldest boy in the Shepard family was becoming a good baseball player, starring in sandlot games around their new hometown of Clinton.

Life was getting easier for him in other ways. He taught himself how to cut hair and became known as "the traveling barber," giving haircuts in people's homes for ten cents. One family was an especially lucrative account—a father and six

17

kids. With that seventy cents, the young man who was blossoming into a sure-enough ball player could treat himself to a White Castle hamburger for a nickel, a chocolate malt for another nickel, and a trip to the movies for a dime, and still have some money left to give to his mother.

Things were improving for his father, too. He was able to save up and buy a Model T Ford—for five dollars. He drove it for two years and then made a hefty profit by selling it for seven dollars.

Baseball's lure proved too strong for Bert by the end of his junior year in high school in 1937. He'd heard that California was the place to go if you wanted to be a baseball player. The weather was good all year long, so there were more teams, more games, and more chances to become good enough to make it as a professional ball player.

With a pal, Bert hopped a freight train out of Clinton bound for Terre Haute, then found another that went all the way to St. Louis. As a paternal send-off, Bert's father provided the strongest financial support he could by giving his son all the money he had in the world—fifty cents.

Bert's odyssey included ten days in jail in Amarillo, Texas, after railroad detectives spotted him, prompting him to hitchhike the rest of the trip. He made it to California by working along the way as a busboy in restaurants to get his meals and a few cents to finance the next leg of his journey.

In California, a job at a tire retread plant at ten dollars a week for a six-day week supported him while he played baseball on every playground and in every league he could find. With that steady salary, he could even afford a copy of *Life* magazine when it published a spread of pictures showing the pitching form of Johnny Vander Meer of Cincinnati in 1938, when he became the only man ever to pitch two consecutive no-hit games. From those pictures and with the mirror in his rooming house, Bert was able to teach himself the crude elements of a pitcher's windup.

With his newly gained prosperity and realizing the importance of a good education—it was becoming harder to get ahead in life without a high school diploma—Bert bought a bus ticket home, worked as a barber in a camp of the Civilian Conservation Corps, and made thirty dollars a month. When

payday came at the end of each month, Bert hitchhiked the fifteen miles home and emptied his pockets to Mom. She always gave him a little something back so he could make it through the next month.

As the New York Yankees were dominating the baseball world with four straight World Series championships, Bert was building a baseball world of his own. A scout for the Chicago White Sox, Doug Minor, signed him to a contract to play for the Chicago farm team in Longview, Texas, for sixty dollars a month, plus a train ticket to Longview.

It was a memorable time. Bert got to ride on a train as a paid-up passenger for the first time. He even got to enjoy a fried chicken dinner in the dining car, although the lemonade after the meal tasted weak and he couldn't understand why the waiter had brought the lemon and water in a bowl instead of a glass, but he drank it anyway.

The fun of baseball and the high excitement of such magical discoveries as eating on a train continued even though Bert, like many left-handed pitchers, struggled to improve his control. He was walking too many hitters, a sure way to keep yourself out of the big leagues. Because of his control problems, Longview released him, and so did three teams in Louisiana and some in Wisconsin.

Although his pitching ability wasn't what he would have preferred, his hitting was—good enough that he was in the lineup at first base on the days when he wasn't pitching. And he always was a fast man on the bases.

In February of 1941, after going back to high school and getting his diploma the previous June, Bert answered an ad in the newspaper to drive a new Chevy across the country to Seattle. That was close enough to California and another try at baseball, so he drove the car—forgetting to take his driver's license with him—and worked his way from Seattle down the Pacific Coast to Anaheim.

There he talked himself into a tryout at the spring-training camp of the Philadelphia A's, got to meet their legendary owner and manager, Connie Mack, laughed at the antics of comedian Joe E. Brown at the A's annual spring-training banquet, and had his prayers answered when the A's offered him a contract to pitch for their minor-league team in Anaheim.

19

The same problems with control plagued him there, too. He was released, but he proved he still had the ability to come up with a job, by traveling to Bisbee, Arizona, and signing a contract with that team in the Arizona-Texas League.

Shepard's 1941 season gave him reason for encouragement. His control was a little better, not much but some, and his hitting continued to improve. He began thinking he might be able to make it to the big leagues after all, maybe as a first baseman instead of a pitcher.

While Bert Shepard was striving toward his dream, Hank Greenberg's was ending. "Hammerin' Hank," the slugging first-baseman-turned-outfielder of the Detroit Tigers, already the American League's Most Valuable Player twice and producer of 249 home runs in eight seasons, was drafted nineteen games into the season.

It was a cruel blow to one of America's most popular celebrities, and at the zenith of his career. He turned thirty on New Year's Day of 1941. Not quite three months earlier, he and his brother Joe had stopped off in Geneva, New York, on their way home from Detroit after the World Series and registered at a local school so Hank could avoid the publicity that was sure to come if he registered at his own draft board in New York City.

Then he took a vacation in Hawaii, returning to a crowd of reporters and photographers when his ship docked in California on February 11. His draft number had been picked in Detroit. Why Detroit? Because when he registered, he listed his address as Leland Park there. His brother put down the family home, 663 Crotona Park North in the Bronx.

After reporting to the Tigers' spring-training camp at Lakeland, Florida, Hank was declared 1-A—physically fit for military service—even though the examining physician noted that he had flat feet. Later he was ordered to report for duty on May 7.

It was especially unfortunate timing. The Tigers had won the pennant in 1940 but lost the World Series to the Reds in seven games. The team was hoping to repeat as American League champions and win the Series in '41. As for Hank, he

20

was hoping to duplicate what he did in 1940 when he led the league in home runs with 41 and both leagues in runs batted in with 150, while also hitting .340, fifth highest in the league.

And he didn't cool off in the World Series. Detroit's second highest hitter with a .357 average, he was only three points below Bruce Campbell, and tied with his teammate, Pinky Higgins and Cincinnati's Jimmy Ripple for the most runs batted in on either team with six. He hit six singles, two doubles, a triple, and a home run in seven games.

Greenberg, after almost breaking Babe Ruth's single-season home run record with fifty-eight in 1938, was what today we could call a superstar, right up there with Bob Feller, Joe DiMaggio, Ted Williams, and the rest of the American League greats and Johnny Mize, Dolf Camilli, and Arky Vaughan in the National.

Despite his stature—and the deep slash in income from $55,000 a year to $21 a month—Greenberg told a reporter for *Life* magazine, "It wasn't as much of a sacrifice as it appears. After all, the government takes most of that fifty grand. I never asked for a deferment. I made up my mind to go when I was called. My country comes first."

Senator Joshua Bailey of North Carolina was moved to remark, "To my mind, he's a bigger hero now than when he was knocking home runs."

On the day that Hank Greenberg reported to the Army, his Tiger teammates did more than play the day's game. At the Detroit ballpark, then called Briggs Stadium for the Tigers' owner, Walter "Spike" Briggs, they also raised the 1940 American League pennant.

The patriotism of Mulcahy and Greenberg in 1941 was displayed by others, too, even those who could legitimately have been deferred from the draft. Dom DiMaggio of the Boston Red Sox was one such case.

This was Dom's second year in the big leagues, one he remembers fondly because of the achievements of his brother Joe and his pal next to him in the outfield, Ted Williams, and his own accomplishment—making the American League all-star team for the first of eight times.

21

One of the few big leaguers wearing glasses in those years, Dom flunked his draft physical because of poor eyesight. Still, as he remembers today, "There was no rejoicing if you were declared 4-F. Every man in his twenties or thirties wanted to do his part in helping America prepare for whatever dangers we would face. . . ."

After getting flunked by the Army doctors, Dom requested an exam by the Navy physicians, was told he might be acceptable for service, and was called to active duty after the '42 season. He served three years—peak seasons gone from his athletic career—but years he sacrificed for the same fundamental reasons expressed by Mulcahy, Greenberg, and others who followed.

Even baseball players who weren't Americans were subject to the military draft, and other pressures. The Cuban and Venezuelan players were vulnerable, and that posed a grave threat to us Washington fans. The Nats' owner, Clark Griffith, had loaded up on Latin American talent, and the expectation was that they would not be drafted because they were not American citizens.

That hope didn't last long. Players like Roberto Ortiz and Alex Carrasquel of the Nats and Bobby Estalella, the former Washington outfielder who had just been traded to the St. Louis Browns, had a problem. The Justice Department notified Griffith that he would be required to post a bond guaranteeing that his Hispanic players "will not become public charges." The government didn't want those guys drawing welfare checks if they didn't make the team.

Toward the end of the war, the Hispanic players were destined to face a far worse dilemma—either register for the draft and take your chances, or go home to Cuba and Venezuela.

Three weeks after Hank Greenberg reported for duty, President Roosevelt addressed the nation in a radio broadcast on national defense. The whole country used to come to a halt when FDR spoke on the radio, so effective was he in projecting his personal magnetism over the airwaves with a voice that was authoritative yet reassuring and a delivery whose pace and timing would have made the most talented entertainer envious.

On this night, May 27, 1941, the president's address was broadcast everywhere, including the Polo Grounds in New York where the Giants were playing the Boston Braves. The game was a pitcher's duel, with Manuel Salvo of the Braves battling Hal Schumacher. It was a 1–1 game after seven innings when time was called so everyone could hear FDR's rich tones flowing from the public address speakers.

His address lasted forty-five minutes. Both managers, Casey Stengel of the Braves and Bill Terry of the Giants, lifted their starting pitchers in the eighth. The Giants won, 2–1, behind their relief pitcher for the night, the immortal Carl Hubbell, who drove in the winning run with a single in the ninth.

The mood of America was changing. FDR was increasing his effectiveness in mobilizing public support for his national defense program. Only two years earlier, three months after Hitler's storm troopers invaded Poland to start the war in Europe, two-thirds of America's citizens surveyed by the Elmo Roper polling organization said they opposed our involvement in the war. One of the leading isolationists in Congress, Senator William Borah, derisively called it "that phony little war."

But Roosevelt was in the process of reversing that national opinion to one of support for his program. He and Great Britain's new prime minister, Winston Churchill, met on a ship in the North Atlantic and signed the Atlantic Charter, pledging the cooperation of both countries on long-range objectives toward "the final destruction of the Nazi tyranny."

In his efforts, Roosevelt had another strong new ally, the brightest new star in broadcasting—reporter Edward R. Murrow of the Columbia Broadcasting System. In August of 1940, when Hitler's air chief, Hermann Goering, sent his fighters and bombers, the *Luftwaffe*, to England every night in the London Blitz, Murrow began a nightly report on CBS radio.

It was called "London after Dark." The intrepid thirty-two-year-old correspondent boldly climbed to the city's rooftops in the middle of the nightly air raids and began his broadcast every evening in the same deep, somber tone: "This . . . is London."

We didn't know it, but we were hearing not only the beginning of a war but the beginning of broadcasting history.

We sat as close as we could to the family radio—most families had only one—while Murrow told us of the destruction and terror being rained down before his eyes on London and her people from the planes with the Nazi swastikas on their sides. The drama, and the fear of what might be in our own future, were heightened by the noises in the background from Murrow's rooftop every night—sirens wailing up and down, the actual sounds of exploding bombs, and through it all, Murrow calmly describing the horrible sights on the streets below him.

Even with accounts like these, there was still doubt in the minds of many Americans over whether we should get involved. Isolationists like Senator Borah and Senator Burt Wheeler of Montana got all the help they needed from influential colleagues like Father Charles Coughlin of Detroit, the "radio priest." Coughlin was a persuasive reactionary who called Roosevelt a "scab president" and whose weekly orations on nationwide radio screamed harsh criticism against FDR and his policies.

Public-opinion polls showed one-third of all Americans were still opposed to getting involved in the war. But that was a noticeable improvement from the two-thirds opposition of late 1939. Roosevelt was making progress in changing American attitudes, aided by events such as the London Blitz.

In the light of all this, the 1941 observance of the Fourth of July took on a slogan—"A Birthday Present for the United States"—and Americans showed their red, white, and blue in celebrations marked with more enthusiasm and national pride than any since the days of "the war to end all wars" twenty-three years before.

As evidence of Hollywood's perfect timing on such things, a new movie, *Sergeant York*, was released all over the country. It starred Gary Cooper in the true-life story of a peace-loving Tennessee sharpshooter, Alvin York, who single-handedly killed more than twenty German soldiers, wounded several

24

others, and captured 132 prisoners in a one-man coup during World War I.

Even the baseball fans who went to the traditional July Fourth doubleheaders—every major-league team always played a doubleheader on Memorial Day, July Fourth, and Labor Day in those years—turned the trip to the ballpark into a service to America. In Los Angeles, a minor-league city in baseball terms then, the fans who came to the Los Angeles-Oakland doubleheader in the Pacific Coast League filled two dump trucks with aluminum to support the national defense program.

As much as Americans have always loved their baseball, it wasn't the only escape from the war news coming out of Europe in 1941. Hollywood was turning out quality viewing such as the classic *Citizen Kane,* starring the young genius Orson Welles, plus *The Grapes of Wrath,* with Henry Fonda, and another Gary Cooper hit, Ernest Hemingway's *For Whom the Bell Tolls.*

For those who liked the "swing" music of the period, and anybody born since World War I seemed to fall into the category, there was *Sun Valley Serenade* with Glenn Miller and Sonja Henie. Bob Hope, Bing Crosby, and Dorothy Lamour starred in a picture that we kids could enjoy, too: *The Road to Singapore.*

But Hollywood managed to provide us with war films, as well, whether we wanted them or not, and most of us did. We made box office successes out of a Tyrone Power and Betty Grable movie, *A Yank in the RAF, Dive Bomber,* starring Errol Flynn and Fred MacMurray, and a comedy about Army life called *Buck Privates,* featuring the new team of Abbott and Costello.

The radio programs were just as popular as the movies. Kids and parents enjoyed what *McCall's* magazine later called "togetherness" as we sat in our living rooms—nobody had "family rooms" or "rec rooms"—and stared at the wooden box with the yellow celluloid dial in front of us while we laughed at Jack Benny, Edgar Bergen with Charlie McCarthy, Fred Allen, and Fibber McGee and Molly.

We smiled often, chuckled at other times, and howled

sometimes as Dennis Day and Rochester drove Benny crazy, W. C. Fields insulted Charlie McCarthy, and Molly shouted a frantic warning to McGee, always a split second too late to prevent the ear-shattering crash when he opened the closet door.

It wasn't all comedy on radio. Older brothers and sisters and our parents, too, shared the tension during the dramatic episodes of "Inner Sanctum," "I Love a Mystery," "The Shadow," and even "Little Orphan Annie." And for music there was always the "Lucky Strike Hit Parade," the "National Barn Dance," and a new show called "Grand Ol' Opry."

Drama was even available in the afternoon on daily fifteen-minute programs usually sponsored by the soap companies. People called them "soap operas"—"Portia Faces Life," "Ma Perkins," "Stella Dallas," and "Just Plain Bill."

As historic as the year 1941 was in world terms, baseball seemed determined to make it memorable in its own way. Ted Williams entered the final day of the season assured of being the first player to reach the magical level of a .400 batting average since Bill Terry hit .401 for the Giants in 1930—if he took the day off. But Ted turned thumbs down on an offer from his manager, Joe Cronin, to sit out the day and see his average rounded off to an even .400, and instead went 6-for-8 in a doubleheader against the A's in Philadelphia. The result was an average of .406, and Williams remains the last man to hit .400—fifty years ago.

Joe DiMaggio accomplished what no hitter in baseball has done before or since, hitting safely in fifty-six games in a row beginning on May 15 until Ken Keltner of the Indians stopped him with two sensational plays at third base in Cleveland on July 17. Williams hit the most dramatic home run in the history of All-Star Games, a three-run shot off Claude Passeau in the bottom of the ninth inning in Detroit that gave the American League a come-from-behind 7–5 victory.

Other baseball news, good and bad, was also historic. Lefty Grove, striving eagerly for the top of the pitcher's mountain—three hundred victories in a career—reached that peak on July 25 with a 10–6 victory over the Cleveland Indians

26

when Dom DiMaggio hauled in Lou Boudreau's fly ball in Boston's Fenway Park for the final out. DiMaggio's catch made Grove the twelfth pitcher in history to win three hundred games. He never won another.

Tommy Henrich, one of baseball's best hitters in 1941, and Mickey Owen, one of baseball's best catchers in 1941, both missed a big, breaking 3–2 pitch from Hugh Casey of the Dodgers with two outs in the ninth inning of the fourth game of the World Series.

It would have ended the game and tied the Series at two wins each. Instead, Henrich reached first base on what has become the most famous "strikeout" in history. The Yankees, as they always seemed to do, jumped all over the opportunity. They rallied for four runs after being behind, 4–3, and won the game that day and the Series the next.

Lou Gehrig, one of the most revered players in the history of any American sport and the holder of one of the most remarkable achievements in any sport with 2,130 consecutive games over a period of fourteen seasons, finally succumbed to the ravages of amyotrophic lateral sclerosis—ALS. The death of the man who only two years before was still called the Iron Horse gave the disease its familiar name, Lou Gehrig's disease. He was thirty-seven.

Events in baseball and in the country seemed intertwined. One of the big song hits of the year, "Joltin' Joe DiMaggio," was recorded by Les Brown and his Band of Renown and had America actually singing about the Yankee Clipper's batting streak. Minor-league teams were cutting back on the number of night games, which they started playing in the early 1930s, to conserve oil and electricity needed to operate our farms and factories. And the departure of young men for military service continued even though we were not yet at war.

President Roosevelt seemed to be talking to us in the movie newsreels every week about the worsening international situation and the need for us to prepare for the inevitable. In those days before television, the newsreels were the only way Americans had to see their leaders and celebrities up front and personal. Stars from the entertainment world, sports, business, and politics were on the screen and we could see what they looked like, how they talked, and actually witness their news-making events—on film a week later.

They came on as part of the "extra added attractions" when we went to see other movies like *Man Hunt*, starring George Sanders and Walter Pidgeon, and *Honky Tonk*, with Clark Gable kissing Lana Turner in a scene that bored us ten-year-olds. You hoped for two extras any time you went to the movies—a newsreel and a cartoon.

Roosevelt declared a state of national emergency in 1941, so there was something else new at the movies. Before the first showing of the day—the one o'clock matinee—the house lights went out and everyone stood at attention in the dark for the playing of our national anthem while the American flag filled the screen.

3

A GEORGIA BOY
AND MEL OTT

AFTER THE '41 BASEBALL SEASON ENDED AND OCTOBER'S golden leaves dropped from their branches and the trees took on their bareness of winter, the world continued to careen toward a full-scale world war. On the other side of both of our oceans, events seemed to be controlling nations, instead of the other way around.

Because of the growing international urgency, Thanksgiving Day that year was no holiday for the American secretary of state, Cordell Hull. He met in Washington with the ambassador from Japan, Admiral Kichisaburo Nomura, and presented him with documents which set forth the U.S. position on the differences between the two countries. It was a last-ditch effort to avoid a war. In Tokyo on the same day, Premier Tojo said Japan remained determined to enforce her national policies. The adults around us seemed to despair of any real hope that we could avoid war.

The day after Thanksgiving, November 28, the *New York Times* told its readers on page one, "All United States efforts to solve differences with Japan appeared exhausted yesterday, and the next move—either diplomatic or military—seemed up to Tokyo."

Four days later—December 2—the Japanese government rejected Hull's proposals. At the same time, Tokyo radioed a coded message to one of its senior officers, Admiral Nagumo, who was commanding six aircraft carriers, two battleships, three cruisers, and nine destroyers steaming eastward in the Pacific.

In code the message said:

CLIMB MOUNT NIITAKA.

Translation:

ATTACK PEARL HARBOR.

As FDR and Secretary Hull worked around the clock to cope with "the foreign situation," others were trying to keep pace with events. On December 5, while Hank Greenberg was being discharged from the Army because men twenty-eight and over were being granted deferments, the House of Representatives approved an additional eight billion dollars for defense to increase the size of our Army to two million men and women.

The members of the House, and the Senate too, were aware not only of the crisis but of the perceptible swing in public opinion toward supporting a "war effort." A Gallup Poll in August showed that 85 percent of Americans thought we would be drawn into the war in Europe. Another poll toward the end of the year showed that two-thirds of Americans thought we would be at war with Japan soon.

On December 6, the Secretary of the Navy, Frank Knox, issued a report declaring, "The American people may feel fully confident in their Navy. . . . The U.S. Navy is second to none."

On the same day, the New York Giants hired Mel Ott as their new manager to replace Bill Terry. Ott, the five-foot-nine-inch slugger who hit 511 home runs in twenty-two Hall of Fame years with the Giants, appeared at a press conference at the Giants' offices on Forty-second Street with owner Horace Stoneham and secretary Eddie Brannick.

30

Ott predicted a first division finish for the Giants in 1942. In the December 7 *New York Times,* reporter John Drebinger editorialized in his news article that Ott " . . . carried off the interview with surprising ease. Melvin Ott, in the short space of four hours, seemed at least to have scored a sweeping social triumph."

As if afraid he didn't have his readers convinced, Drebinger went on, "By his engaging frankness, even temper and pleasing personality, the 32-year-old 'boy wonder' of the Polo Grounds seemed to convince one and all that here indeed was a Major League skipper who would never be difficult to approach or interview."

The major leagues were holding their annual winter meetings at the Palmer House in Chicago, where owner Clark Griffith of the Washington Nationals was reported to be seeking an increase in the limit on night games from seven—one against each team in your league—to fourteen.

Drebinger, in a separate article on the meeting, wrote, "The National League is certain to move solidly against this, and in the American only the Browns are looked upon as likely supporters of Griffith's plan."

On the morning of December 7, the front page headline of the *Times* said:

ROOSEVELT APPEALS TO HIROHITO

FDR sent a personal message to Hirohito for peace in the Pacific. The sense of urgency in his message was based on the concern caused in Washington by reports received in the State Department that 125,000 Japanese troops were concentrated on the Indochina border. An attack on Thailand appeared imminent.

In Europe, German troops were trapped along the southern front in the Soviet Union, cut off without supplies or reinforcements. Hitler's bold—some said crazy—decision to invade Russia seemed about to blow up in his face.

The next day's headline in the *Times,* at the top of page one and in type far bolder than its usual bannerlines, told of Hirohito's defiance against Roosevelt's appeal:

31

JAPAN WARS ON U.S. AND BRITAIN;

MAKES SUDDEN ATTACK ON HAWAII;

HEAVY FIGHTING AT SEA REPORTED

Another story on the front page appeared under a headline that said:

ENTIRE CITY PUT ON WAR FOOTING

The second paragraph reported, "One of the first steps taken here last night was a round-up of Japanese nationals by special agents of the Federal Bureau of Investigation, reinforced by squads of city detectives acting under FBI supervision. More than 100 FBI men, fully armed, were assigned to the detail." The article said "hundreds" of Japanese Americans were sent to Ellis Island that night, only hours after the attack on Pearl Harbor.

Mayor Fiorello LaGuardia, who was also New York's civil-defense chairman, spent that Sunday evening ordering guards to take up positions at the city's bridges, tunnels, and factories, and alerting his 115,000 air-raid wardens.

Most Americans confessed later that they didn't even know where Pearl Harbor was. I didn't either, but then I had a good excuse—geography bored me more than any other subject except arithmetic in Sister Edward Paul's classes at Nativity School.

In Washington the next day, that champion of isolationism, Senator Burt Wheeler, became an instant convert to what we now, more than ever, called "the war effort."

I heard Wheeler quoted on the radio during the day. At dinner that night, I piped up from my junior seat among us seven kids and our two parents and said with boldness, "Senator Wheeler says we have to kick hell out of 'em."

Mom didn't even tell me to go wash my mouth out with soap.

On December 9, star pitcher Bob Feller of the Cleveland Indians, with 107 victories and still only one month past his twenty-third birthday, put aside his 3-C draft deferment as his family's sole support and enlisted in the Navy. Feller was in a class with Hank Greenberg, Joe DiMaggio, Ted Williams, and Buck Newsom as baseball's highest salaried players, and he was protected by the draft because of his family responsibilities. His father was dying of cancer on the family farm at Van Meter, Iowa, and young Bob was supporting his parents and his kid sister.

When a reporter asked him after the war why he turned down the opportunity to continue his career and keep earning the big bucks, not to mention the safety of working in a baseball stadium instead of on a warship, Feller put it bluntly. "We were losing the war," he said. "We needed heroes—fast."

Feller served first in Gene Tunney's physical-fitness program, but became itchy for action after only six months and requested transfer to gunnery school. He got it, and served on the battleship *Alabama* as chief of a gun crew of twenty-four men, first in the icy waters of the North Atlantic as the *Alabama* escorted American ships against the threat of German submarines, and later in eight invasions in the South Pacific. He was gone for almost four seasons.

Hank Greenberg made the same kind of decision. Having been out of the Army for only two days when Pearl Harbor was attacked, he reenlisted, even though he, like Feller, might have been able to sit out the whole war. But Americans, including their baseball players, didn't think in those terms in 1941 or at any time during the war that followed.

Greenberg was thirty years old then, and he knew what he might be sacrificing. He was gone as long as Feller, serving as a captain in the China-Burma-India theater and returning for the second half of the 1945 season, a few weeks ahead of Bob.

When he voluntarily reentered the Army on December 9, he told the Associated Press, "We are in trouble and there is only one thing to do—return to service. I have not been called back. I am going back of my own accord. . . . Baseball is out the window as far as I'm concerned. I don't know if I'll ever return to baseball."

The mood in Washington became still more serious. We were told to be ready for air-raid drills, practicing for what could be the real thing at any time. The lights on the Capitol

Building and the rest of the city's landmarks went out. We bought "blackout curtains" and dark shades for our houses so the lights wouldn't be shining through the windows even when there was no drill.

The librarian of Congress, Archibald MacLeish, moved swiftly to transfer our founding documents, the Declaration of Independence and the Constitution, to "places of greater security," along with the library's copy of the Gutenberg Bible and one of three copies of the Magna Carta.

Washington was at war. We were scared that the Germans might bomb our city, and other cities in the East like New York or Boston. On the West Coast, the people were afraid of the same thing from the opposite direction, air attacks from the Japanese. In the case of both coasts, that fear produced immediate panic.

On the night of December 8, sirens suddenly sounded in New York and a million people hurried to their basements and other shelters until the "all-clear." The Army said it was a false alarm.

In San Francisco, the Army said it had received a report from the Associated Press that two squadrons of enemy planes—fifteen to a squadron—crossed the coastline west of San Jose and flew over the Bay Area and other sections of California.

Radio signals in San Francisco were silenced. Lieutenant General John DeWitt, commanding general of the Fourth Army and the Western Defense Command, declared emphatically, "I don't think there is any doubt that the planes came from a carrier."

The panic produced automobile accidents and traffic jams. No planes were spotted, not even by the searchlights scanning the night sky, but General DeWitt was still cautioning the citizens the next morning: "Death and destruction are likely to come to this city at any moment."

While her husband presided over an emergency meeting of his cabinet on December 8, Eleanor Roosevelt spoke on the radio and told us, "I have a boy at sea on a destroyer. For all I know, he may be on his way to the Pacific. Two of my children are in coast cities in the Pacific. Many of you . . . have boys in the service . . . you cannot escape anxiety, you

34

cannot escape the clutch of fear at your heart, and yet I hope that the certainty of what we have to meet will make you rise above those fears."

Fear even gripped the Midwest. A Chicago air-raid warden said the atmosphere created by the blackouts and the drills "does something to you. It is a personal experience. . . . There is no physical fear. But the war is no longer far off in London or Chungking."

In Washington we kids always loved Christmas and for more than the usual reasons. The national celebration was held right in our own hometown. We had the national Christmas tree, and it stood not in front of one of thousands of city halls but on the grounds of the Ellipse, between the White House and the Washington Monument. And its lights were always turned on not by a mayor or a town alderman but by the president of the United States. The Christmas season in Washington, just like the baseball season, always began in major-league style.

Christmas of 1941 was different. The reminders of the war were all around us, especially in the number of uniforms. The presence of Prime Minister Churchill was another reminder. He was in our town for meetings with FDR and to address Congress, so he joined Roosevelt in turning on the tree lights.

Washington was a city of red, white, and blue, and more and more of the people on our streets were wearing the Army's appropriately named "olive drab," the Navy's blue, or the Marine Corps' green.

Parents whose kids wanted ice skates that Christmas could buy them at Irving's Sports Store at Tenth and E Streets for $3.29. And if the parents wanted a shot of rye to toast the season, they could buy a bottle at Eagle Wine and Liquor in Georgetown for $1.69.

The growing number of Army officers in the nation's capital could buy a new trench coat at Fogel's Military Outfitters at Tenth and D for $11.95. If Dad wanted to buy Mom a rebuilt Eureka vacuum cleaner, he could pick one up at the Clean-Rite Vacuum Store at 925 F Street. The price was $12.95, but the store offered "liberal terms." For holiday

35

entertaining, a host or hostess could display a hand-hemmed five-piece luncheon tablecloth and napkins set from the Esther Shop, 1225 F Street. The set would cost $1.99, but it was a "regular $4 value."

On our first wartime Christmas Eve, in addition to the traditional carols, we were also singing "God Bless America," the song Irving Berlin wrote in 1918 and then forgot about as it lay in a trunk until Kate Smith asked him to write a patriotic song for her. He remembered his 1918 number, which he hadn't done anything with, dug it out of his trunk, and gave it to her.

Two days before Christmas, our Pacific commander, General Douglas MacArthur, began pulling back, directing his forces to the island of Bataan off the coast of the Philippines.

The *Washington Post* published a front-page "Greeting to Marines on Wake," who were suffering heavy casualties and in danger of losing the Wake Island to the Japanese onslaught. They were commanded by a local boy, Major James Devereux of Washington. The headline included three dots and a dash, the Morse code for the letter *V*, representing the new battle cry being heard and seen all over the United States: "V for Victory."

The article said, "We all know, because of you, that a Christmas will come when there will be Peace on Earth, Good Will to Men! Merry Christmas, Marines . . . and give them HELL!" Reporter Jack Norris wrote, "The undying story of Wake Island's heroic Marines appeared last night to be nearing its inevitable outcome. . . ."

Back home, the mother of George Fones got a letter from her son in the Navy. He was writing to let her know his ship was back in port now after a long cruise. "Honolulu is still dull," he wrote. He said he hoped to be back in D.C. for Christmas. After he mailed the letter, he was killed on the *Arizona* at Pearl Harbor.

For those who had the time to read the sports page, or any other part of the paper, on Christmas Day, there was an Associated Press story from Riverdale, Georgia. Cecil Travis, Washington's all-star shortstop and a man who finished with a higher batting average than Joe DiMaggio in 1941 even though DiMaggio hit in those fifty-six straight games, had been drafted.

For Washington's baseball fans, the story was the latest disaster in the war. Their team, winners of the American League pennant in 1924, '25, and '33, plus the World Series title in '24, had fallen on lean times in the second half of the 1930s. They weren't quite as bad as the old vaudeville gag, "Washington—first in war, first in peace, and last in the American League," because they had never finished last since Clark Griffith became their owner in 1912.

Still, they were bad enough. The Nats and the Philadelphia A's, owned and managed by Griffith's friend and fellow American League pioneer Connie Mack, were being outpaced in the 1930s and into the '40s. The wealthier teams were passing them by with their more up-to-date managerial methods including the extensive farm systems of the Yankees, Dodgers, and Cardinals. As Shirley Povich wrote in the *Washington Post* in later years, Griffith was running a "five-and-ten-cent-store operation in the supermarket era."

The 1941 season was typical. The Nats finished in seventh place under Bucky Harris, just ahead of Mack's A's, for the second straight year. Since winning its last pennant in 1933, Washington had finished in the top half of the eight-team league only once—fourth place in 1936.

In spite of such dismal performances year-in and year-out by their team, the Washington fans could at least thrill to the individual exploits of their few stars, and Cecil Travis was the brightest of them all. He was a consistent all-star, elected to the midsummer "dream team" for his excellence as a short-stop and his superior performance as a hitter.

Travis was a quiet, drawling Georgian who hit well above .300 every year but one from the time he broke in to play eighteen games on the 1933 pennant winner until that dreaded draft call at Christmastime 1941. His only sub-.300 season was .292 in 1939. Otherwise his averages were among baseball's best, ranging from .319 in his first full season in '34 to .359 in 1941.

In spite of their historic seasons in '41, neither Williams nor DiMaggio led the major leagues in hits that year. Travis did, with 218. That was 32 more than Stan Hack's high figure for the National League.

Travis, a six-foot-one-inch left-handed natural hitter, was on course for a plaque in the Hall of Fame when the war erupted. Like Feller, Greenberg, Mulcahy, and others, he lost all of the 1942, '43, and '44 seasons and all but the final fifteen games of 1945 to wartime military service.

When he came back to the Senators, his all-star reflexes were gone. He retired in 1947.

On New Year's Eve, thousands of native Washingtonians and the thousands more who were in the city now as part of the war strolled along the city's main drag, F Street. The usual ear-shattering sound of blaring noisemakers and honking automobile horns was diminished in 1941. People wanted to be sure they could hear the air-raid sirens.

The *Post* article reported that "many persons left the streets shortly after midnight to return home and rest up for work in the morning." More than half of the city's working citizens were scheduled to be at work on New Year's Day.

In his *Post* article, reporter Ben Gilbert described the subdued celebrations on the night of December 31, 1941, in Washington better than anyone:

New Year's Eve merrymakers remembered Pearl Harbor.

Part Two

1942

4

A FAN AT THE TOP

WE SANG A NEW HIT SONG IN 1942, A RALLYING CRY CALLED "Let's Remember Pearl Harbor," while we were wrestling with upheavals in every phase of our lives. Parents, children, even entire industries and professions were uncertain of their fate. In the face of the confusion, the commissioner of baseball had the same question as everyone else: What should we do?

The commissioner was a hard-as-nails, white-maned former federal judge named after a Civil War battle—Judge Kenesaw Mountain Landis. There were many things that Judge Landis didn't approve of, and President Roosevelt was one of them.

It is an indication of the times that Landis swallowed his pride, and his opposition to FDR's third term, and wrote to the president in January asking for guidance on how to operate the 1942 baseball season, or whether to operate it at all.

Describing baseball's dilemma, Landis asked, "What do you want it to do? . . . If you feel we ought to continue, we would be delighted to do so. We await your order."

FDR responded on January 15, "I honestly feel that it would be best for the country to keep baseball going." He added a plug for more night games, which might reveal the

41

fine hand of his Washington friend, Clark Griffith, the Nats' owner, in the presidential decision.

"I hope," the president wrote to the commissioner, "that night games can be extended because it gives an opportunity to the day shift to see a game occasionally." Given this presidential priority, games were played at night and the question of blackouts and dimouts took a backseat.

On the subject of the players being drafted, the president told Landis candidly:

As to the players themselves, I know you agree with me that individual players who are of active military or naval age should go, without question, into the services. Even if the actual quality of the teams is lowered by the greater use of older players, this will not dampen the popularity of the sport.

For his action in getting what has come to be called "the green light letter" from Roosevelt in the first month of the war and the new year, history has credited Judge Landis with saving baseball for the duration. But history is wrong says Shirley Povich of the *Washington Post*.

By the time 1942 arrived, Povich had been a Washington reporter and columnist for nearly twenty years. His reliable sources included Griffith, who told Povich that his personal friendship with FDR, resulting from all those opening games and other visits to Griffith Stadium by President Roosevelt, was what saved baseball during what we were now calling "World War II."

Roosevelt made so many trips to the ballpark, and always seemed to bring the Nats good luck, that he told Griffith he considered himself the team's mascot. Griffith told Povich that he simply mentioned to FDR that baseball should be allowed to continue during the war because it would be good for the morale of the people on the home front. The baseball fan in the White House readily agreed.

Besides, Griffith told Povich, Landis couldn't have saved baseball or anything else with Roosevelt. "Landis," Griffith said, "wasn't much more welcome at the White House than the Japanese ambassador."

42

Roosevelt, the successful politician who was so skilled at gauging public opinion, correctly foresaw the continued popularity of major-league baseball even without all of its prewar stars. The FDR green light, in fact, contributed to more than just morale on the home front. The GIs overseas told us, in letters to the folks back home and in interviews in the movie newsreels, that being able to follow the pennant races and read about the individual players in clippings from home and stories in *Stars and Stripes,* the GI newspaper, pumped up their morale.

FDR didn't have to worry about major-league baseball players serving if called. By the time the 1942 season started, there were sixty-one major-league players in the armed forces, forty-one from the American League and twenty from the National.

Many of them, like Feller and Greenberg, didn't wait to be called, volunteering for duty instead. Others went promptly—Feller's roommate, "Soup" Campbell, Outfielder Sam Chapman of the A's, Catcher Ken Silvestri of the Yankees, Outfielder Buddy Lewis and Third Baseman George Archie of the Senators. Others were living in the big leagues on borrowed time after being classified 1-A. Ted Williams was placed in that category even though he was the sole support of his mother. He joined the Navy after the '42 season. Johnny Sturm, the Yankees' first baseman, was 1-A even though he was married right after the '41 World Series. He enlisted in the Army in January 1942.

Four of the top vote-getters in the balloting for the American League Most Valuable Player Award for 1941—Williams, Feller, Travis, and Chapman—were either in the service already or classified 1-A. The MVP himself, Joe DiMaggio, was destined to be gone after the '42 season. And the man who won it in 1940, Greenberg, was gone, too.

The manpower shortage was here.

The National League's personnel supply was in better shape for the time being. However, Hugh Mulcahy, discharged at the same time as Greenberg because he also was over twenty-eight, was recalled to active duty and was driving an Army truck at Fort Devens, Massachusetts. The Giants were in danger of losing First Baseman Babe Young, but they felt relatively secure with slugger Johnny Mize, classi-fied 3-A, ready to play after being traded by the St. Louis Cardinals. The Dodgers were sweating out the fate of their twenty-one-year-old "phee-nom," Pete Reiser, the National League's 1941 batting champion, who was being told by his draft board in St. Louis that he, too, might be classified 1-A.

The draft became a new criterion to be factored into pre-dictions and expectations about a team's prospects for the coming season, and it quickly became the most important consideration of all. The truth is that you couldn't make any predictions anyhow. Even after seeing which teams escaped the ravages of the draft in the off-season, no one could anticipate which teams might lose stars during the season.

That's what happened to the Yankees in 1942, when their star right fielder, Tommy Henrich, was ordered to report for duty in the Coast Guard at the end of August, just as the Yankees were in their annual fight with the Boston Red Sox, this time to defend their 1941 pennant. But as the stars went away to war, those who took their places, although often lacking in the baseball skills of their predecessors, neverthe-less possessed certain redeeming features of their own.

One such player was Ellis Clary.

He entered our lives in 1942 as the new second baseman of the Washington Nats, 4-F because of a bad back but blessed originally with so much speed that he could run, to use his own description, "like a scalded six-legged cat."

He hit .275 for our team that year, but he never played more than ninety-six games a season even among his fellow 4-Fs. He appeared in only twenty-six games in 1945, after Griffith traded him to the St. Louis Browns, and then was gone from the major leagues forever.

As a player he really wasn't much, but as a source of laughs and entertainment, he was an all-star. He describes himself during his wartime career in the major leagues, starting as a twenty-five-year-old, by saying, "I couldn't stop a grounder, and I couldn't catch a fly ball. I was nearsighted, and I couldn't run because I had the gout. Other than that, I was one hell of a player."

44

The truth is that he *could* run, especially in his "scalded cat years," when he was in the minor leagues. He remembers playing for a manager named Wild Bill "Raw Meat" Rodgers with Sanford, Florida. In a game against De Land one afternoon, Clary beat out a bunt, stole second on the first pitch to the next hitter, and then third on the following pitch.

When he slid into third, Raw Meat simply hollered at him, "Hell, go on home!"

So on the next pitch, Clary stole home. Three stolen bases on three pitches after beating out a bunt to start it all. "Raw Meat used to introduce me," Clary says, "as the guy who stole first, second, third, and home on four pitches."

He even raced our U.S. Olympic champion, Jesse Owens, and he later described his experience to St. Louis columnist Bob Broeg. "I beat the gun, ran in Jesse's lane twice—making him run 110 yards instead of 100—but he went by me so fast I don't think I could have beaten him on a Harley-Davidson."

His defensive skills—if that's the right word—were another story. "I had the same glove for eight years," he said after his playing days, "and it was always brand-new because I ain't touched anything with it yet." Clary has claimed over the years that the only reason that glove isn't in the Hall of Fame was that the Lipton Tea Company bought it to use as the world's first flow-through tea bag.

Ellis was talking to me from his home in Valdosta, Georgia, one night. When I told him I seemed to remember an in-the-dirt brawl involving Johnny Peacock, the Red Sox catcher, and him, he verified the memory with no trouble. "I beat the living hell out of him." But then he minimized it. "He just said the wrong thing at the wrong time, and I just whipped hell out of him," he said. "I tore his mask off with one hand and hit him with my other."

The Senators' radio broadcaster, Arch McDonald, called him Chigger, and Walter Masterson, a Washington pitcher, remembers that his teammates called him Goat. We were chuckling about that. "Hell," he said, "they had a different name for me in every town."

He played on three teams with Early Wynn, at Sanford, Florida; Charlotte, North Carolina; and with the Senators. Wynn made the Hall of Fame. During his induction speech

45

at Cooperstown in 1972, he told his audience, "I won three hundred games. If Clary hadn't been playing second base, I'd have won six hundred."

Clary swears attendance was so poor when he was playing for the Browns in 1945, his wife walked up to the ticket booth and asked the ticket seller what time the game started, and he told her, "When would you like it to start, lady?"

Over his many years in baseball after his playing days—fifty-two years in all as player, major-league coach, minor-league manager, scout, and storyteller par excellence—Clary has always been a willing foil for a gag.

Like the time as a scout when he was watching a spring-training game in Lakeland, Florida, between the Tigers and the Minnesota Twins. He suffered a heart attack.

As they were placing him carefully but quickly into an ambulance for the emergency trip to the hospital, with the chest pains continuing and concern for him growing, Clary called out to anyone who might hear, "Somebody make sure to get the mileage."

On the home front in 1942, the news we heard remained grim. The war dominated every newspaper and every radio newscast. Men—there weren't any prominent women newscasters—who brought us the news were becoming our newest celebrities, especially Gabriel Heatter, who seemed to want to cheer us up at the beginning of his nightly reports by reassuring us, "Ah, yes—there's good news tonight."

In the early going, there wasn't any good news at all. We were getting pushed back in the Pacific, with the Japanese army overrunning our soldiers and marines and capturing strategic islands like Wake, Bataan, Corregidor, and the Philippines. MacArthur was forced to flee to Australia and set up headquarters there to begin mapping the road back, if we could stop the Japanese long enough.

The toll in American lives was staggering, and local newspapers began publishing a daily list of casualties—killed, wounded, and missing in action—accompanied by the rapidly climbing totals. Kids our age and older, and the adults, didn't just read the front page, sports, and the comics anymore. We looked for the day's casualty list to see if we knew any of the names. From time to time, everyone did.

The news on the home front wasn't any better. The luxury ocean liner *Normandie* caught fire and sank in New York, just as her conversion into an aircraft carrier was nearing completion.

In Washington, someone with the same hatred of the Japanese that many Americans were feeling and expressing in different ways reacted in an unusual manner. He, or she, chopped down four of the 3,000 cherry trees lining the Tidal Basin that had been donated to the people of the United States by the people of Japan in 1912. The annual Cherry Blossom Festival, Washington's rite of spring that ushers in the season and features the beauty of those 3,000 trees that rim the Tidal Basin and the Jefferson Memorial, was canceled.

More sad news on the home front came in the first days of 1942 when one of our biggest movie stars, Carole Lombard, was killed on a TWA Skyliner that plowed into Table Rock Mountain near Las Vegas. She was returning from a speech in Indianapolis in which she raised two million dollars in the sale of defense bonds and stamps. Her mother, press agent, and nineteen others, including fifteen Army fliers, were also killed.

The shock over a movie star's death was compounded by the patriotic conditions surrounding it and the fact that she was married to another Hollywood giant, Clark Gable. The Secretary of the Treasury, Henry Morgenthau, sent a telegram to Gable saying, "Your wife died in the service of her country. Her brilliant work for the Treasury this week in selling defense bonds in Indianapolis will be long remembered and honored by us all."

Her death brought expressions of shock and sympathy from the biggest names in films—Spencer Tracy, Gene Tierney, Walter Pidgeon, Robert Taylor, Marlene Dietrich, Rita Hayworth, Ida Lupino, Betty Grable, and Pat O'Brien.

One other expression of sympathy came from a seventeen-year-old student at Culver Military Academy in Indianapolis, Cadet Dave McElroy. During the bond rally, he had bet his schoolmates two dollars he could get a kiss from her.

He worked his way up to the popular actress and told her of the wager. She told the boy, "Well, you won, honey."

When he learned of Miss Lombard's death, he told a reporter he would use the two dollars to send flowers to her funeral.

On April 9, my eleventh birthday, Dad didn't make it home for my ice cream and cake. He worked all night in the Agriculture Department in the same office he occupied as an illustrator before the war. Only he wasn't working for the Agriculture Department now. He was reassigned with the start of the war, transferred to something new called the Office of Strategic Services—O.S.S. After the war it was succeeded by a now more familiar set of initials—the C.I.A.

We didn't find out until the war was over why he didn't make it to my birthday party in 1942. He worked all that night on secret maps for President Roosevelt.

Something far more serious than my turning eleven happened on that birthday evening in '42. Bataan fell. General Wainwright was forced to withdraw to Corregidor. The infamous Bataan Death March began for more than twelve thousand Americans and sixty thousand Filipinos. Ten thousand of them died in the punishment.

There was a crisis of a different nature facing the people along the East Coast and the Gulf of Mexico. German submarines—U-boats—were sinking ships, too many of them, right there along our beaches, sometimes in full view of people on shore.

The subs traveled in "wolf packs." One of their first successes occurred on the night of January 14, one month after America's entry into the war, when a British tanker was sunk twenty-seven miles south of Long Island. The island's residents could see the flames and smoke produced by the explosion of the *Coimbra's* eighty thousand barrels of oil.

Some estimates were that the Germans were sinking a ship a day along our shores, even near Panama and other Caribbean locations. The supply of oil on our East Coast began to dwindle. Gas stations in seventeen eastern states were ordered by the federal government to reduce their hours of operation to conserve the supply of oil and gasoline.

Our wartime production capacity was being jeopardized by

the loss of oil and gasoline. England's dependence on our shipping both essential items for her people and equipment for her battle against Germany was also gravely threatened.

The Germans called their project "Operation Drumbeat." In 1942, the operation's commander, Admiral Karl Donitz, informed his superiors, "Our U-boats are operating close inshore along the coast of the United States of America, so that bathers and sometimes entire coastal cities are witness to the drama of war. . . . "

In the first six months of 1942, the U-boats sank 397 Allied freighters and tankers in what author Michael Gannon called our "Atlantic Pearl Harbor." By June, one of our most prominent and most respected military leaders, General George C. Marshall, the Army chief of staff, said the German successes along our shores "now threaten our entire war effort."

In his 1990 book, *Operation Drumbeat,* Gannon, a historian and war correspondent, called the disaster "the American nation's worst-ever defeat at sea."

The grim figures support that contention. In addition to the ships, more than five thousand Allied lives, many of them American, were lost. Only when the U.S. Navy began escorting our merchant ships with convoys of war vessels did the attacks and sinkings stop, beginning in the second half of 1942.

We kids learned a new word—*rationing.* The government quickly slapped limits on all kinds of food, clothing, and other essentials. One of the first items to become scarce was sugar. Beginning in April, you couldn't buy more than ten pounds at a time because the shipments from the Philippines were stopped. Now we were getting our sugar only from Cuba and Puerto Rico.

In May our parents went to our neighborhood schools to get a new item in our lives, ration books, with little stamps that you had to give to the man at the grocery store if you wanted to buy sugar. And you couldn't buy much—eight ounces per person a week. Across the country, a million teachers handed out the books to twenty million parents.

The list of rationed items quickly grew long—meat, butter, fats, oils, coffee, canned foods, gasoline, even shoes. Ham was fifty-one cents a pound, plus seven ration points. Pineapple juice was twenty-two points for a forty-six-ounce can. Hamburger was seven points, too.

Rationing wasn't the only problem in trying to buy something now. Other items were restricted because production of civilian goods was being converted to make war materials. The production of most electric appliances was discontinued on May 31—toasters, coffee percolators, waffle irons.

In those days before our homes were heated by forced air, we were kept warm by radiators with hot water inside, and all of a sudden you couldn't buy them, either. It was the same with plumbing fixtures, flashlights and batteries, even garbage cans.

The manufacture of toys was cut back sharply. Typewriters were "frozen" to be available for government priority work. Hearings aids became scarce, and so did spare parts for cars. The government announced that after July 1 there would be no new vacuum cleaners or irons—or steel caskets.

Production of razor blades was limited to the 1940 level, and this was in the days when Santa Claus and actor Monty Woolley were about the only men who wore beards. Tea sales were reduced to 50 percent of the 1941 total. The production of toothpaste and shaving cream was ordered back to 1940 levels—and when you bought a new tube, you had to turn in your old one.

There was a paper shortage. When the ex-wife of George Preston Marshall, the owner of the Washington Redskins, wrote a book saying "nobody knows what I went through" during their marriage, Shirley Povich wrote in the *Post,* "Oh yes we do. She went through three hundred pages during a paper shortage."

5

<hr>

HINDSIGHT

THE BIGGEST INCONVENIENCE OF ALL WAS THE RATIONING of gasoline. The program was ordered into effect not only because gasoline and oil were scarce but also because rubber was, too. When FDR asked one of his chief advisers, Bernard Baruch, how the nation could save rubber, he was told to ration gasoline so Americans wouldn't drive their cars as much. We couldn't import rubber from Burma and other exporters anymore, so we needed to conserve what we had.

Gasoline rationing went into effect for the entire country on December 1. It was drastic all right, four gallons a week—later it was cut to three—if you were issued an *A* sticker for your windshield. The government estimated an *A* sticker would allow sixty miles a week for your "necessary" driving such as shopping, getting to work, and trips to the doctor or church. If you were a war worker in an essential occupation, you got more with a *B* or *C* sticker. Truck drivers displayed *T* stickers.

In January of '43, only one month after ordering gasoline rationing on a national scale, the government banned all pleasure driving. If you wanted to go to a ball game, you might leave your car home and take the bus or streetcar to save your precious gasoline.

A national speed limit of forty miles an hour was put into

effect in 1942, reduced to thirty-five by December as America's "victory speed."

On February 19 Roosevelt ordered the immediate round-up of 125,000 "nisei"—second-generation Japanese. The nisei were native American citizens whose parents came to this country in earlier years. Those rounded up were relocated from their West Coast homes to nisei camps in the interior of the country, where they were confined to temporary barracks behind barbed wire and guard towers. Many responded to this shocking and frightening turn in their lives with grace. A sign in a store window in Los Angeles early in 1942 read:

MANY THANKS FOR YOUR PATRONAGE. HOPE TO SERVE YOU IN THE NEAR FUTURE. GOD BE WITH YOU TILL WE MEET AGAIN.

MR. AND MRS. K. ISERI

Hindsight has convinced many Americans that Roosevelt's decision on the nisei question was not a wise or fair course of action, but that same hindsight shows that his decision on baseball was both.

Mickey Owen, the catcher for the Brooklyn Dodgers, told me recently, "In 1942 we filled the ballpark every day. On Sundays the sidewalks near Ebbets Field would be filled with people for several blocks, walking away because they couldn't get in—and the ballpark hadn't even opened yet."

The season began with the usual red, white, and blue bunting around Washington's Griffith Stadium, but the effect of the war was evident there, too. The headline in the *Washington Post* on April 15 might have sounded like an insult against Vice President Wallace, who threw out the first ball the day before, but it wasn't intended that way. It just told the story of life in the United States during a world war:

COLOR LACKING AS PRESIDENT IS FORCED TO MISS OPENER

Wallace's pitch sailed over everybody except Buddy Hassett, the Yankee first baseman. The rest of the afternoon went just as well for the Yankees. They won, 7–0.

The night before, we had our first big air-raid drill. The story in the paper the next day described it by saying:

Washington seemed to disappear from the face of the earth last night when a blast of sirens signaled the beginning of the Capital area's first full-dress air-raid test.

Some 75,000 civilians participated, including Dad, who patrolled our 5800 block of Seventh Street in the Brightwood section in a white helmet with the civil-defense logo on the front, a pyramid of red and white diagonal stripes. He showed no favoritism in enforcing the blackout.

The drill lasted only fifteen minutes, but he found time to bang on his own front door and shout in to his own wife and kids, "Douse that light!" Our house was completely dark. "That light" was the little red one on our radio dial.

They said downtown was so quiet the people around the Treasury Department could hear the trains coming into Union Station fifteen blocks away. The chief of police, Ed Kelly, told reporters, "We had a total of 4,135 regular and auxiliary police on duty, and they haven't turned up a thing." No crimes or accidents were reported.

Among the stories on the sports page about the Opening Game was an ad announcing that the Young Men's Shop on F street would now be open all the way to nine o'clock every Thursday for its new "victory store hours." The Burlington Hotel on Vermont Avenue near Thomas Circle was offering a five-course lunch for fifty cents. Dinner was more expensive, of course—ninety cents.

The Palais Royal on G Street at Eleventh featured a sale of "better dresses" for $9.90. If you needed a front-end check for your car, you could get one at the Firestone store at Twelfth and K for ninety-five cents. Chambers Funeral Home was offering "beautiful funerals" for $95.

In what must have been the last great bargain before the wartime housing shortage created havoc in Washington, a young couple bought a "bungalow" in Bethesda for $6,750.

Baseball's minor leagues were one of the first casualties of the first wartime baseball season, and that had a direct impact on the career hopes of Bert Shepard. Minor leagues were folding for lack of players, including the Arizona-Texas League, so Bert remained home in Clinton, Indiana. It didn't make any difference, because he was soon drafted anyway.

He was inducted into the Army in May at Fort Benjamin Harrison, Indiana, and sent to Daniel Field near Augusta, Georgia, where he quickly applied for pilot training. The same young man, still only twenty-one years old, who was brave enough to hop freight trains across America, was eager for the thrill of flying.

While he waited for an opening in flight school, he played first base for the Daniel baseball team, but he got even more satisfaction out of his brief football career. He was such a gifted athlete that he made the post team even though he had never played football before.

"The coach saw me playing baseball," Bert was saying to me over the phone from California a few months ago, "and he thought I had some ability as an athlete so he asked me where I was from. I told him Indiana, and he thought I meant the University of Indiana."

The result was the coach gave Shepard a tryout. When Bert heard that the team used the Notre Dame shift in its offense, he went to the camp library and looked at pictures of the shift in a book and then practiced it behind the barracks at night. The boy from Indiana made the football team as its starting fullback.

Against Jacksonville Naval Air Station, which had six players from the National Football League, Bert intercepted three passes, made eleven tackles, and threw several crunching blocks. The next day, while he was at the peak of his football fame, his orders for pilot training came through, transferring him to Williams Field in Chandler, Arizona.

He still laughs about it today. "The local paper said the team was going to miss my 'valuable experience,'" Bert says through his laughter. "Nobody ever knew it was the only game of football I ever played in my life."

While Private Bert Shepard was playing first base in the Army, the major-league season, like everything else, was beginning to take on a different look, and not just because

54

players like Cookie Lavagetto of the Dodgers, Billy Cox of the Pirates, Detroit's Fred Hutchinson, Mickey Harris of the Red Sox, and Washington's Walt Masterson joined baseball's honor roll of those who answered "the call to the colors." Other things were changing, too.

There were two All-Star Games, one at the Polo Grounds in New York and one the next night in Cleveland, to raise funds for Navy Relief and the Armed Forces' Ball and Bat Fund. The game at the Polo Grounds was followed exactly two minutes later by a citywide blackout as part of an air-raid drill. The players, coaches, and managers had to stay right where they were—still on the field or in the dugout or the clubhouse—until the all-clear was sounded by the civil-defense sirens twenty minutes later.

Shirley Povich of the *Post* put on a big-time promotion at Griffith Stadium, an exhibition between the Nats and a team of Navy all-stars from Norfolk and Newport News in Virginia. The Washington team was outmatched by the Navy team with the likes of Bob Feller while he waited to ship out to the North Atlantic, Phil Rizzuto, Benny McCoy, Don Padgett, and Dom DiMaggio.

Povich, the last guy in the world you would cast as a showman, attracted thirty thousand to Griffith Stadium, which didn't hold any more than that anyhow, and raised two million dollars in war bonds to pay for a navy cruiser. It was the second largest amount of money ever raised through a sports event until then, topped only by the second Dempsey-Tunney fight.

Shirley managed his achievement by recruiting some of the biggest names in show business. He got Kate Smith to stand behind second base and sing "God Bless America." Bing Crosby sang some of his hits, and Babe Ruth trotted out of the Washington dugout as the grand finale.

"I didn't know I was such a showman," Povich told me years later.

One of the most emotional moments of the year came when Washington's Buddy Lewis flew off to war as a new pilot, destined for the China-Burma-India theater of operations, where he flew more than three hundred cargo missions over "the Hump," the Himalaya Mountains, in a

C-47 cargo plane. The C-47 was the military designation for commercial aviation's DC-3 and was nicknamed the Gooneybird by the fly-boys of the war.

We were talking not long ago about his farewell salute to his old teammates. Lewis, a consistent .300 hitter as a third baseman-outfielder with the Nats since 1935, flew to Washington on a weekend flight from Lawson Field, Georgia, and visited his old teammates at Griffith Stadium. On his final handshakes, he told them to watch for him. He was going to give them a salute they would never forget.

"I never did forget it, either," Walt Masterson said. Walt was awaiting imminent call-up to the Navy himself. "Buddy had to leave before the game started. Not longer after that, a plane came near the ballpark and we looked up and saw him coming so low we knew it was Buddy."

How low was he? Lewis laughed when I asked him. "I could almost read the letters on their uniforms." Flying restrictions over wartime Washington were strict, with pilots required to keep their planes in designated areas and avoid classified locations.

"We had to stick to corridors," Buddy said. "Well, I didn't do that. I didn't stick to the minimum altitude either."

He tipped one wing of the twin-engine plane and headed off for war, but not before George Case returned the salute. He was the American League's stolen base champion for five years in a row. He and Buddy Lewis and Walt Masterson were more than teammates. They were pals, close ones.

"When Buddy came in low like that and tipped his wing," Walt says today, "George was in the batter's box. He stepped out and threw his bat in the air."

Then Lieutenant Lewis pointed the nose of his Gooneybird south. Not long after that, he flew to his assignment in the China-Burma-India theater. To get there, with the C-47 cruising speed of 150 miles an hour, he had to fly from West Palm Beach, Florida, to Puerto Rico, then to South America, then to Ascension Island, then to Africa, then across the Red Sea, then over the Indian Ocean, and finally to Karachi. The flight took two weeks.

6

ROOKIES

ONE HUNDRED ROOKIES DOTTED THE ROSTERS OF THE MAJOR-league teams in 1942, the most in baseball history, as something we were hearing about every day—"the manpower shortage"—had a sudden impact. Most of these young players would be gone with the end of the war, unable to compete against the prewar likes of DiMaggio, Williams, Mize, and Feller. But not all.

Johnny Pesky was a rookie shortstop with the Boston Red Sox that year. He reached one of the hitter's levels of excellence—over 200 hits—with 205 as a rookie. But he was classified 1-A for the draft even though he was supporting both of his parents and three siblings.

He went away to war in the Navy immediately after the season ended. When he got out in time to play the 1946 season and had to compete with the other returning players, he left no doubt that he belonged in the big leagues, war or no war. He got 208 hits. Then he topped 200 for the third straight season in 1947 with 207. He led the American League in hits in all three years and became the only player in baseball history to get over 200 hits in each of his first three seasons.

Allie Reynolds was another player who broke in during the

'42 season and made it as a star himself when the others came home from the war. He wasn't a kid as a rookie. He was already twenty-seven when he appeared in two games for the Cleveland Indians, pitched five innings, and had no won-lost record.

He was a fastballing six-foot right-hander whose speed earned him the name of one of our star trains of the forties—Superchief. He came out of Oklahoma, one-quarter Creek Indian, the son of a fundamentalist minister, and a superb athlete who starred in track and football. He won a track scholarship to Oklahoma A & M, where the football coach, the legendary Hank Iba, encouraged him to try out for the football team. He did, and he became one of the best running backs in the Missouri Valley Conference.

After graduation in 1939, he was drafted by the New York Giants of the NFL as well as the Indians. He chose baseball and then proceeded to pay his dues in the minor leagues with stops at Cedar Rapids, Wilkes-Barre, and Springfield, Ohio. He wasn't just a pitcher in those towns. He was a catcher and an outfielder, too.

Reynolds not only survived the postwar competition, but had his best years then. During his four wartime seasons, he was 0–0, 11–12, 11–8, and 18–12. In 1945, wrestling with the same problem that other fastballers have—control—he led the American League by giving up 130 walks. After the war and a trade to the Yankees for Joe Gordon, he continued to win in double figures. He never won fewer than eleven games in his entire career, led the league in winning percentage, strikeouts, and earned run average, and became a twenty-game winner as a mainstay on the powerful Yankee pitching staff with Vic Raschi, Ed Lopat, Frank Shea, and Joe Page.

Another star arrived when a future Hall of Famer played his first full season with the St. Louis Cardinals after getting twenty hits in twelve games in 1941. That was Stan Musial, who says the biggest thrill of all for him in a baseball career that included seven National League batting championships, a lifetime batting average of .331, and three Most Valuable Player Awards was "putting on the uniform every day."

Musial remembers more than just his own success and his team's. He remembers the way of life, too. "That was the good era," he says. "We still rode trains and had lots of time to talk. There were only eight teams in each league then, and things were slower and more peaceful."

He remembers another key difference: "When I played, it was very unusual for whatever anybody said in the clubhouse to leak out. We didn't take our problems to anybody on the outside. Today the players talk to the press and say things about the manager. . . . I just couldn't put up with all that."

Musial adopted what came to be called his "peekaboo" stance, crouching slightly, bending his front knee, holding the bat straight, and almost peeking at the pitcher over his front shoulder. Another Hall of Famer, Ted Lyons, the old White Sox pitching great, said, "He looks like a kid peeking around the corner to see if the cops are coming."

With a wife and a baby, Musial was making $750 a month as a big-league player in 1942. He hit .315 in a season when most of the good pitchers were still around, led both leagues in hitting the next year with .357, and was off on his way to a plaque in Cooperstown. When he came home from the Navy in 1946, he led both leagues again, this time with a .365 average.

He did it for a lifetime. When he hit .330 in 1962, he was forty-one years old. He retired after the '63 season, twenty-two years after getting those first twenty hits in 1941.

Another position was won by a rookie in 1942: the manager's job in Cleveland. There had been trouble there since 1940, when the Indian players staged a "revolt" and demanded the firing of their dictatorial manager, Ossie Vitt. He had alienated too many players—and failed to win the American League pennant, something many observers, including the players, thought they were capable of achieving.

The players made their demands in June of that year, following a road trip, when a delegation of regulars, including twenty-one-year-old Bob Feller, met with the Indians' president, Alva Bradley. The executive was sympathetic, but he refused to fire Vitt during the season. But the end of the season was different. He fired Vitt and replaced him with Roger Peckinpaugh, an American League shortstop for seventeen seasons and now the Indians' manager for the second time. He had been their skipper from 1928 through 1933.

But his term this time turned out to be for only one season. On November 25, 1941, after the Indians finished fourth with a 75–79 record and failed to win the pennant for the twenty-first straight year, Peckinpaugh was replaced by Lou Boudreau, their twenty-four-year-old shortstop. Peckinpaugh was named vice president and general manager. Boudreau was destined to be one of the last of a now-vanished species, the playing manager. He was also the youngest manager in the history of big-league baseball.

Gordon Cobbledick wrote in the Cleveland *Plain Dealer* that Boudreau's appointment "was a complete surprise." He said it was generally believed that Bradley had decided Boudreau's "youth and inexperience made it inadvisable to burden him with the manager's duties and responsibilities."

Despite Americans being warned by the U.S. Consulate in Tokyo to leave Japan for their own safety, and despite the German army storming toward Moscow, the biggest news of the day in Cleveland was the hiring of Lou Boudreau. The *Plain Dealer* ran an eight-column bannerline in bold capital letters across the top of its front page proclaiming:

BOUDREAU SIGNS TO MANAGE INDIANS

Below the bannerline was a smaller headline, only six columns wide and not in capital letters, that reported:

NAZIS REACH MAIN MOSCOW ROAD

No one argued with the *Plain Dealer*'s news judgment.

Boudreau became one of the great stars and respected leaders in the postwar years, topped by his classic season in 1948 when he led his team to the world championship as both its star player and its manager and won the Most Valuable Player Award.

He became a Hall of Fame player on the frailest ankles in baseball after a college athletic career as star of the University of Illinois baseball team and captain of its basketball team.

He broke his right ankle so many times that his draft board examined him twice and declared him 4-F twice.

By '42 Boudreau was in his third full season as a player, and his abilities at shortstop, especially on those brittle ankles, amazed people throughout the American League. Paul Richards, then a catcher with the Detroit Tigers and later an opposing manager, said during the war, "Lou is the slowest infielder in the American league, but he is Mr. Shortstop."

Another Tiger, Pitcher Dizzy Trout, was even more enthusiastic. "The guy is amazing," he said. "He can't run, his hands are small, and he has practically nothing to recommend him except the greatest baseball instincts of any shortstop since Honus Wagner."

All of Boudreau's abilities and instincts, however, didn't produce any noticeable improvement in the Indians in 1942. They finished fourth again, and with the same won-lost record as they had the year before under Peckinpaugh.

As the manpower shortage worsened, the presence of older men in the big leagues was reflected in the list of the National League's top hitters in 1942. Musial hit .315 in his first full year, the third highest average in the league. His teammate Enos Slaughter was second with .318. But the man with the leading average was thirty-four years old, the catcher for the Boston Braves, Ernie Lombardi.

Hitting was something Lombardi could do with the best of them, and that batting title in '42 didn't come to him just because there was a war on. He won the championship in peacetime too, with a .342 average in 1938.

"Lom" was a big man—six three and 230 pounds, with a nose whose size earned him the nickname Schnozz. The kidding didn't bother him. He got used to it right away, beginning with his rookie year in Brooklyn in 1931, before he was traded to Cincinnati.

Someone brought comedian Jimmy Durante into the clubhouse at Ebbets Field after a game. Photographers took a picture of the two beaks together, and Durante told them, "Lom's is bigger, but mine is more educated."

He was voted the National League's Most Valuable Player in 1938, finished with a .306 lifetime average over seventeen

61

years, and was one of the most feared hitters of his time. The remarkable thing abut Lombardi's batting averages was that he achieved them—those two league-leading marks plus such numbers as .333, .334, and .343 in his ten .300 seasons—with agonizing slowness afoot. The man simply couldn't run at all.

A right-handed hitter, he once hit the left-field wall in Cincinnati with a line drive and was thrown out at first base, the result of both his slowness and his power. The screaming drive hit the wall so fast that the outfielder, knowing Lombardi's inability to run, was able to make the play. On another occasion, sportswriter Harold Rosenthal wrote, "Lombardi hit the left-field wall for a double and ran it into a single."

Because of his slowness, he never had the luxury of bunts or "leg hits" on infield dribblers. For the same reason, he never got as many extra-base hits as other hitters would have with his talent. On more occasions than anyone knows, Lombardi had to settle for a single on hits that would have been doubles or even triples for anyone else in the league.

Columnist Arthur Daley of the *New York Times* remembered the game in 1935 when Lombardi hit four doubles in four consecutive innings off four different pitchers. Daley wrote, "Considering the fact that Lombardi always had to hit the equivalent of a triple to make a double, you can picture what sort of clouts all of them were."

His teammate, pitcher Johnny Vander Meer, remembers how slow Lombardi was. "He was a seven-second man to first base," Vandie says, in a profession where 4.3 seconds from home to first is average for a right-handed hitter. "The infielders would play him twenty-five feet back on the outfield grass. Billy Herman always played him thirty feet behind second base."

There was another dimension to Lombardi as a hitter, and that was his ability to avoid the strikeout, the out that kills so many rallies. Vander Meer likes to point out in defense of his teammate that Lombardi, even though he was a power hitter with that big swing characteristic of long-ball hitters, averaged only fifteen strikeouts a year.

Lombardi could do more than just hit. He could catch and he could think. Vander Meer told me once it was no accident that Lombardi was his catcher in both games when he pitched his back-to-back no-hitters in 1938 and became known to this day as Johnny "Double No-Hit" Vander Meer.

"He made an extremely quick, intelligent decision in my second no-hitter," Vandie was remembering. After he walked the bases loaded with one out in the ninth inning against the Brooklyn Dodgers in the first night game played at Ebbets Field, Vandie got Ernie Koy to hit a grounder to Lew Riggs at third base. Riggs threw home, Lombardi tagged the plate, and there were two outs.

"Lombardi was ready to try for the double play at first base, but he saw Koy running inside the baseline. He knew Koy was fast, and he knew that by running inside the line, a throw from home to first might hit Koy. So he held the ball rather than taking a chance of either hitting Koy or throwing the ball into right field."

The next hitter, Leo Durocher, hit a routine fly ball to Harry Craft in center field, and Johnny Vander Meer became a baseball legend.

There is additional evidence of Lombardi's intelligence. He considered involved managerial strategy against hitters to be overrated. "I once told every batter in a game what the next pitch would be," he said, "and we still won."

Lombardi knew what it was like to play in the big leagues during the Depression years of the 1930s. A bleacher seat in Cincinnati's Crosley Field cost only fifty cents, but people didn't have even that much to spare. "The crowds were so scarce," Ernie said, "that we used to call off a Wednesday game and move it to Sunday so we could play a doubleheader and get maybe four thousand people into the ballpark. We did it so often we'd find we'd have ten days off at the end of the season."

The Reds' great catcher and hitter grew unhappy in Cincinnati, even after helping his team win the 1940 World Series with a .319 average during the season. He got into only two games in the Series, came to bat only three times, and got a double plus a walk. The word was he wasn't happy with General Manager Warren Giles. He was sold to the Braves for the '42 season, at a $6,000 cut in salary.

While he was getting his revenge against the Reds with his league-leading batting average, the catcher who replaced him in Cincinnati, Ray Lamanno, told him the effect Lombardi was having on his old manager, Bill McKechnie.

"Man, you're driving McKechnie crazy," he said to Lombardi. "He's pulling his hair out."

Unhappy over his deep pay cut, Lombardi was traded to the Giants for Hugh Poland and Connie Ryan at the start of the '43 season, and played in New York for the rest of the war and until his retirement after the 1947 season.

With the Giants he enjoyed something he didn't always have on other teams—a roommate, pitcher Bill Voiselle. "Nobody would room with me," he admitted in later years. "They said I snored too much."

How could Voiselle put up with the snoring when nobody else could? "I've got bad ears. I can't hear him."

The question arises why a player of Lombardi's star credentials was so long in being elected to the Hall of Fame. The answer, some feel, lies in the Cincinnati turf where Crosley Field's home plate once was.

On that spot in the fourth game of the 1939 World Series against the Yankees, Charlie Keller slammed into Lombardi and scored the second run of a three-run rally in the tenth inning. It was the most horrifying inning in World Series history, with the Reds making four errors that gave the Yankees the game and a clean sweep of the Series.

As Lombardi lay stunned in the dirt near the plate, the ball on the ground a few feet from him after Keller dislodged it with the force of his slide, Joe DiMaggio also scored, on the same play that he started with a single.

Even though the run was not decisive, the writers and others came down hard on Lombardi. They said he was caught "snoozing" at home plate. No less a figure than Grantland Rice criticized Lombardi and wrote harshly, "The afternoon was insufferably hot and big Ernie was tired."

The play haunted Lombardi for the rest of his career and the rest of his life. He became a sad and lonely figure in later years, and as the chances for his election to the Hall of Fame seemed to grow dimmer, the speculation began that the rap hung on him for his alleged "snooze" in '39 was the reason.

The Reds players came to his defense over the years, including the pitcher of the moment, Bucky Walters, who had an answer for the members of the baseball media of that time. "It was a silly rap," he said, "but the Yankees beat us four straight and they had to pick on something, I guess. You can blame part of the thing on me. I was pitching, and I should have been behind home plate, backing up Lombardi. But the run didn't mean anything anyway."

Vander Meer adds, "I'll give you the true story on that. The throw from the outfield came in a short hop and hit Lom in the cup. You just don't get up too quick. Somebody put out the word that Lombardi went to sleep, took a snooze.

"He was paralyzed. He couldn't move. With anybody but Lombardi they'd have to carry him off the field."

Vander Meer is still strong in his support of Lombardi and bitter that he was not elected to the Hall of Fame until after his death. When I reminded him that Lombardi was elected to Cooperstown, Vandie said, "Yeah, nine years after he died. That bothered me."

The civilian population was rallying to the war cause on the home front during the '42 baseball season. By July there were seven million volunteers in the civil-defense program, whose enrollment reached twelve million by the next year, matching the number of men and women in the armed forces. Forty thousand civilian pilots joined the Civil Air Patrol to scan the skies for enemy aircraft and help provide backup air transportation.

Even the ball players who were destined for military service were performing volunteer "war work" in the meantime. Dom DiMaggio was leading the American League's center fielders, including his brother Joe, in putouts and assists, as well as hitting .286, while still finding time to serve as an aircraft spotter. Several other members of the Red Sox, including player-manager Joe Cronin, did the same thing.

Dimouts and blackouts became part of our routine. New York City conducted its first dimout in June. San Francisco staged seven blackouts by early in the year. Electric outdoor signs for advertising were forbidden. The lights went out at Coney Island and in Times Square. The Latin Quarter nightclub said its business dropped 25 percent.

Beaches at Ocean City, New Jersey, and in other locations

were closed at sundown, although bathers everywhere got at least one break. They were getting an hour more of sunshine every day with the enactment of year-round daylight savings time. Only we didn't call it "Eastern Daylight Savings Time." It was "Eastern War Time."

There was growing concern about the threat of runaway inflation, always a possibility in a booming wartime economy. It seemed ironic to all of us, grown-ups and kids alike. A few years before, we were in a deep worldwide depression and singing one of the hit songs "Brother Can You Spare a Dime?" Now we were worried about inflation. Roosevelt had the answer. To keep stability in the national economy, he froze prices and wages as of September 15.

Irving Berlin made another contribution to our wartime morale. He wrote "White Christmas" for a movie called *Holiday Inn* and all of the songs for a box office smash hit on Broadway, *This Is the Army,* which became an equally big hit as a movie the next year.

This Is the Army was a Hollywood extravaganza with more stars than you could think of, but the real stars were the 350 singing soldiers. Song-and-dance man George Murphy was one of the actors. Another actor told the group of performers in the show-within-a-show that they had been invited to perform at the White House in front of the president. The actor who read that line was Ronald Reagan.

Yet when Bing Crosby sang Berlin's sentimental words "I'm dreaming of a white Christmas, just like the ones I used to know," echoing the feelings of the GIs away from home and the folks back here, and other recording stars entertained us with other hits by Berlin and the rest of the wartime composers, we couldn't call the disc jockeys and ask them to play our favorites on the radio. The government wouldn't allow requests on the radio because of the possibility that some of the messages might be coded communications being sent by the enemy.

Weather forecasts on the radio were discontinued until the middle of 1943 so announcers would not accidentally provide useful information for an air strike against the United

States. Baseball announcers were forbidden from mentioning when it was raining. Every radio network began carrying a weekly government information program for the citizens called "This Is the War." The National Association of Broadcasters announced a voluntary code banning all radio programs "which might unduly affect the listener's peace of mind."

In their patriotic zeal, announcers and masters of ceremonies occasionally fluffed their lines, creating some of the best wartime "bloopers." At a small-town rally to sell war bonds, the town's mayor, flustered with excitement, introduced one of Hollywood's most respected actors, Walter Pidgeon, by saying, "Mr. Privilege, this is indeed a Pidgeon."

7

SHOCKING
NEW YORK'S
WRITERS

THE MILITARY ESTABLISHMENT WAS HARD AT WORK ON THE
home front as well as overseas. Its new headquarters for all
the branches of the service, something the country never had
before, was completed in Arlington County, Virginia, just
across the Potomac River from downtown Washington. This
five-sided building has never been called any military name.
From its completion in 1942 it's always been the Pentagon, an
enormous layout that provided office space for 35,000 uniformed and civilian personnel.

People marveled at its size, and when someone asked President Roosevelt what in the world we would do with a military
headquarters that big when the war ended and we wouldn't
need it anymore, he said it could be used for storage.

"Victory gardens" were introduced by the Secretary of
Agriculture, Claude Wickard, and they were popping up all
over the place. We had one in our backyard, growing corn,
tomatoes, beans, peas, and anything else we could cultivate.
The neighbors had them too, under strong encouragement
from the government so our crops could help to meet our
growing food needs.

Victory gardens appeared everywhere, not just in the

backyards of the nation's cities. There was one at the zoo in Portland, Oregon. In Chicago you could find one at a racetrack and another at the Cook County jail. By the end of 1943, there were twenty million victory gardens producing forty percent of all the vegetables grown in the United States.

Scrap drives become a popular project. Citizens turned in old items from around their house or farm to be melted down or otherwise "recycled," as we would say today. There was such a project in Boston in 1942, and, befitting Boston manners, it was marked by a black-tie affair. A shoemaker in Seattle saved the rubber heels from his repair jobs and eventually had six tons of them for the war effort.

The '42 baseball season gave us something resembling normality to cling to, beginning with spring training. Things looked even more normal with the Yankees and Dodgers leading their leagues.

Brooklyn got off to a quick start and stayed strong through its first hundred games, winning seventy-one of them. But the St. Louis Cardinals got hotter later, when the pennant was on the line. They were ten games out of first place on August 6, thanks to Brooklyn's strong first half, but then they simply refused to lose.

St. Louis won thirty of thirty-six games, sweeping its way into first place on September 13. The Dodgers tried to take things back into their own hands on the strength of an eight-game winning streak, but it was no help. The Cardinals, after taking over the top spot on the 13th, won ten of their next eleven.

St. Louis finished the season with 106 victories and beat out the Dodgers by two games. The issue was in doubt until the last day of the season, the first time since 1934 that a pennant race in either league was not decided until the final day.

The Cards defeated the Cubs, 9–2, in the first game of a doubleheader on September 28. Ernie White disposed of the Cubs on a five-hitter. Stan Musial caught Clyde McCullough's long fly ball in left field to end the game and wrap up the National League championship for the Cardinals.

The Yankees were not quite as dramatic, beating the Boston Red Sox by nine games. When the World Series arrived,

69

the tendency was to belittle the Cardinals' chances. After all, they were taking on the mighty Yankees. But there was a clue in the statistics at the end of the season: the Cardinals won three games more than the Yanks. Any team that won 106 games in the days when the teams played 154 games shouldn't have been dismissed going into a series where you needed to win only four.

When the World Series started in St. Louis on the afternoon of September 30, however, the Yankees were a strong favorite to win it. After all, they had won their last eight.

Even before it started, the World Series was notable for two reasons: it was the first to be broadcast to American armed forces around the world by shortwave radio, and it was the first since 1918 whose proceeds would go in part to the Army's Emergency Relief Fund.

It looked like more Yankee domination when Red Ruffing had a no-hit game with two outs in the eighth inning and finished with a seven-hitter and a 7–4 victory, the first pitcher in history to win seven World Series games. The Cardinals did not go quietly, however. They scored four runs in the bottom of the ninth. That must have been an omen. The Yankees never won another game.

The Cards picked right up again with two runs in the first inning the next afternoon, added another run in the seventh, and had a 3–0 lead going into the eighth. But the Yankees tied it up with three of their own, two on a home run by Charlie Keller.

The Cards came right back in the same inning, as they did all Series long, and evened the Series at one win each on a double by Enos Slaughter and a single by Stan Musial. Slaughter, the North Carolina farm boy nicknamed Country, contributed even more to the win by throwing out Tuck Stainback when Stainback tried to go from first to third on a single with nobody out in the Yankee ninth.

Johnny Beazley, a twenty-four-year-old who was one of the sensations of the National League that year with twenty-one wins, went the distance, even though the Yankees got ten hits, and beat another route-going pitcher, the veteran Ernie "Tiny" Bonham.

When the scene shifted to Yankee Stadium, it didn't make any difference. Ernie White, the first left-hander to face the Yankees, pitched a masterful six-hit shutout for a 2–0 victory, the first time New York had been shut out in a Series game since 1926.

The Cardinals' center fielder, Terry Moore, helped to insure their win with one of the great World Series catches. In one of Joe DiMaggio's last turns at bat before joining the Army over the winter, he sent a long fly ball to left center. Stan Musial made a diving try for the ball, and Moore leaped over him and made the catch backhanded in midair to the astonishment of 69,123 fans.

The manager of the Cards, Billy Southworth, called it "one of the most thrilling moments in baseball."

By the end of the fourth game the next afternoon, the Yankees were in a hole with only one win against three losses. Mort Cooper, pitching to his brother Walker behind the plate and coming off a twenty-two-win season, was no great mystery to the Yankees. He lost the first game and was in danger of losing again in the fourth game when his brother helped to win the game and keep Mort off the hook.

Mort gave up a run to the Yankees in the first inning, but his teammates scored six in the fourth and it looked like another Cardinal victory and Mort's first World Series win. But the Yankees came swinging back with five runs of their own in their sixth, including another homer by Keller, this time with two on.

Brother Walker came to the rescue by scoring Slaughter with a single in the seventh to break the 6–6 tie. Two more runs gave the Cards a 9–6 win and now the Yankees were the ones being intimidated.

In the fifth game, on October 5, it was Red Ruffing again, facing Johnny Beazley. New York again scored a run in the first inning, only to fall behind. St. Louis scored single runs in the fourth and sixth and two in the ninth on a home run by rookie third baseman Whitey Kurowski. The Cardinals won 4–2. As a result, Ruffing was not able to increase his all-time total of World Series victories. Instead, he lost to Beazley, who pitched a seven-hitter for his second Series win.

71

It was a major World Series upset, the first defeat for the Yankees in the World Series since they lost it in '26—to the Cardinals.

Kurowski remembers that there was no champagne in the dressing room, and no beer either. Tommy Henrich says the same thing about World Series celebrations in the Yankee dressing rooms: "We never had any champagne, and if there was any beer the club would charge us for it."

Whitey was hoisted to the shoulders of his teammates in the clubhouse, and he did something no one had ever dared try—he rearranged the white mane of Judge Landis. "I messed up his hair pretty good," Whitey told me, "and that was a first."

No one would ever think of doing that to the stern commissioner. "When he came around," Kurowski said, "the players jumped. When they heard he was coming to town, they straightened up. They were afraid of him. And the owners were afraid, too. He didn't take any stuff."

As we talked, Whitey remembered that his off-season appearances consisted of one guest spot on the radio with Fred Waring and his Pennsylvanians, with Johnny Beazley. "I got twenty-five dollars," he said, "and a record album."

Kurowski was honored with a parade in his hometown of Reading, Pennsylvania, and Beazley was mobbed by autograph seekers down home in Nashville, Tennessee.

Their common fate ended there. Whitey was declared 4-F because his right arm was four inches shorter than his left. Doctors had removed that much bone after Whitey fell off a fence when he was seven years old and cut the arm on a piece of glass. Osteomyelitis, the same bone disease that hampered Mickey Mantle in his knees and kept him out of the Army, set in.

The condition put a premature end to Kurowski's career in 1949 after nine years with the Cardinals. He was only thirty-one, but he couldn't throw anymore.

Beazley entered the Air Corps before the start of the 1943 season and missed three full seasons. He never regained his '42 form and won only seven games with the Cards in '46 and two the next year with the Braves.

72

In 1948 and '49, his last two seasons in the major leagues, the pitching star of 1942 didn't win a game.

The New York writers seemed to have trouble coping with the loss. Joe Williams of the *World-Telegram* started his report in the paper the next day by writing, "The capitalistic system took another kick in the pants today when the aristocratic and well-fed Yankees were forced to bend the knee to the Oakies of baseball, the under-privileged St. Louis Cardinals."

Williams wrote that the Yankees "did not have what it takes. . . . The Yankees were blown up by their own special brand of dynamite. The poor man's team from the Missouri Metropolis, little fellows who relied on little hits and their great speed, knocked the Bombers out cold with home runs."

Dan Daniel raised some eyebrows among the readers of the *Sporting News*. Daniel covered the Yankees for the *New York World-Telegram* and also wrote about the team for the *Sporting News*, the weekly baseball newspaper.

In that paper's columns he wrote what surely is one of the all-time great examples of what sportswriters and broadcasters call a "homer" article, an article favoring the home team. Daniel wrote that obviously "many of the Bombers went into the classic fighting the war and not the Cardinals. . . . The Cardinals conceivably were not bothered as yet by the wartime considerations."

Today, Walker Cooper gives a far more fundamental explanation. The Cardinals were good, he claims, and they were confident. "We could beat anybody then," he said over the phone from his home in Scottdale, Arizona. "We hardly ever lost two in a row. The Yankees were a good ball club, but we were just that much better."

As the manpower shortage worsened, the government established women's auxiliaries for the branches of the services. The first was the WAC (Women's Auxiliary Corps) of the Army, followed by the WAF (Women's Auxiliary Ferrying Command), and the branch with the longest name, the WAVES (Women Appointed for Voluntary Emergency Service) in the Navy.

There weren't any women's auxiliaries for the baseball

73

teams, although the Boston Red Sox might have wished there were. They became the first classic example of how a team's fortunes could rise or fall dramatically from one season to the next during the war simply because of how badly they were hurt, or not hurt, by military call-ups.

After their second-place finish in 1942, the Sox lost Ted Williams, Johnny Pesky, and Dom DiMaggio to the armed forces in the fall. Williams did everything that year. He won baseball's triple crown by leading the American League in hitting, home runs, and runs batted in.

Pesky had the league's second-highest batting average and the most hits and led the league's shortstops in assists. DiMaggio led the league's center fielders in putouts and assists while finishing with a .286 batting average and hitting fourteen home runs as Boston's leadoff hitter.

The Red Sox lost all of that offense and defense in one off-season. Williams became a Marine Corps fighter pilot, and Pesky and DiMaggio entered the Navy. The Red Sox plunged to seventh place in 1943 and lost twenty-five more games than in '42.

Johnny Mize joined the Navy too, and Joe DiMaggio entered the Army. Tommy Henrich, Enos Slaughter, and Johnny Beazley were also gone after '42, missing all of the next three seasons because of their military service.

Henrich enlisted in the Coast Guard during the season and was told to await notification of when to report. In the meantime, he was free to continue playing right field for the Yankees. Slaughter volunteered for duty on July 27 and was told the same thing.

Henrich was called to active duty on August 30. When the public-address announcer at Yankee Stadium informed the fans during a game against the Tigers that this would be Tommy's last time at bat before going away to war, the ovation was so thunderous that Dizzy Trout, the Detroit pitcher, refused Henrich's request to throw his first pitch.

Trout wanted Henrich to enjoy the salute, then added to the genuineness of the moment by giving Henrich nothing but fastballs, knowing Henrich's ability to murder them. Henrich got a single and was off to boot camp, lost to the Yankees for the always-critical September pennant drive and the World Series, too. The Yankees were losing more than just their starting right fielder and one of their best hitters. Henrich was a star and a leader.

Slaughter was more fortunate, and so were the Cardinals. He wasn't called to active duty until January, and so was able to stay with the team throughout its stretch drive against the Dodgers. He had the second-highest batting average in the National League that year behind Ernie Lombardi and also topped the league in hits, triples, and total bases. He finished second in runs scored and was third in slugging average and runs batted in.

In the World Series, "Country" continued to contribute significantly to his team's success. He made that game-saving throw to get Stainback in the ninth inning of the second game, singled home the all-important second run in the Cardinals' 2–0 win in the third game, scored the tying run in the fourth game, and hit a home run in the fifth game, which they won by only two runs for the championship. He also robbed Keller of a homer with a leaping catch at the fence in the seventh inning of the third game.

Would the Cardinals have won the 1942 World Series if Slaughter had been called to active duty at the same time as Henrich, or instead of Henrich? Even with the Cards' luck in retaining Slaughter's skills, would the Yankees have been able to win the Series with Henrich still in their lineup?

Baseball was important to Americans during World War II, but nobody, outside baseball or in, ever argued that it was essential. There were too many grim reminders every day in the news and those telegrams and visits by uniformed officers.

Families with members in the service proudly displayed a white satin flag with a red border and gold trim in the front windows of their homes, a blue star in the middle for each member in uniform. Those with someone who paid the last full measure of devotion took down the window flag with the blue star and sadly replaced it with one showing a gold star.

The month after the '42 World Series ended, the Sullivan family of Waterloo, Iowa, suffered one of the most devastating events in the history of American wars. The five sons of

Mr. and Mrs. Thomas Sullivan —George, 29, Francis, 26, Joseph, 23, Madison, 22, and Albert, 20—enlisted in the Navy on January 3, but only on the condition that they be allowed to serve together. The Navy granted their request.

In the fall, General MacArthur began a strategy of "island-hopping" to win back strategic Pacific islands from the Japanese one at a time. In November, the Marines invaded Guadalcanal. On November 13, during the fierce and bloody battle that followed, the Sullivan boys' ship, a new cruiser named the U.S.S. *Juneau,* was sunk.

All five sons were lost.

Part Three

1943

8

WARTIME PRIORITIES
FOR ALL OF US

Comin' in on a Wing and a Prayer,
Comin' in on a Wing and a Prayer,
Tho' there's one motor gone,
We can still carry on.
Comin' in on a Wing and a Prayer.

HAROLD ADAMSON WROTE THOSE WORDS IN 1943 FOR A MEL-
ody by Jimmy McHugh. Eddie Cantor recorded the song,
and it became one of our most uplifting, confidence-building
songs as we headed into our second full year of war and life
on the home front.

Maxene Andrews remembered the feeling on the home
front during World War II, aided by songs like Cantor's hit,
in an interview with ABC for an episode of its 1980s series
"Our World" about the year 1943. On the series, hosted by
Linda Ellerbee and Ray Gandolf, Maxene said, "It was like
having—almost having a big love affair or a big love-in, and
you'd always get the feeling that people were standing and
holding hands, encircling the whole country. There was a
marvelous, marvelous kind of unity."

A kid from New Jersey named Frank Sinatra produced his
own kind of unity. He was the latest craze among our pop
singers, employing a new style called crooning. By 1943 he
was the darling of America's teenage girls, the "bobby-

soxers," who wore white bobby socks and loafers and swooned at Sinatra's vocal renditions. When he appeared at the Paramount Theater in '43, he required more police protection from the swarming mobs than any other American entertainer of the time.

While Sinatra was becoming our newest star on records and on the stage, women were becoming our newest stars on the job. By 1943, surveys found that women were qualified for eight out of every ten jobs held solely by men before the war. Some 280,000 women were working as "government girls" in Washington. Sometimes called "G-girls" for short, they were making $1,600 a year. Two million women were working in defense jobs, building our airplanes, warships, tanks, guns, and ammunition while we sang a musical salute to them, "Rosie the Riveter."

The rapid increase of women in formerly all-male occupations did more than help to win the war. It also set in motion social changes which extend to this day. Janet Doyle, a welder during the war, told "Our World," "I feel that it was the beginning of the women's liberation movement. Maybe they didn't realize it at the time, but it was, because we showed that we could do a man's job and that there weren't that many differences."

As the major-league baseball teams prepared for spring training before the 1943 season, Bert Shepard did, too. He was playing first base for the team at Williams Field while learning to be a pilot. We joked about that recently. Only a few cadets in pilot training had flown an airplane before. A few more in those days had flown as passengers.

Bert was in an even smaller category. "Hell," he said with a laugh, "I had never even *seen* an airplane."

The war had another profound impact on major-league baseball that season. Commissioner Landis ordered the teams to train near their homes and discontinue the annual—and always popular—trip to Florida or California for six weeks of sunshine, warm temperatures, and balmy breezes.

An Associated Press story on January 5 reported that Landis drew up "a sharply defined area in which they [could]

80

do their spring training, with the understanding each club would condition at home, or as close as possible, in the interest of curtailing rail travel."

Landis laid out specific boundaries—above the Mason-Dixon Line north of the Potomac and Ohio rivers and east of the Mississippi except for the St. Louis teams, which could choose a location in Missouri.

As another part of his decision, Landis telescoped the season, cutting back the number of trips each of the sixteen teams made to the other cities in their league from four a season to three while retaining the traditional 154-game schedule. He said the total package would save five million miles of railroad travel.

Landis worked out his program with Joseph B. Eastman, director of the government's Office of Defense Transportation, and his announcement drew a rave review from Eastman, who issued a statement through the Office of War Information saying he was "greatly pleased by the action baseball has taken."

Eastman pointed out that he set no minimums because he didn't know enough about baseball to make such a decision. "In these circumstances," he said, "the action which the major leagues have taken on their own initiative is most gratifying. It shows a real and keen appreciation of the very troublesome travel problem which our country has under present war conditions, a problem which is bound to grow in difficulty and seriousness."

The teams went from the sublime to the subfreezing. The two Boston teams stayed in New England, a sacrifice for a baseball player in February and March. The Red Sox trained at Tufts College in Massachusetts, while the Braves tried to get their muscles loose at Choate Prep School in Wallingford, Connecticut. The Cubs and White Sox went to a resort in French Lick, Indiana.

Tony Cuccinello, a thirty-six-year-old infielder with the White Sox for most of 1943 and all of '44 and '45, whose body was the victim of too many collisions at second base on double plays, found a fringe benefit in the requirement to train in the North.

When we were talking about the inconveniences and

hardships of trying to get into condition in an environment of snow and ice, "Cooch" said he never felt better than when he trained with the White Sox at French Lick. He learned that there were warming, healing groundwaters under the hotel. He soaked in them in a tub in the hotel basement every day, followed by a hot shower to wash off the black dirt, then a rubdown from the trainer and a nap.

"It made me alert, rejuvenated," he said.

Certain improvisations were necessary. The Cubs and the White Sox worked out together. They did what they could to get into shape, including playing basketball in a gym. They practiced their baseball fundamentals outside on most days, in the Indiana March temperatures, and jogged at the end of each day's workout—after brushing the snow off the bridle path.

The New York teams stayed close to home, the Yankees training at Asbury Park, New Jersey, the Giants at Lakewood, New Jersey, and the Dodgers braving the temperatures at Bear Mountain near West Point.

Lou Boudreau remembers that he took his Indians to Lafayette, Indiana, home of Purdue University. He prepared his team through indoor workouts in a field house where the Boilermakers had "beautiful equipment."

The one-time kid manager remembered, "They dropped a huge net around us so we could practice the fundamentals—pickoff plays, rundowns, and so on. And we could take batting practice and not interfere with their physical-education program."

Our Washington team might have been the most patriotic, traveling only as far as the suburbs. The Senators, who were still being called the Nats most of the time, especially by headline writers who prefer the shortest name possible, trained at the University of Maryland in College Park, just across the D.C. line and only five miles out Route 1 from the center of town. Their choice of sites was another step in destiny's plan to bring Bert Shepard and me into each other's lives, and into Shirley Povich's too.

Transportation wasn't the only wartime problem that baseball was coping with for the new season. The manpower shortage was getting worse, and not just at the major-league level. The world-champion Cardinals, once the proud operators of one of baseball's mightiest farm systems, placed an ad in the *Sporting News* in February calling urgently for minor-league players.

The Associated Press said the ad was "probably without precedent in the history of baseball," describing openings on Cardinal minor-league teams for free agents with previous professional experience. The organization had lost 265 minor-league players to military service.

Two minor-league teams, the Memphis Chicks of the Southern Association and the Toledo Mud Hens of the International League, had similar ads in the same paper. The president of the Cardinals, Sam Breadon, explained the need for his ad in a masterpiece of understatement: "These are unusual times."

Breadon's fellow major-league executives could confrim his assessment. In 1943, there were 219 major-league players in military uniforms, including such new departures as Red Ruffing, the Yankee pitching star, Outfielder Taft Wright and Pitcher Ted Lyons of the White Sox, Shortstop Pee Wee Reese of the Dodgers, Pitcher Hal Schumacher of the Giants, and three key players for the Tigers—Outfielder Barney McCosky, Second Baseman Charlie Gehringer, and Catcher Birdie Tebbetts. The Indians lost two promising prospects, Catcher Jim Hegan and First Baseman Eddie Robinson.

Clark Griffith, having been badly damaged in '42 with the loss of Travis, Lewis, and Walter Masterson, fared better in '43, prompting him to remark with an ironic bit of wartime optimism, "The rest of the league is coming back to us."

Steve O'Neill, the manager of the Tigers, who saw his team's chances suffer a severe blow with the departures of McCosky, Tebbetts, and Gehringer, said, "Nobody is intimidating anybody. The two leagues are leveling off, and as we go along, the tendency toward that process will increase. . . . The top clubs will lose five players and have to take on five who are about on a level with the five the cellar team acquired to fill in."

The major leagues were suffering from not being included in a long list of occupations whose workers could be granted deferments from the draft. The government published the list in October 1942. Secretary of War Stimson announced a goal to increase the strength of the military from 4.2 million to 7.5 million men and women by the end of 1943.

In support of that goal, the commissioner of manpower, Paul McNutt, issued a list of occupations whose workers could be deferred and those which couldn't. Baseball wasn't on either list.

Instead, McNutt, maybe mindful of FDR's position on the baseball question yet still trying to support Stimson's goal, said, "The usefulness of the sport is a separate question from the 'essentiality' of individuals who play it. Thus it may well be that it is desirable that Blankville have a ball team. But Blankville may lose certain members of that team to higher priority industries—even members that might be 'essential' to winning the pennant. The pennant is not 'essential.'"

The president of the National League, Ford Frick, a former New York sportswriter, responded to McNutt's statement with one of his own: "He wants able-bodied men whose work could be done by older males or women to get into war industry or the Army. I don't believe anybody in Washington thinks the major leagues could be manned by old veterans and girls."

Branch Rickey had a similar reaction. "If Bob Hope and Fred Allen and Jack Benny and others can do a better job carrying a rifle than they are doing right now," Rickey said, "then, of course, essentiality compels them to change their jobs overnight. And if these four hundred players now classed as 3-A can do a better job for our 130 million people at anything other than playing this game this coming summer, then we want to know the way to do it and we are anxious to do it."

The movie industry as a whole did not suffer this way. The director of Selective Service, General Lewis Hershey, ruled that movie production was "an activity essential in certain instances to the national health, safety, and interest, and in other instances to war production."

Hershey ordered California's draft boards to grant deferments to "actors, directors, writers, producers, cameramen, sound engineers, and other technicians."

In Washington, the wartime atmosphere was unmistakable and becoming even more pronounced amid the sea of military uniforms, the daily hardships caused by the scarce housing, and the constant complaints about buses and streetcars that ran late as they groaned under their burdens of too many passengers.

One family was going to have a home in Washington no matter what happened—the Roosevelts. The government built an air-raid shelter for President Roosevelt underground at the east end of the White House grounds. The layout included a backup Oval Office.

The Washington office shortage was as severe as the housing shortage. "Tempos," those eyesores that marred Washington's beauty in World War I, were imposed on our landscape again. They were "temporary" office buildings, some still standing and in use from World War I. Twenty-seven new ones were built in less than a year at a cost of $850,000 each, providing more than three million square feet of critically needed office space but lacking air-conditioning for Washington's hot and sticky summers.

The ugly things plagued downtown Washington's appearance for the next thirty years, giving rise to the truism that, "In Washington there is nothing so permanent as a tempo."

They lasted through the end of World War II, the Berlin airlift, the Korean War, and almost all of the Vietnam War until they were demolished during the Nixon administration. There was widespread rejoicing as Washington's scenery, especially the Mall between the Washington Monument and the Lincoln Memorial, was made beautiful again.

Tempos didn't solve Washington's space crisis, so the federal government began a program of relocating various agencies. The Patent Office was moved to Richmond, Virginia; the Rural Electrification Administration was transferred to St. Louis; and the Farm Credit Administration went to Kansas City. Parts of the Civil Service Commission, what today is the Office of Personnel Management, were moved to Raleigh, North Carolina, and several elements of the Social Security Administration went to Newark, New Jersey. The Army's personnel records and the massive amount of paperwork and personnel who accompany them were moved to St. Louis.

The weapons of war were all around us as we kids were growing up. Antiaircraft guns, painted brown, stood in some of Washington's parks, silent but effective reminders that while we were at play, our nation was at war. On the roof of the Capitol Building there were fake wooden guns and wooden soldiers, presumably to scare off any enemy planes before they dropped their bombs on us.

Blood for surgery and other forms of medical treatment was in shorter supply than ever. One ad in the *Washington Post* on August 1, 1943, said:

WE CAN'T LET HIM DOWN NOW!
YOUR BLOOD WILL HELP!

The ad was not from the Red Cross. It was from Milstone's Liquor Store on Pennsylvania Avenue.

We saw propaganda posters everywhere—in our schools, in office buildings, on the streetcars and buses, on billboards. They encouraged Americans not to miss any time from work, not to reveal anything about their jobs that might aid the enemy, to buy war bonds and stamps to support the war effort, and to avoid traveling when we didn't have to.

We were used to the posters, the billboards, and their slogans:

A SLIP OF THE LIP MAY SINK A SHIP
BUY BONDS TODAY
IS THIS TRIP NECESSARY?

The one that made the most profound impression on a kid who wasn't even a teenager yet showed a sinking American ship, its bow pointing into the air and the rest of its hull submerged already, with a caption below in the murky waters that said in a chilling reminder:

SOMEBODY TALKED!

In Detroit, the Tigers were headed for a fifth-place finish, which is no cause for a team's fans to rejoice, but their followers were thrilled instead by the individual exploits of their players. Dick Wakefield, with a bonus of $52,000, the highest in history, proved his worth in his first full season by leading the league in hits and finishing with the second-highest batting average, behind only the veteran Luke Appling, the Hall of Fame shortstop of the Chicago White Sox.

Rudy York led the league in home runs, runs batted in, and total bases. The Tiger pitchers were among the league leaders in almost every department. Dizzy Trout was fourth in winning percentage, Tommy Bridges and Trout were three and four in earned run average, Trout tied Spud Chandler of the Yankees for the most wins with twenty, Hal Newhouser, Virgil "Fire" Trucks, and Bridges were in the top five in strikeouts, and Trout tied for third in complete games and tied for first in shutouts and second in games pitched.

Despite all of those individual numbers, Detroit finished behind New York, the surprising Washington Nats in second place, and the Cleveland Indians and Chicago White Sox, who were third and fourth respectively.

The biggest story in Detroit that summer was not about baseball. It was an enormous tragedy spawned by racial tensions, which were on the rise in many American cities that summer, the same tensions that led to demonstrations in Washington against the Capital Transit Company for failing to hire black bus drivers and streetcar operators. Detroit became both the flash point and the focal point for this story.

On June 20, a Sunday when the temperature reached into the nineties, a large number of black workers and their families spent the day picnicking on Belle Isle, a parklike island covering a thousand acres in the Detroit River. Many of them were residents of a ghetto neighborhood ironically called Paradise Valley, where they were forced to use outdoor toilets and were faced with other hardships and ignominies.

As the group walked home across the bridge connecting the island with shore, something happened. To this day nobody knows for sure what it was. Some said later that maybe some of the teenagers in the crowd of blacks bumped a white sailor and his girl on the bridge.

Whatever the cause, a scuffle broke out, and the fight immediately became a full-scale race riot that spread to the north and east sides of the city. The rioting continued into the next day, when ten thousand white people formed a mob and roamed up and down Woodward Avenue, the city's main thoroughfare, beating up any blacks in sight.

The toll in human and dollar terms was staggering. Thirty-four people were killed, twenty-five of them black. Eight hundred were injured. Police arrested five hundred persons. Damage was estimated at two million dollars. Officials calculated the loss in productivity at two million man-hours.

Riots also occurred that summer in Beaumont, Texas, another city where martial law had to be declared, and in Los Angeles, where the outbreak was the worst in a generation. There was a "hate strike" in Mobile, Alabama. Tense moments developed in the Philadelphia suburb of Chester, Pennsylvania, and in New York City's Harlem.

In the middle of the long, hot summer of 1943, the first nighttime All-Star Game in history was played, only ten years after the tradition was started by sports editor Arch Ward in Chicago. Shibe Park in Philadelphia, the home of the A's and Phillies, was the setting. The game was the first to be broadcast to our troops overseas by shortwave radio.

Vince DiMaggio of the Pittsburgh Pirates was the hitting star with a single, triple, and home run for the National League, and Cincinnati's Johnny Vander Meer, destined for military service after the season, tied an all-star record with six strikeouts, but their team lost, 5–3. Bobby Doerr of the Red Sox, a future Hall of Famer who was also destined for duty in the armed forces in the Pacific, hit a three-run homer in the second inning that was enough to carry the American League to victory.

The manpower shortage was affecting the Brooklyn Dodgers so much that Leo Durocher tried a comeback. After breaking in with the Yankees as a teammate of Babe Ruth and Lou Gehrig in 1925, the thirty-eight-year-old Durocher played six games at shortstop before conceding the job to Arky Vaughan. The Dodgers called up an eighteen-year-old fireballer named Rex Barney and a first baseman who was ineligible for the draft because he was too tall—Howie Schultz, six feet, six and a half inches.

None of this helped. The Dodgers finished third, twenty-three and a half games behind the Cardinals, who won their second straight National League pennant.

Mickey Owen said recently that Durocher was a different kind of manager during the war because he realized the shortcomings caused by the manpower shortage. Durocher, Mickey told me, was "more patient" during the war, realizing that his players were not always the most talented or most experienced. He also placed more emphasis on teaching, using two of his coaches, Charlie Dressen and Freddie Fitzsimmons, as instructors.

The war's impact was reflected in the American League standings, too. The Yankees won again, setting up a return match against the Cardinals in the World Series, but it wasn't close in their league, which was never a surprise where the Yankees were concerned. What was a surprise, however, was the identity of the second-place team—Washington.

The Yankees finished 13½ games ahead of Washington, but there the Nats were, ahead of the league's other teams. They got there with Mickey Vernon, George Case, Gerry Priddy, and Stan Spence leading their offense and a pitching staff that included a future Hall of Famer, Early Wynn, who won eighteen games, and four eleven-game winners—Dutch Leonard, Milo Candini, Mickey Haefner, and Alex Carrasquel.

Washington's Clark Griffith was being proved right. The rest of the American League was dropping back to his team's level of play. It was a strange development, but then strange developments were becoming a way of life for all of us.

There was deepening concern that the war would continue and baseball would simply run out of men to play the game. Out of that came something called the All-American Girls Professional Baseball League, encouraged by Phil Wrigley of the chewing gum family, owners of the Chicago Cubs. The league, formed in 1943, was composed mainly of smaller cities in the Midwest like Battle Creek, South Bend, Kenosha, and Rockport, 450 of them. Some of the teams had former Major League stars as their managers, including two future Hall of Famers, Max Carey and Jimmie Foxx. The league outlasted the war, operating through 1954. Some observers now refer to the players from that unique undertaking as "the girls of summer."

9

NEW PLAYERS
AND NEW PILOTS

BASEBALL FANS WERE LEARNING THAT THEIR SPORT COULD help them forget race riots as well as a war, and the cast of characters was changing. In fact, even the ball was changing.

As early as the first war year, Joe DiMaggio noticed a difference in the ball and its reaction when hit hard. He points out today that his average dropped fifty-two points in 1942, and that Ted Williams lost an even fifty points from 1941. DiMag blames such sharp drops on "the simple reason that they didn't have that good wool in the ball."

DiMaggio and Bobby Doerr of the Red Sox, another Hall of Famer, talked about the strange and frustrating change on ESPN's "Major League Baseball Magazine" in 1987. Doerr confirmed Joe's memory: "I remember hitting some balls . . . when I thought, 'Man, that's as good a ball as you'll hit,' and you thought it was out of the ballpark. Then the outfielder would go back to the wall and pretty soon he'd take three or four steps in and catch the fly ball."

For the 1943 season, with strategic materials such as rubber no longer available, the baseball itself was becoming a scarce item. The Spalding Company came to the rescue, or so it thought, by developing something called the "balata ball" for use in the major leagues.

The Spalding substitute was a combination of nonstrategic materials including balata, a substance obtained from the milk of tropical trees. But the experiment went over like, well, a lead ball.

Frank McCormick of the Cincinnati Reds, with 488 extra-base hits in his career, could hit a ball as far as anyone, but not the balata ball. He remembered after the war, "It was like hitting a piece of concrete. It reminded me of when I was a kid. I used to practice by hitting stones."

Mickey Owen of the Dodgers said the balata ball was "the biggest thing I remember about wartime baseball. You'd have to hit it twice to get it out of Ebbets Field."

Warren Giles, the president of the National League in later years, said he suspected someone was using "ground up bologna." The problem was solved shortly thereafter when researchers developed synthetic rubber.

Adjustments were starting to be made to allow for the difference in playing talent. "You had to work with the pitchers harder," Owen said, "because they weren't as experienced and didn't have the control that the prewar pitchers had."

One of Owen's fellow catchers, Hall of Famer Rick Ferrell, agreed. His instructions to his pitchers were basic: "Let's just don't walk anybody."

Lou Boudreau, in only the second season of his managerial career, was aware of changes he had to make in his handling of players. "There was a lot of shifting about with the manpower shortage," he said.

Did he manage differently?

"No, but there were certain things you couldn't do. You couldn't press their ability. You had to be more patient."

Johnny "Specs" Podgajny was one of names we were reading about now. He was a right-handed pitcher for the Phillies at the start of the war and was traded to the Pirates on June 15, 1943, for another pitcher named Dutch Dietz.

Podgajny turned twenty-three five days before he was

traded. He entered the service after '43 and returned in '46 to pitch only nine innings in six games. Over his career, he won only twenty games in five years, but he led the league in one department—temper.

Specs appeared in 115 games and seemed to get thrown out of most of them. When he blew his stack, he played no favorites. Even his teammates were vulnerable to attack.

"I remember one time when I was with the Phillies and we were playing the Cubs at Wrigley Field," he said after he retired as a player. "I got myself in a jam, and Merrill May, our third baseman, walked over to me and said something about not giving up.

"I misunderstood him, because I thought he said I *was* giving up and not giving my best. Anyway, I grabbed him by the neck and was ready to work him over until some of the guys separated us. May was the most surprised guy on the field. And I felt pretty silly."

That same candor allowed Podgajny to tell another story which explained why he turned down an offer to become a scout after his playing days were over. "I would have taken the job," he said, "but I realized I wasn't much of a judge of talent. I once said Stan Musial would never be a hitter, and I also said Bob Lemon would never be a pitcher."

Some of the strangest things in baseball were happening in Washington, maybe because the war influenced everything there more than it did anywhere else. In one of the strangest cases, an infielder for the Senators was the owner's son.

Sherry Robertson was Clark Griffith's adopted son and a decent minor-league ball player when Griff surprised the Washington press corps by announcing in 1940, "I've just bought Sherrard Robertson because I've changed my mind about him. I've decided he's going to be a ball player after all."

Sherry was a member of a unique baseball family. Griffith was his uncle, and Robertson and his six brothers and sisters were raised by Griff when their father, Jimmy Robertson, Griffith's partner, died at an early age. Griffith formally adopted two of them and gave them his name: Calvin Griffith—who succeeded the senior Griffith as the head of the Senators and then moved the team to Minnesota to become the Twins—and Calvin's sister, Thelma.

The baseball atmosphere in the family became even stronger when Thelma married one of Washington's pitchers, Joe Haynes, and another sister, Mildred, married Joe Cronin, the Boston Red Sox shortstop, field manager, general manager, and later American League president.

Griffith brought Robertson up to the majors from the team's farm club at Charlotte, North Carolina, in time to appear in ten games in 1940. He was back in the minors in '41, coming up for only one game, but in '43 he was able to make it to the bigs for fifty-nine games as a substitute third baseman behind Ellis Clary.

When he was killed in an automobile accident in 1970 at the age of fifty-one, one obituary recalled, "He probably was the most booed player in the Senators' history, starting in 1940. . . . The fans never let him forget he was the nephew of the club owner. Surprisingly, Robertson held up well under the boo barrage."

He was a nice guy to us kids, always willing to talk and give us his autograph. His attitude on his strange situation showed his class. "I guess it's the fans' privilege if they want to jeer me," he said. "I really wish my uncle would trade me. I know I could do better with another club. Whenever I have a bad day, I know the fans will bring up that uncle business."

Shirley Povich came to Robertson's defense in his *Washington Post* column, urging the fans, "Holy smoke, give the guy a break. He can't pick his relatives."

It didn't help any when Robertson made a wild throw over First Baseman Mickey Vernon's head that was so high it sailed into the stands and struck a fan in the head. The man walked out of Griffith Stadium under his own power a few minutes later, went to the emergency room at Garfield Hospital only a few blocks away—and died overnight.

Robertson never was a real success in the majors, but he lasted ten seasons with a .230 career average. Griffith relented and sold him in 1952 to his friend Connie Mack of the Philadelphia A's, who expressed an interest in Robertson several times. By then it was too late in his career to help him. He finished the season with the A's, hit an even .200, and was gone from the majors after that.

Robertson went into the Navy following the '43 season, and strangely enough, that's where he achieved his greatest baseball success, and against major-league competition at that. He was stationed in Hawaii, and he was one of the stars against fellow sailors like Johnny Mize, Schoolboy Rowe, Dom DiMaggio, Phil Rizzuto, Fred Hutchinson, Walter Masterson, Rollie Hemsley, Ferris Fain and Hugh Casey.

Hutchinson, a veteran of twenty-three years in the major leagues as a manager and a pitcher with ninety-five wins before and after the war, knew talent when he saw it. "I always thought," he said in later years, "that Robertson was going to develop into a great ball player. He wore the pitchers out in the service, and I figured Washington was lucky to have him. I know Detroit tried to get him a few times. It always puzzled me that he didn't make it."

Bobby Estalella was making a name for himself with the Nats in 1942 and the A's in '43. He was one of Clark Griffith's Cuban imports, and his is one of wartime baseball's most intriguing stories.

Griffith's main scout in the minor leagues, Joe Cambria, began mining the sugar fields of Cuba and the other fertile lands of Central and South America years before the war started. People laughed at Griffith, accusing him of avoiding the expense of operating a big-time minor-league system and trying instead to sign Cubans as cheap labor.

Whatever his reasons, history shows that Griffith was decades ahead of his time. Since the 1960s, many of baseball's brightest stars have been Hispanic—Roberto Clemente, Luis Aparicio, Pedro Guerrero, Fernando Valenzuela, and a long list of others.

Griffith was the one who pioneered the entrance of Hispanic stars into major leagues, and his first pride and joy was Estalella.

Estalella had the ability to put people in Griffith Stadium's seats with home runs over the left-field wall, something few major leaguers could do consistently because of the distance involved—405 feet down the foul line. It helped Griffith's gate receipts even more that his squat little third baseman–outfielder had a storybook beginning in baseball.

Estalella looked more like a fireplug than a ball player, only five feet six inches tall and 185 pounds. But his name was a variation of "little star" in Spanish, and when Cambria spotted him in Cuba, that's what he saw in Estalella's future, and Washington's.

He was from Cardenas and was twenty-four years old when Cambria discovered him playing baseball in his bare feet on a sugar plantation outside Havana. It cost the Griffith organization the princely sum of seventy-five dollars to get Estalella's name on a contract, what with steamship fare to the mainland and hotel bills. In the discussions that led to the contract, Estalella needed an interpreter. He spoke no English.

Actually, the cost to Griffith was higher than the papers reported. Another Washington scout, Ed Liberatore, who has spent a lifetime in baseball as a scout and adviser to the Dodgers and Reds and now the Orioles, was with Cambria when they met Estalella in Baltimore to escort him on the last leg of his trip to Washington for his debut in the major leagues.

Liberatore told Cambria that their new prospect was hungry and needed meal money. Cambria cheerfully gave him fifteen cents—and told Estalella, seriously, "Don't eat too much." Fifty-five years later, Liberatore still remembers Estalella's "meal"—a milkshake for ten cents and a pack of peanut butter crackers for the remaining nickel.

Shirley Povich described Estalella's appearance and the reaction of the five thousand fans at Griffith Stadium when they saw their new third baseman for the first time, on September 7, 1935: "They laughed when he jogged on the field. . . . He was funny looking . . . his underslung chassis conveyed by a bow-legged duck-waddle that made his appearance even more ludicrous. . . . The 5,000 fans in the stands made no attempt to suppress their mirth."

Povich also mentioned that this unlikely looking third baseman had "forearms that would make a sissy out of Tarzan." Those forearms helped him lead the New York–

Pennsylvania League in home runs and hit .320, and on that September afternoon in Washington, they helped him again.

Against the St. Louis Browns, he doubled over Ray Pepper's head to the left-field wall and hit two other screaming shots right at Pepper, all right there in front of no less a figure than the ambassador from Cuba himself. Estalella still wasn't a household name, though. While he hadn't learned much English, the *Washington Post's* headline writer hadn't learned much Spanish—and misspelled Estalella's name in the headline the next morning.

As a third baseman, he was a joke, and everyone knew it, but those forearms saved him from time to time. He had difficulty with grounders of either kind, hard-hit smashes or slow rollers. But his arm was strong enough to get the runner at first even if he muffed the ground ball at the start of the play.

"If there's a stronger arm in the American League," Povich wrote in his column, "This Morning with Shirley Povich," the next spring, "it belongs to Jimmie Foxx." As for Estalella's power at the plate, Povich described a ball he hit in Philadelphia, one of his two homers in fifteen games with Washington the September before: "The home run that he socked over both decks of the Shibe Park grandstand last year was a feat that no other Washington player has ever approached."

Still, his fielding and batting averages looked too much alike after fifteen games in '35 and thirteen in '36, and he dropped back to the minor leagues until being called up in '39. His ups and downs continued with another year in the minors in 1940, a one-year trade to the Browns in '41 for only forty-six games, and then a far more successful season in Washington in 1942 as a draft-exempt player in baseball's first wartime season.

Estalella got to play in 133 games back with the Nats that year and hit eight home runs, plus twenty-four doubles and five triples. His batting average was .277, his highest since his rookie season. His bat wasn't able to change things for Washington, however, and the Nats finished seventh again, ahead of only the A's.

After that, he was gone from Washington for good. Griffith's friend Connie Mack remembered that home run over everything in Shibe Park in '35 and made another of his many trades with his friend in Washington.

During the 1943 spring-training season, Mack obtained Estalella from the Senators, and Bobby could feel complimented in the price Mack paid to get him. The A's sent the Senators "Indian Bob" Johnson, who was thirty-six years old by then but had been a home-run star with the A's for ten seasons, hitting 252 home runs. With the new wartime economy, the price for Bobby Estalella had gone up. Now he was just what his name said, a "little star."

He lasted through the end of the war with the A's, hitting eleven home runs in 1943 but only seven and eight in the two seasons that followed. He was hitting for average even better than for distance, with marks of .298 and. 299 as a starter in '44 and '45.

After '45, now thirty-four years old and with the stars marching home from the war, Estalella dropped out of the majors again. He resurfaced briefly four years later, playing in eight games with the A's in 1949, and getting only five hits in twenty times at bat, all singles.

Even so, the man they laughed at in Washington in 1935 could point to nine years in the major leagues, forty-four home runs, and a career that he might not have dreamed possible when he was a kid playing baseball in his bare feet.

Another colorful Cuban in the war years was Roberto Ortiz, one of Estalella's teammates in Washington.

Ortiz was the exact opposite of Estalella. By Cuban standards he was a giant of a man—six four and two hundred pounds. He could pitch, play the outfield, and hit home runs. He had a brother, "Baby," another six-footer, who was Roberto's teammate on the Senators for one year during the war, started two games, lost them both, and was never heard from again.

Roberto's story was different, and so was Roberto himself. He was another Joe Cambria product who came up through the Washington farm system. The Cuban players were frequently lonely, their different culture and the language barrier separating them from their teammates. But Ortiz had a friend who helped him through his lonely days on the Senators' minor-league team at Charlotte, North Carolina.

His constant companion there was a yellow dog named Yellow Dog. Ortiz gave him that name because he thought it suited the dog perfectly, and no one could argue the point.

Unlike his master, Yellow Dog was something of a runt. He was skinny, too, the result of living a scavenger's life around the Charlotte ballpark on Magnolia Avenue, scrounging for whatever scraps he could find—until he met his master.

Home for Ortiz wasn't a whole lot better. He had a cramped apartment under the left-field bleachers. Yellow Dog slept at his door. When the ball player walked to a nearby diner for his meals—which were always hamburgers because the only words he knew were *hamburger* and *hello*—he always saved a bite or two for Yellow Dog.

Three times a day the two ate hamburger, Ortiz at the diner and Yellow Dog on their way home.

As they say in sports, the two were friends on the field and off. At the end of his turn in the cage during batting practice, Ortiz would run the bases. Yellow Dog, with ears that flapped in the wind, ran right behind him. Ortiz, the gentle giant when he was in Yellow Dog's company, taught his dog to tag the bases and even how to slide. Columnist Herman Helms once wrote, "The sight of that little mutt turning his fanny toward the base and doing a rolling slide into it broke up the players on the Charlotte team."

Yellow Dog was confined to quarters during games, sleeping in their apartment under the bleachers while his master hit home runs and earned growing respect around the Piedmont League, but one day the inevitable finally happened.

After one of Roberto's long drives hit the left-field fence, he was racing around the bases trying for all he could get, maybe a triple. All of a sudden, there was Yellow Dog, too. He had escaped from the apartment earlier without being noticed and was somewhere in the vicinity when Ortiz began to circle the bases in the routine that Yellow Dog knew so well.

Columnist Helms wrote in later years that as Ortiz rounded second base, so did Yellow Dog. As the throw came into third, the ball player slid into the bag, and so did the dog. Ortiz barely beat his dog to the bag. The umpire gave the safe sign—twice.

The official scorer that day, who was either burdened by a scrupulous conscience or blessed with a refreshing sense of humor, wrote Yellow Dog's name into the box score for the game, with an X beside it and this notation below, "Ran with Ortiz in 9th inning."

The box score in the paper the next day carried Yellow Dog's name and the information that he ran in the ninth inning, making him the only dog who ever got his name in a baseball box score.

Ortiz made it to the majors with Washington in 1941 but played in only twenty-two games that season and twenty the next, hitting only one home run each year. In 1943, he made it up from the minors for only one game with the Senators, but he was able to hang around for eighty-five games in '44.

Like Estalella, he vanished from the majors with the return of the stars in '46, playing instead in the new Mexican League. Also like Bobby, he made it back briefly at the end of the forties, when Commissioner Happy Chandler granted amnesty to those who had jumped to the Mexican League after Chandler prohibited their participation.

Ortiz played part-time in '49 with Washington and again in '50, when he divided his season between playing for Clark Griffith and then for Griffith's friend Connie Mack in Philadelphia.

As a pitcher, he could throw hard, but that was all. At the plate, he could hit the long ball, but not often. In 659 at bats in his major-league career, he hit only eight home runs. His most commendable achievement may have occurred in a fight instead of as a result of his baseball skills.

When Tom Turner of the St. Louis Browns got into a heated argument with little Mike Guerra, one of Ortiz's fellow Cubans on the Senators, a brawl was threatened, one that surely would be a mismatch. Turner was five inches taller than Guerra and outweighed him by sixty pounds.

Shirley Povich described Turner as a "big Cuban-baiting catcher," and Ortiz obviously felt the same way. He rushed into the confrontation, hollered at Turner, "You no fight Mike—you fight me," and then, in Povich's words, "beat the daylights out of him."

It was more than a favor to Guerra. It was a service to all Cuban players. Their big man was putting the whole league on notice that Cuban players were not to be messed with, because if they were, they were willing to fight.

For the rest of his career, Ortiz had the respect of his fellow Cuban players—and those nice memories of his friend Yellow Dog.

The Cuban players weren't the only newcomers attracting attention as the war reached its midpoint, not even in Washington. The Yankees and Senators made a deal in January that sent Pitcher Bill Zuber and $10,000 to New York in exchange for Second Baseman Gerry Priddy and another pitcher, a rookie right-hander named Milo Candini.

Priddy became a solid starter for Washington, but Candini became a sensation. After a minor-league apprenticeship that included service in El Paso, Norfolk, Waxahachie, Binghamton, Oakland, and Kansas City, Candini made it to the Yankees' top farm team, the Newark Bears in the International League, in '42. But he came down with a sore arm caused by adhesions near the shoulder and won only four games.

When the Yankees and Nats made their deal, it was in reality a Zuber-for-Priddy exchange. Candini was a throw-in to sweeten the pot for Griffith.

During spring training and the first two months of the season, the Senators' manager, Ossie Bluege, was unsure what to do with his sore-armed prospect. To the rescue came the Senators' trainer, another old Griffith pal, Mike Martin. He worked on Candini's arm every day, and by June the rookie was ready to pitch. After a couple of relief appearances—he was the winning pitcher in both—Candini became a starting pitcher in Bluege's rotation.

With that, Candini reeled off five more wins, telling reporters, "My arm never felt better in my life. If I get licked, it's my own fault." It was a career year for Candini. His seven straight wins propelled him to an 11–7 season, the most games he ever won in an eight-year career that lasted through his 1951 season with the Phillies.

Trainer Martin got his own reward—a new suit from Griffith.

Neither league had a close pennant race—for either the top spot or the bottom. While the Cardinals were winning their second straight National League championship, the Giants were finishing last, 49½ games out of first place and 8½ behind the seventh-place Phillies.

The American League had even more space at the top and bottom. While the Yankees were winning the title by 13½ games over the Senators, the A's were 49 games behind first place—and 20 games out of seventh.

In the World Series, the Yankees went about the business of getting revenge against the Cardinals in a professional, workmanlike manner. The teams played the first three games in New York that year and were scheduled to play all the remaining games in St. Louis, baseball's way of again cutting down on unnecessary travel. Until 1943, the traditional schedule was to play the first two games in one city, the next three in the other city, and then return to the first city for the rest of the Series.

The Yankees won the first game, 4–2, at Yankee Stadium, lost the next day, and then won three in a row. The Series was not without its moments, though, and the decisive moment came in the third game and involved Whitey Kurowski of the Cardinals and Johnny Lindell of the Yankees.

With the Cardinals leading, 2–1, in the eighth inning and the Series tied at one victory each, Al Brazle was in command with a three-hitter, maintaining the upper hand over the ace Yankee right-hander, Hank Borowy. Then things began to happen, when Lindell singled and went to second after Harry "The Hat" Walker juggled the ball while picking it up in center field.

Joe McCarthy, New York's manager, sent George "Snuffy" Stirnweiss up to the plate to pinch hit for Borowy. Stirnweiss bunted to Ray Sanders at first base, who threw across the diamond to Kurowski in an attempt to get Lindell at third.

As Kurowski went to apply the tag, Lindell came crashing

into him. Kurowski dropped the ball, and Lindell was safe. But still no damage was done when Tuck Stainback flied out to Danny Litwhiler in left as Lindell held at third and Stirnweiss scooted down to second.

Southworth ordered Brazle to walk Shortstop Frankie Crosetti intentionally. Then Billy Johnson, New York's third baseman, playing in his first World Series, tripled to clear the bases and lead the Yankees to a five-run rally. The game was over and so, some thought, was the World Series. The Cardinals never recovered.

The next two games were close enough, victories of 2–1 and 2–0 for the Yankees, but the Yankees gained revenge for their upset loss to the Cardinals the year before.

Kurowski still remembers the Lindell play. "He came in pretty high," he said when we were reliving the Series, "more like a body block." He said Lindell and the ball arrived at third base at the same time. "If the ball had gotten there a split second sooner," he said, "the whole thing might have been avoided."

Was it a dirty play by Lindell? The first word of Whitey's response was drawn out—"Weelll, I don't know if it was or not. He came in high. That was just his way of sliding."

The memory of that play lingers with other Cardinals, too. When we were talking about it not long ago, I asked Walker Cooper if he still remembered it. "Oh, Lord yes," he said.

Did he think Lindell went into Kurowski harder than necessary?

"I know he did—but he got results."

Did the Cardinal players hold it against Lindell for the rest of the Series?

"No. That's just baseball. You play hard."

The biggest story to come out of that Series, in addition to New York's success, wasn't a fight. It was the inspiring performance by the "brother battery" of the Cardinals, Pitcher Morton Cooper and his brother and catcher, Walker, in the second game.

The Cooper brothers were Missouri boys from the rural town of Atherton, near Independence and across the state from St. Louis. Mort was two years older—thirty in 1943—and made it to the team of the brothers' dreams, the Cardinals, in 1938. Walker, right on schedule, made it two years later.

Individually and together they were stars. Mort was a major-league pitcher for eleven seasons, the National League's Most Valuable Player in '42 with his league-leading 22 victories and the league's best again in '43 with 21 wins. In all, he won 128 games.

Walker was a star for eighteen seasons, served in the Navy in 1945, hit 173 home runs, finished with a lifetime batting average of .285, and was especially tough in the World Series with an even .300 average for three of them. On defense he was widely recognized as one of the most intelligent and capable catchers in baseball.

His power popped the eyes of Tommy Holmes, the Braves' center fielder, when "Coop" hit a home run over the center-field fence in Braves Field, against the wind on a drizzly night when the air was heavy. It was a grand slam—in two ways. Cooper's homer cleared the loaded bases, but it also came on a swing that broke his bat apart in three pieces.

The Coopers' most memorable moment as the "brother battery" moved a nation. It happened in that second game of the '43 Series. Their father, a rural mail carrier for thirty-nine years and a pitcher himself when he was young, died that morning.

"Dad used to sit on the floor to put his shoes on," Walker was recalling for me. That's what he was doing when he suffered a heart attack that morning. "He just fell over while putting his shoes on," he said.

Their brother Robert called the Cardinals' hotel in New York and got hold of their manager, Billy Southworth, who broke the news to Walker. Then the two wondered whether to tell Mort before or after the game.

Together they decided they should tell him before. After they did, the brothers had to decide whether to catch the first plane back to St. Louis or stay for the game. They decided to stay, with Mort saying, "I think that's the way Dad would want it."

103

There was no talk between the brothers before or during the game about winning one for their father. Instead, they put on a workmanlike performance. With Walker calling the pitches, Mort pitched a six-hitter and defeated the Yankees, 4–3, the only St. Louis victory.

In the dressing room after the game, Walker said, "We gave that one to Dad."

A new name and an old one were the batting champions in 1943, Stan Musial in the National League and Luke Appling for the second time in the American. But an outfielder for the Chicago Cubs was winning increasing recognition as one of the stars of wartime baseball.

He was Bill Nicholson, and he played right field for the Cubs. He won the nickname Swish from the Wrigley Field faithful because that's what they yelled when he took his patented from-the-heels swings. The Cubs didn't do much that year. They finished in fifth place under Jimmie Wilson with seventy-four wins and seventy-nine defeats, but Nicholson provided enough entertainment for Cub fans.

As a six-foot, 205-pound left-handed hitter, he led the league with 29 home runs and 128 runs batted in, while also hitting .309, seventh highest in the league. He was second in total bases behind only Musial.

Johnny Cooney, who started his major-league career only three years after World War I, was still playing in the big leagues during World War II. After Nicholson's year in '43, Cooney, by then forty-two years old and playing for the Dodgers, offered a reason for Swish's success.

Cooney was talking to another senior citizen, Paul Derringer, thirty-eight years old and pitching for the Cubs after spending most of his career with the Reds. "Nicholson is the most determined player in the game," Cooney told Derringer. "He may have had some faults when he was breaking in, but he has worked hard to cure them. He's out there practicing fielding ground balls when the pitchers take their batting practice long before the game starts."

He got no argument from Derringer, who was able to appreciate Nicholson's 1943 performance because it helped him to win ten games and save three others for the Cubs. "He gets his base hits, knocks in a lot of runs, and hits plenty of homers," Derringer said. "He just gets out there and plays a great game—and never yet has said 'boo' to an umpire."

Casey Stengel may have paid the highest compliment of all to Nicholson. Stengel was managing the Braves that year, and before one of the Braves-Cubs games he came out of the Boston dugout and went over to Jimmie Wilson, pointed to Nicholson in right field, and said, "Take that guy out of there."

When the blank expression on Wilson's face showed he didn't have the vaguest idea what Casey was talking about, Stengel went on: "Take him out and I'll let you play two men in his place, and I'll agree to use only eight men against your ten. Just take him out."

Two years later, other National League managers were ready to suggest the same thing, and so was Detroit's Steve O'Neill in the 1945 World Series.

Mary Carolan Kunovit was in charge of the hostesses who provided companionship for servicemen at Macy's department store in New York during the war. When she was interviewed by ABC's "Our World" in 1986, she remembered that 1943 was one of the most active, eventful years of the war, and that women were right in the thick of it.

"When I retired," she said, "I was sure I was going to write a book. . . . I was going to have the title *We Fought Too,* because, believe me, in our own way, we did. Nineteen forty-three—it was a busy year. It was right in the middle of everything."

It was a busy year for Bert Shepard, too—now Lieutenant Shepard, P-38 pilot. He completed his flying training and got his silver wings and gold bars, then passed the Christmas season in a way he still remembers—a Christmas Eve bus ride from Chandler Air Force Base, Arizona, to Los Angeles, a four-day ride on a troop train to New York, and two weeks on a troop ship, the *Aquatania.* Several thousand officers and enlisted men were crammed aboard the World War I transport ship when it left Pier 88 in zero temperatures and steamed across the North Atlantic alone weaving a zigzag course to dodge the German submarines.

105

Shepard was destined for the European theater of operations—the E.T.O.—but he and his fellow flyers were issued tropical gear. "It was to throw the enemy off," he remembers. "The Army always took every precaution against word leaking to the enemy. We knew where we were going and that we didn't need that tropical gear we were carrying, but we didn't want the enemy to know it."

What was the mood aboard ship? Was everybody scared stiff? "Not at all," Bert says today. "We wanted to get over there and get into the action so we could get everything over with. I figured the sooner we could end this thing the sooner I'd be back playing baseball."

As Shepard prepared for his service as the pilot of our new and fast bomber with a double fuselage, another pilot—this one fictitious—was becoming a national hero. He was the product of songwriters Mack David and Vee Lawnhurst.

David's words told the story of a boy who was ridiculed in school because he got too many zeroes on his tests, but when he grew up and started collecting another kind of zero—Japan's most famous kind of warplane—his standing among his friends soared just like his fighter plane:

> The kids all called him Johnny Zero.
> In school they always used to say,
> "Johnny got a zero, Johnny got a zero.
> Johnny got a zero today."
>
> The kids all laughed at Johnny Zero
> And they would tease him when they'd play,
> "Johnny got a zero, Johnny got a zero.
> Johnny got a zero today."
>
> He couldn't concentrate on studies,
> His mind was always in the sky.
> When he grew up he left his buddies
> And Johnny learned how to fly.

Now they still call him Johnny Zero
And all the pilots proudly say,
"Johnny got a zero,
He got another zero,
Johnny got a zero, hooray!
Johnny Zero is a hero today."

It was a bittersweet year. American fathers, sons, husbands, and boyfriends were being killed in massive numbers in strange waters and faroff places we'd never heard of before. But we had held our own through 1942, and in '43 we were beginning to win. We began to believe in ourselves.

Ray Gandolf of ABC News and I were about the same age—twelve—in 1943. He remembers the effect that the war years had on us as a people, that we became united in more than just our country's name and seemed to mature together in what was, after all, the most maturing kind of experience life has to offer. On "Our World," he remembered that we seemed to grow up in 1943, as a nation of people and as the kids he and I were:

It was a profoundly lonely time. Every person had his own thoughts, his own fears. What the war effort did was let us bury that in a common purpose. It energized us, made doers of us all. It was not a good way to grow up, but it worked.

Luke Appling's wife offered a reason for optimism when her husband left for the service after the '43 season. Mrs. Appling could have expressed the sorrow of it all, that her Luke was going away to war just after winning the championship. Instead she gave all Americans reason for hope.

"The war will soon be over," she predicted, "because outside of baseball, Luke never held a job for over two weeks."

Part Four

1944

10

OPENING DAYS

FOR BERT SHEPARD, THERE WERE TWO OPENING DAYS TO THE 1944 baseball season—the one he read about in *Stars and Stripes,* the daily GI newspaper, reporting the major-league season beginning back in the States, and the opening day for his own team in England.

He was assigned to the Fifty-fifth Fighter Group of the U.S. Eighth Air Force, piloting one of the new and fast P-38 Thunderbolts, a sleek bomber with two engines, two tails, and even two fuselages, the pilot seated between them. The new aircraft was what pilots called "a hot plane," one capable of great speeds and aerial maneuverability. Lieutenant Shepard was having a high old time, logging thirty-three missions including one that made headlines—the first daredevil raid over Berlin in daylight, on March 2.

Between missions Bert pursued his other love by assembling a baseball team to compete against teams from other airfields in the English countryside. Opening Day was set for May 21, two weeks before an opening day of a different sort, D-Day. Everything worked out perfectly. Shepard flew a mission two days before and was available to play and manage on Opening Day.

That morning, a Sunday, another mission was scheduled

to bomb Berlin. When he heard about it, Bert volunteered, even though he wasn't due to fly until the next day. "It was going to be a rough mission," he says. "We were scheduled to do low-level bombing and strafing, so I knew we'd need as many pilots as we could get. Besides, we'd be back in time for the ball game."

Just before reporting for takeoff, Bert received a phone call from his English girlfriend. She was worried about him. She'd had a dream the night before that something terrible happened to him. He calmed her down. "I'm just fine," he told her. "I'm going on today's mission and then I'll be back here for the game. After that I'll be able to come to town tomorrow and see you."

The formation pounded a Luftwaffe airfield in the Berlin suburbs and other military targets. As the mission, Bert's thirty-fourth, neared its end, he spotted one more target for his machine guns, a German plane parked on the runway like a sitting duck, the kind of target that no self-respecting wartime pilot can pass up. He didn't.

Shepard came in low, only twenty feet off the ground, and destroyed the enemy plane with repeated bursts of machine-gun fire. But enemy gunfire got even. German bullets pierced Shepard's plane and shot his right foot off. He was hit in the chin, too. As he slumped forward, sliding into unconsciousness and feeling the warm blood running down from his face, he actually radioed to his flight commander in the lead plane, "Tell the boys I guess I won't make it back for the game."

Then he passed out, just before his plane crashed into the ground at 380 miles an hour, fracturing Bert's skull. The plane caught fire and exploded, but the Germans rescued him in time. He didn't wake up until two days later, as a prisoner of war in a German hospital. With a lifetime of adventures already behind him—riding freight trains to California, playing professional baseball, becoming a fighter pilot with thirty-four combat missions, and now a P.O.W.— he was still only twenty-three years old.

"When I opened my eyes," Bert remembers, "there were all these German doctors and nurses around me. They're always worried about how a patient might react when he wakes up and discovers he's lost a limb. The emotional response can be devastating."

In the case of Shepard, they were dealing with the world's most confirmed optimist. With his dreams of becoming a big-league baseball player obviously shattered, he was still able—and willing—to smile and say, "Thank you for saving my life."

In the big leagues that Shepard now might never reach, fans found more truth than ever in the old vendor's cry, "You can't tell the players without a scorecard." They were coming and going almost faster than the printer could change the names and numbers on the rosters.

More than 60 percent of the starting players in the major leagues in 1941 were in the service by 1944. In all, 470 major leaguers were in the armed forces. The Yankees lost more of their stars after '43—Charlie Keller, Bill Dickey (even though he turned thirty-seven that year and suffered from a bad sinus condition), and Joe Gordon, plus Outfielder Roy Weatherly, Third Baseman Bill Johnson, and Pitcher Marius Russo.

Dan Daniel was not overstating things when he wrote, "The Yankees have lost a ball club." Every starter from their 1942 pennant winner was in the armed forces.

But it was still baseball, and the fans of America still wanted it, including the men and women in uniform, even those who had been wounded in the fighting overseas. Author Richard Goldstein, in his research for his book *Spartan Seasons,* found the results of a survey taken in the recreation hall of Walter Reed Army Hospital in Washington at the beginning of the 1944 season. In a landslide, the wounded GIs expressed their support for the continuation of baseball. The vote was 300–3.

The manpower losses were felt by every team. The Senators lost one of their all-time favorites, Mickey Vernon, who could play first base better than anyone and was developing fast as one of the American League's best hitters, reaching his peak after the war when he won the batting championship twice. The most colorful catcher in the league, Jake

Early, was gone too, and so was their new second baseman acquired from the Yankees, Gerry Priddy.

In St. Louis, the Cardinals were more fortunate than the Yankees. They still had five starters from the '42 team that upset New York in the World Series—Catcher Walker Cooper, First Baseman Ray Sanders, Third Baseman Whitey Kurowski, and two outfielders: Stan Musial and Johnny Hopp, who also filled in at first base from time to time. They had Danny Litwhiler, who fielded 1.000 for the Phillies in left field in 1942. Danny was a twenty-six-year-old left fielder from Ringtown, Pennsylvania, who developed the skill to achieve that perfect fielding average by practicing in the infield as well as the outfield. He's quick to admit that his manager deserves some of the credit.

We ran into each other in St. Petersburg, Florida, in March of 1991 at the annual reunion for former players sponsored by the Major League Baseball Players Alumni Association. When we started talking about his 1.000 season, Danny mentioned the kicker—the year before, his first full season in the majors, he led the National League's outfielders in errors. All but one were on ground balls.

He also led them in putouts, but the errors bothered his manager, Hans Lobert, so much that he ordered Litwhiler to take drastic action. At the start of the 1942 spring-training season, he told Danny, "If you don't take infield practice with the second unit every day beginning now and all through the season, it will cost you fifty dollars."

Litwhiler told me, "So I took infield every day. I didn't want to lose that fifty dollars."

Harry Brecheen was on his way to being a left-handed pitching ace, and five-foot-nine-inch right-handed relief pitcher Ted Wilks broke into the majors that year. Brecheen won sixteen games, and Wilks won seventeen. And they still had right-hander Mort Cooper and left-hander Max Lanier, two of the National League's best starting pitchers, from their '42 championship team.

The Cardinals were vulnerable to Uncle Sam's call, too. They lost four good pitchers—Al Brazle, Murray Dickson, Howie Krist, and Ernie White—who won thirty-two games among them for the Cards in 1943. The Cincinnati Reds lost their strikeout king, Johnny Vander Meer, and their second baseman, Lonny Frey, who had just introduced a new kind of fielder's glove, one with a solid leather web between the thumb and the fingers. In our neighborhood, any kid with a Lonny Frey model had the newest status symbol and was envied as much in the summer as were those who owned Flexible Flyer sleds in the winter.

The other St. Louis team, the Browns, finished sixth in the American League in '43, eight games below .500 and twenty-five games behind the first-place Yankees. But the draft gods were about to smile on the '44 Browns.

The draft was concentrating on younger men now, the ones in their twenties, so the trend in baseball was to sign older players, those in their mid- to late-thirties—and older. The Browns, destined to win their only pennant in '44, were an example of the trend toward senior citizens, including some who were more senior than others.

Their team included First Baseman George McQuinn, thirty-five years old, Don Gutteridge, thirty-two, at second base, and thirty-year-old Mark Christman at third. Shortstop Vern Stephens, only twenty-four years old but 4-F, was the baby of the infield.

The pitching staff included thirty-four-year-old Steve Sundra, thirty-six-year-old Al Hollingsworth, and George Caster, who turned thirty-seven in August. Then there was Sig Jakucki, thirty-five when the season started, who hadn't pitched in the major leagues since 1936, when he appeared in seven games and had a record of no wins and three losses for the Browns.

Eight years later, under their wartime standards, the Browns brought Jakucki back. He won thirteen games for them, saved three more as a relief pitcher, and tied Detroit's Rufus Gentry for the third most shutouts in the league with four. He won twelve more games for the Browns in '45, then was gone from the majors after the war.

To handle their aging pitchers, the Browns obtained a young veteran—not a baseball veteran, a real veteran. He was Frank Mancuso, whose older brother Gus was a star catcher in the National League from 1928 until the war ended. Frank hadn't been that successful—he played only four seasons in the big leagues—but he was lucky enough to be available in 1944. The war gave him his chance to play in the majors, and he earned it in advance.

Frank had already served his country as a second lieutenant in the Army, but he broke his leg as a paratrooper making his fifth jump and was discharged in time to play in eighty-eight games as the Browns' starting catcher.

A report from United Press said, "The 25-year-old player, disappointed because he wanted to go overseas, believes it is his responsibility to help baseball weather the manpower crisis because he is convinced his ex-buddies want it to continue."

Even with such an apparently safe strategy of going with older players, the Browns got a scare. Outfielder Chet Laabs, who had hit forty-four home runs for them over the two previous seasons, received a notice from his draft board to report for induction into the Army on April 15, just as the season was starting.

He and his team got a reprieve on April 9 when the draft regulations were changed to exempt any man who was twenty-seven or older and was also married and working in a defense plant. With help from the Browns' general manager, Bill DeWitt, on that last item, Laabs qualified on all counts.

DeWitt found jobs in St. Louis defense plants for Laabs, and Galehouse, too. It was a distinct improvement for Laabs, who had worked at a defense plant in his hometown of Detroit the year before, even though he was classified 4-F because of severe headaches, the result of a brain concussion caused by a beaning in 1938.

When he was rejected for military service, his draft board warned him that a defense job might be a good idea in case he was called again. During the '43 season, Laabs commuted to the Browns on weekends from Detroit. "I'd catch the midnight train to St. Louis," he remembered in later years. "Priorities went to servicemen, which was absolutely right. But it meant I either sat in a chair car or had to sleep on the floor or stand."

With his new St. Louis defense job taking priority, Laabs was able to play in only sixty-six games in 1944, mostly on weekends during his days off from the war plant. As things

President Roosevelt throws out the first ball in
Washington to open the 1941 baseball season.
UPI/Bettmann News Photo

Pitcher Hugh Mulcahy of the Philadelphia Phillies (second from right) shows his fellow soldiers at Camp Edwards, Massachusetts, how he grips his fast ball, in March 1941. Mulcahy was the first major league player drafted in the military buildup before World War II. *UPI/Bettmann News Photo*

A Navy recruiting poster in Benton Harbor, Michigan. *John Vachon, FSA*

Babe Ruth hits a home run off Walter Johnson in an exhibition at a packed Yankee Stadium to promote war bonds in 1942. It was the last time the two immortals faced each other. *AP/Wide World Photo*

Rookie Stan Musial rounds third
base for the Cardinals at Ebbets
Field in Brooklyn in 1942.
*National Baseball Library,
Cooperstown, N.Y.*

Members of the Brooklyn Dodgers, who received 10 percent of their salary in war
bonds like all major leaguers, bought an extra bond apiece here. American Women in
Volunteer Services member Valerie Harding
(left) presents his bonds to Leo Durocher
while Betty Leggatt gives his to Johnny
Cooney. Other Dodgers, from left: Kirby
Higbe, Buck Newsom, and Mickey Owen.

Store sign in Los Angeles after its Japanese-American owners were uprooted by the U.S. government and sent to a "nisei" camp. *Russell Lee, FSA*

Chicago White Sox Shortstop Luke Appling becomes Private Luke Appling right after winning the 1943 American League batting championship. *AP/Wide World Photo*

The 1943 All-Star Game, played at Philadelphia's Shibe Park, was the first to be played at night. *UPI/Bettmann News Photo*

The Giants limber up in cold-weather spring training in Lakewood, New Jersey, in 1944. *National Baseball Library, Cooperstown, N.Y.*

Three blue stars in the window show that this family in Oswego, New York, has three members serving in the armed forces. *Marjorie Collins, OWI*

Giants Manager Mel Ott, like many of the wartime players and managers, tours Europe in the off-season and autographs a ball for a GI.

Chet Laabs, who spent part of the war working in a defense plant during the week and playing baseball on weekends, crosses the plate with the home run that won the 1944 pennant for the St. Louis Browns. Greeting him is Mike Kreevich, number 12. *UPI/Bettmann News Photo*

One-armed Pete Gray sends a hard ground ball to Detroit Shortstop Skeeter Webb in his first time at bat in the big leagues in April 1945. *UPI/Bettmann News Photo*

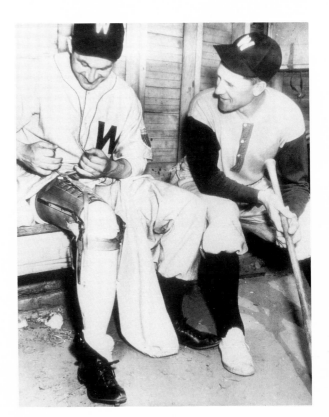

War hero and Pitcher Bert Shepard of the Washington Senators laces on his artificial right leg. Manager Ossie Bluege watches. *AP/Wide World Photo*

General Dwight D. Eisenhower talks baseball on his triumphant trip to New York's Polo Grounds after Victory-in-Europe Day in 1945. Ike visits with Braves Manager Bob Coleman, Mayor Fiorello LaGuardia, and Manager Mel Ott of the Giants. *AP/Wide World Photo*

Children wait in line at their school in New York in 1942 to buy stamps to be redeemed for war bonds. *Marjorie Collins, OWI*

Baseball player and spy Moe Berg (center) on one of his secret overseas trips for the government.

Cleveland's star pitcher, Bob Feller (second from right), is discharged from the Navy in August 1945 after almost four years of duty and eight Pacific invasions. *AP/Wide World Photo*

Two stars of baseball's last wartime season, Detroit's Hank Greenberg (left), whose grand slam home run won the 1945 pennant for the Tigers, and First Baseman Phil Cavarretta of the Chicago Cubs, the National League's Most Valuable Player. *AP/Wide World Photo*

Tommy Holmes (center) of the Boston Braves shows teammates Jim Tobin (left) and Mort Cooper the bat he used to set the National League record for hitting in the most consecutive games. The record lasted thirty-three years. *UPI/Bettmann News Photo*

President Truman visits Washington's Griffith Stadium and throws out the first ball in a game between
the Senators and the Browns in September 1945, a
month after Japan surrendered. It was the first presidential trip to a game since before the war.

turned out in October, that was enough to make a difference. In the meantime, he was inspecting pipes made at the defense plant—ten, twelve, and fourteen inches in diameter. After the war he learned the pipes were shipped to Tennessee as part of the atomic bomb project.

The biggest jolt of all on the manpower front was felt by the Washington Senators, 1943's second-place finishers in the American League. On April 10, 1944, just before the season began, the Associated Press reported, "Pennant hopes of the Washington Senators, bright and rosy just twenty-four hours ago, took a downward tumble today as Uncle Sam's draft men took a cut at the contingent of Latin-Americans the club had assembled for the 1944 campaign."

Clark Griffith had no fewer than eighteen players from Cuba, Puerto Rico, Venezuela, and Mexico in spring training at the College Park campus of the University of Maryland, where I was thrilled to be among the spectators. The wartime requirement for the teams to train near home was a bonus for us kids. On Easter vacation in '44 and again in '45, we were able to ride our bikes from my house in Silver Spring five miles up and down hills to College Park. We packed a lunch of two Vienna sausage sandwiches—heavy on the mustard—and bought a bottle of root beer at the campus drugstore on Route 1 while the Senators were in the clubhouse having their own lunch break.

We followed the routine every day for a week, thrilled every minute of the time, watching our heroes, matching new names with new faces, asking what happened to those missing from last year, and getting every autograph we could. I made sure to get one from a Washington favorite who wasn't even a player—Shirley Povich of the *Post*. Even a war can have its bright side once in a while, especially if you're still only thirteen.

The Selective Service shocked Griffith and his Hispanic players by ruling that they must return home or register for the draft. AP speculated, "Should any of the Latins decide to return home—and some of them unquestionably will do just that—they won't be able to reenter the United States without special permission."

Griffith and his manager, Ossie Bluege, were depending on Third Baseman Gil Torres, Pitcher Alex Carrasquel, Catcher Mike Guerra, and Outfielder Roberto Ortiz as regulars. AP suggested the possibility that Carrasquel, "the towering Venezuelan dancing master who pitches with considerable success when he feels in the mood, probably will stick around. He's in his 30s."

AP was right. Torres, Ortíz, and Guerra quit the team on July 16 after officials of the Selective Service System ordered them to sign up or leave. They were in the United States on three-month visas that began in March. Selective Service extended the visas but then ruled the players were "resident aliens" and must register for the draft within ten days.

All three returned to Cuba, where they were also subject to a military draft. Griffith did not contest the ruling by Selective Service. "Natually I hate to see these boys go," he said, "but it's an order from a war agency, and there's nothing to do but comply."

The owner they called "The Old Fox" was able to see decades and even generations beyond 1944, despite the setback. AP said Griffith "still holds high hopes for Latin American ball players and believes plenty of major-league talent will come from there in future years."

Carrasquel, thirty-two years old, decided to stay and take his chances. He won eight games that year, and the writers and broadcasters appreciated his decision to stay as much as Griffith and Bluege did. From the time he was a rookie in 1939, the writers knew Carrasquel had more than just baseball ability: He was good copy, too.

He was blessed with good size—six one and 180—and he was capable of taking his turn in the pitching rotation every fourth or fifth day. But he was moody as well as short-tempered and never pitched more than 159 innings as a starter, prompting complaints from club officials and other players. Compounding his problem, especially since he was a rookie, was something else that wasn't his fault. He was a foreigner.

Shirley Povich wrote during the war, "Carrasquel had a rough time of it in his early years with the Nats. He wasn't a popular fellow with his teammates. The fault was theirs, not his. Ball players are notoriously narrow-minded anyway. They resented the presence of the South American. They were fed up, in fact, with all of the Latins the Washington club was importing. The 100 percent Americans on the club viewed the influx as bread being taken from their mouths."

Povich recalled that some of the Nats didn't even like Carrasquel's looks, with his padded shoulders and a sharp cut to this clothes, "but the fact that he looked like a Spaniard and couldn't speak English was enough. . . . Somebody once said he looked like a guy off a Spanish galleon who wouldn't be out of character climbing up the side of a pirate ship with a knife in his teeth."

He was excluded from his teammates' card games, which was cruel and unusual punishment in those days of long train trips from Boston to St. Louis or New York to Chicago. In general he was made to live the life of an outcast in a strange land with a strange language and a strange culture.

Eventually the team's brass had enough and stepped into the situation, telling the players to start getting along with the guy, especially after he won five games in a row in 1941. Their treatment improved.

Right from the start, the Senators knew they had both pitching potential and a personality in Carrasquel after their Latin scout, Joe Cambria, signed him to a Washington contract. There was always a mystery about his age. Once he told a reporter he was twenty-five, then told another reporter a few minutes later he was twenty-nine. In 1943 he was listed as twenty-nine on the Senators' roster, but some estimates said he was forty. What did Carrasquel do to clear up the matter? He laughed about it. To him, the uncertainty was fun.

His first manager in the big leagues, Bucky Harris, liked his fastball. He also liked Carrasquel's experience. After he picked off the first two base runners in his first appearance with the Senators at their 1939 spring-training camp, Harris said, "I don't know where he learned it, but this fellow is smoother than any rookie who ever broke in under me."

Bucky later had reason to admire Carrasquel's poise and courage. The first time he went to the pitcher's mound in a big-league game was enough to test the nerves of the most

119

experienced veteran. It happened in Yankee Stadium before a near-sellout crowd. The Yankees had the bases loaded, and the hitter was Joe DiMaggio.

At this critical point, Harris waved Carrasquel in from the bullpen. He struck DiMaggio out.

Not all of the old men were in the majors. Horace "Hod" Lisenbee was a case in point.

Lisenbee turned forty-six years old in 1944, when he decided to make a comeback with the Syracuse team of the International League. He was a rookie with the '27 Senators and later pitched for the Boston Red Sox and the Philadelphia A's in the 1930s, winning thirty-six games and losing fifty-five.

For the first part of the war, he tended his herd of Polled Herefords on his cattle farm in Clarksville, Tennessee, because all the young men who worked for him had gone off to war. But by 1944, Lisenbee was ready to come out of retirement. To any kids on the Syracuse team who might be waiting to be called into the service, Lisenbee could pop their eyes with stories of his earlier days.

"I never had a baseball in my hand until I was twenty-one years old," he said. But that didn't hurt him when he pitched against the feared Murderers' Row of the New York Yankees as a rookie. He faced the '27 Yankees five times, the team rated by many as the greatest of all time, with Babe Ruth, Lou Gehrig, Tony Lazzeri, Frank Crosetti, Earl Combs, Bob Meusel, Waite Hoyt, and Herb Pennock. Lisenbee won all five games, striking out Ruth three times the first time he pitched against him.

He was an eighteen-game winner that year, led the American League with four shutouts, and was fourth in strikeouts even though he was not blessed with an overpowering physique—only five feet eleven inches tall and 170 pounds.

By 1944, seeing others coming out of retirement, Lisenbee decided to do the same. He had eighteen years of experience as a pitcher in the majors and minors and hadn't pitched for two years, but his age and rust didn't slow him down. He pitched a no-hit game for Syracuse, attracted the interest of the Cincinnati Reds, and signed a 1945 contract with them

120

for a bonus of $3,000. He won one game for the Reds and then retired for good at forty-seven when the war ended, one of the oldest pitchers in baseball history.

Washington found at least partial relief from the departure of its Hispanic players in the signing of a former big-league outfielder, but the relief could be only temporary.

Eddie Boland, who started the 1944 season playing right field for the New York City Sanitation Department's baseball team, agreed to come back to the big leagues, where he had played in thirty-eight games for the Philadelphia Phillies in 1934 and '35. But there was a catch.

Boland turned thirty-six in April, and he had a steady job as a clerk in the Sanitation Department. The security meant a lot to Eddie. He told the Senators he'd be able to retire on a nice pension at half pay in nineteen more years.

That was the catch. He wanted to take every precaution necessary to protect his future pension. One of the things he was going to do was play in a big game at Yankee Stadium on September 7 to raise money for the retirement fund. It was the Sanitation Department against the Fire Department, and every year the game drew between 40,000 and 50,000 fans and raised $200,000 for the pension funds of the two departments.

No mere return to the major leagues was going to keep him from that game. He'd play for the Senators all right, but only during his summer vacation. That would last only one month. After that, he'd have to leave to get back to the department or he might lose his job.

True to his word, Boland played in nineteen games in midsummer, hit .271, and then was gone, back to clerking for the department. As Shirley Povich wrote in his column, "There had to be a war before that could happen."

Maybe the baseball purists could find fault with the quality of play by 1944, but the fun was still there. Jim Tobin got things off on a newsmaking note on April 27 by pitching the first no-hitter in the major leagues since Lon Warneke of the Cardinals pitched one on August 30, 1941. It was the first by a Boston Braves pitcher since 1916.

121

Only 1,447 fans were at Braves Field when Tobin, who began his major-league career with the Pirates in 1937 and ended it with the Braves after the '45 season, shut down the Dodgers, 2–0. The feat was especially enjoyable for Tobin for two reasons: (1) a doctor predicted in 1940 that Tobin would never pitch again after injuring his knee, and (2) Tobin wanted to show Brooklyn's manager, Leo Durocher, that he was a better pitcher than Leo seemed to think.

Before the game, Durocher was told that the Braves would not be able to start the scheduled pitcher, Al Javery, because of a sore shoulder. "That's fine with me," Leo said. "I'd rather hit against Tobin any time than Javery."

Phil Weintraub kept the excitement level high three days later with one of the most dazzling hitting displays in one game in the history of baseball.

He was an outfielder–first baseman who shuttled back and forth between the majors and the minors beginning with eight games with the Giants in 1933. Despite several sensational minor-league seasons, including a .401 average at Nashville, he never played more than sixty-four big-league games in a year until he made it with the Phillies in 1938, where he appeared in one hundred games and hit .311 in 351 times at bat. But he was gone again, not to appear in the majors again until winning a job with the '44 Giants as their first baseman.

He was a colorful character, one of baseball's flashiest dressers and reportedly the owner of a wardrobe that included one hundred suits. He was also an enthusiastic accordian player.

Weintraub wasted little time establishing himself. On the last day of April, against the rival Dodgers, Weintraub drove in eleven runs at the Polo Grounds with two doubles, a triple, and a home run. He equaled the American League RBI record for one game and missed the record set by Jim Bottomley of the Cardinals in 1924 by only one.

The final score was Giants 26, Dodgers 8.

After the game, Weintraub was surprised to see baseball's most famous face in the Giants' clubhouse—Babe Ruth. The Babe walked over to the new slugger and said in his booming voice, "Kid, that was some performance! You knocked in

122

enough runs for a month! Some guys don't get that many in a season!"

Right up until his death in 1987 at the age of seventy-nine, Weintraub received a steady stream of fan mail. "I probably get more mail now than I ever got when I was playing," he said when he was sixty-six. "Maybe fifty or sixty letters a month from fans. A lot of them remember that game."

The Yankees had a twenty-five-year-old rookie right-handed pitcher who helped them in 1944 with thirteen wins, but he did more than that. He brought one of baseball's refreshing new personalities into the majors that year.

He was Walter "Monk" Dubiel. He became a hard-luck pitcher and never won that many games again in a seven-year career in the majors that ended with forty-five wins and fifty-three losses. But nobody ever accused him of being a quitter.

His minor-league career included stops at Akron, Erie, Binghamton, Norfolk, Newark, Seattle, Springfield, Los Angeles, Milwaukee, and Toledo. He picked up his nickname at Akron, where the equipment manager issued him a uniform far too small for his one hundred ninety pounds. His teammates told him he looked like "an organ grinder's monkey."

When he was with Newark in 1943, the Bears traveled to Baltimore for a series with the Orioles in the International League. He lost his meal money, but he was too shy to ask the team's traveling secretary for a loan, so he washed cars at the hotel garage.

"I made four bucks washing cars," he said. "That carried me over until the next day when I got some more meal money from the club."

The Dodgers were pinning some of their hopes for '44 on a promising—and towering—new player, Howie Schultz, a twenty-one-year-old first baseman who came up to them from St. Paul of the American Association for forty-five games in 1943, hit .269, and was now expected to be able to take over the first-base job for the entire season. He was draftproof, too, and not because he was too young or too old—he was too tall.

Schultz was six feet six and a half inches tall, a half inch over the Army's height limit. They called him Stretch, to no one's surprise. Reporter Tim Cohane referred to him as "the latest juvenile" to join the club.

He was good enough to make it at first base for the Dodgers that year, playing in 138 games. His batting average was only .255, but he hit eleven home runs and thirty-two doubles and drove in eighty-three runs. He never hit that well again and was gone after the 1948 season, still only twenty-six years old.

In December of '44, after that encouraging first full season in the big leagues, he proved to New Yorkers he could play more than baseball. He returned as the center and star for Hamline College against City College of New York at Madison Square Garden.

A reporter described him as having "speed, coordination, and fine condition." He said Schultz looked "like one of the best tall men seen in the Garden in many years." Schultz's comment: "Don't tell the coach, but I'd rather play baseball."

The war set in motion a series of events that produced social changes and advancements for minorities and women, and baseball itself reflected that wartime change as it did so many others.

An Associated Press item early in the baseball season hinted at the changes beginning to take place in American society that continue to this day:

ST. LOUIS, May 4—The St. Louis major league baseball teams, the Cardinals and Browns, have discontinued their old policy of restricting Negroes to the bleachers and pavilion at Sportsman's Park. Negroes now may purchase seats in the grandstand.

11

PARIS AND ST. LOUIS

OUTSIDE THE BASEBALL FAN'S WORLD, THE YEAR'S BIGGEST news came on June 6 when 187,000 Allied troops landed on the beaches of Normandy in France on D-Day. Even a seventh grader knew that the tide was swinging our way. We were convinced we wouldn't lose the war.

D-Day set off a national celebration. Store owners closed their doors. Horns and whistles shattered the subdued wartime atmosphere in big cities and small towns all over the country. People went to church. The Statue of Liberty, dark since Pearl Harbor, was illuminated again that night for fifteen minutes. President Roosevelt led the American people in prayer on the radio.

When our troops recaptured Paris eighty days later and turned it back to the jubilant French people as General Charles de Gaulle marched triumphantly down the Champs Elysées, another national celebration erupted. Confetti and ticker tape floated from New York office windows. Radio stations played "The Last Time I Saw Paris."

From the scene in Paris, General Patton sent a message the next day to General Eisenhower at his Allied command headquarters in England: "Dear Ike: Today I spat in the Seine."

In the Pacific, MacArthur's "leapfrog" campaign of capturing strategic islands and ignoring the others continued to produce victories. As a result of the success of this strategy over two years, MacArthur waded ashore in the Philippines at the Battle of Leyte Gulf on October 20, to the people to whom he had promised in 1942, "I shall return."

As far as baseball was concerned, MacArthur and Eisenhower couldn't return fast enough. The season was fun, as always, but the playing ranks were running thin with kids like Eddie Yost and Joe Nuxhall, and the clerk from the Sanitation Department, and a staff of starting pitchers in Washington consisting of nothing but knuckleballers whose butterfly pitches were being handled by a balding thirty-nine-year-old veteran of sixteen seasons, Rick Ferrell.

We had an inkling right from the start that things were going to be more unusual with each passing year of the war. After nine games, the Browns—yes, the ones in St. Louis— were leading the American League! Not only that, they hadn't lost a game.

Bill DeWitt told ESPN's "Major League Baseball Magazine" in 1987 that he thought his team's spring training was a factor in its fast start. The team trained at Southeast Missouri State University in Cape Girardeau, one hundred miles south of St. Louis. DeWitt and his staff arranged to have dirt put on the floor of the school's field house, then installed one of the first pitching machines and a batting cage.

When the weather was too cold or too snowy, or both, for other teams, the Browns were able to practice indoors. DeWitt estimates that the innovation enabled the Browns to start the season "at least a week" ahead of the other seven American League teams in their conditioning and practice.

The Browns led the league in another department in addition to wins, and there was definitely a connection. They led the league—both leagues—in the number of 4-Fs with eighteen. By D-Day, the Browns were still in first place, a game and a half ahead of the Yankees and two and a half ahead of the Tigers. The Senators, reeling under the loss of so many regulars and the Cuban fill-ins as well, were last.

In the National League it was no contest. The Cardinals were racing to their third straight pennant and seemed determined to win it by the Fourth of July. By the end of June they had a record of forty-five wins and only fifteen losses, leaving the Pirates and the Reds in their dust.

The Cards were doing it with their stars—Musial, Kurowski, the Cooper brothers, and the rest—but they were getting additional help from a new source, a second baseman who never made it to the Hall of Fame but managed to have a national society named after him as a tribute to his work ethic and day-in, day-out steadiness.

He was Emil Verban—a twenty-eight-year-old rookie from Lincoln, Illinois, with two nicknames, Dutch and The Antelope. Verban was 4-F because of a shattered eardrum, and he filled the vacancy created by the departure of Lou Klein. It's true there was a definite drop-off in the offensive statistics as a result: Klein hit seven home runs in 1943, Verban none in '44. Klein had sixty-two runs batted in, Verban forty-three. Klein hit .287 to Verban's .257. Klein stole nine bases in 1943. Verban didn't steal any in 1944.

But it was in the field that Verban excelled. He performed well at second base during the war and after it, too. He made more putouts and more assists than Klein did the year before and turned in more double plays—"the pitcher's best friend"—leading the league's second basemen with 105. He was proving his worth, and in the World Series he became a genuine hero.

It seemed to be a St. Louis year everywhere, even in the movies. Two of the most popular films of 1944 had a St. Louis flavor. The Academy Award winner for the top film of the year was *Going My Way,* starring Bing Crosby, Gene Lockhart, and Barry Fitzgerald, the biggest box-office success since *Gone with the Wind* five years before. Crosby played a young priest, and when he was working with the teenagers of the parish, keeping them out of trouble by teaching them four-part harmony and how to hit a baseball, he wore a St. Louis Browns warm-up jacket.

Judy Garland and Margaret O'Brien were featured in the Technicolor musical hit *Meet Me in St. Louis,* about that city at the turn of the century.

Other big films of 1944 were about the war. Spencer Tracy

and Van Johnson starred in *Thirty Seconds over Tokyo*. That was a can't-miss production because of the popularity of its subject—Colonel Jimmy Doolittle's raid over Tokyo in April 1942, when his squadron of eighteen B-25 bombers took off from the carrier *Hornet* and bombed the capital city of Japan, giving our armed forces, and us at home, too, a morale boost only four months after Pearl Harbor.

See Here, Private Hargrove was a comedy about life in the Army starring Robert Walker. We also saw *Purple Heart* with Dana Andrews, a grim depiction of Americans held as prisoners of war by the Japanese, and *The Sullivans*, with Thomas Mitchell, about the overwhelming tragedy of the loss of the five Sullivan brothers at the battle of Guadalcanal.

The songs from *Going My Way* and *Meet Me in St. Louis* were among the top numbers on "The Lucky Strike Hit Parade" every Saturday night on the radio, along with other top tunes that reflected the times as much as the movies did. They were girl-misses-boy songs, but they could have been describing the manpower shortage, too, in tunes like "They're Either Too Young or Too Old" and Frank Sinatra's "I'll Be Seeing You."

Advertisers followed the same war theme in promoting their products. Sunbeam Shavemaster told us in a large ad in *Life* magazine that an average of five GIs a day can use the same electric razor. Boeing aircraft took out ads to brag about its new Boeing B-29 Superfortress bomber.

Full-page ads by Ford promised us that when the war was over we'd have "a new Ford that's big, roomy, and sturdy," the ad predicting, "There's a Ford in your future." The company assured us, "Meanwhile, however, the full Ford resources are being used to help bring Victory closer."

United States Rubber Company ads showed a drawing of two kids enjoying the old swimming hole in 1941 with a rubber inner tube—and a pilot's life being saved in the ocean by his rubber life raft during the war. The message at the bottom said, "You had already paved the way for these war-time products when you demanded prewar quality in rubber goods. You had already begun saving the lives of thousands of our airmen when you and your neighbors decided that our peacetime products were important."

Mobilgas, aware that the government had prohibited the production of new cars since 1942, subtly advertised, "Older cars need better oil—See your Mobilgas dealer."

And most of the ads included reminders to do our part in the seven war-bond campaigns conducted by the Treasury Department to pay for the cost of fighting the war—and hold on to them instead of cashing them in. Philco's ad urged us, "Follow through to victory. . . . Keep buying War Bonds and keep the bonds you buy!"

The 1944 All-Star Game, baseball's twelfth, was played in Pittsburgh, and it was a night for Phil Cavarretta to remember. The National League won for the first time since 1940, 7–1, for only its fourth win against eight defeats. The attendance at Forbes Field was only 29,589, which Roscoe McGowen of the *New York Times* regarded as "considerably below pregame estimates."

Maybe the size of the crowd disappointed McGowen, but it was enough to help the Service Men's Bat and Ball Fund, which received $81,275 from the gate receipts. The Fund also got another $25,000, the amount of the radio rights for the broadcast.

Each member of the National League team received a memento based on the number of years he'd been selected for the game. Mel Ott of the Giants received what Tim Cohane of the *New York World-Telegram* described as "a beautiful cigarette case" as a memento for being selected for his eleventh all-star appearance. Dixie Walker and Augie Galan, in their second games, received plaques. The American League was more patriotic. Each player received a fifty-dollar war bond.

The All-Star Game wasn't immune from the effects of the manpower shortage. Thirty members of the 1942 and '43 all-star teams were missing from the '44 game because of military service.

Cavarretta, the Chicago Cubs' first baseman and one of the most popular players of his time, set an all-star record by reaching base five times on a single, a triple, and three walks. His Cub teammate, Bill Nicholson, drove in the National League's first run to tie the game 1–1 in the fifth inning with a double that hit the right-field foul line. Three more runs followed in the inning.

The rally made a winning pitcher of Ken Raffensberger of the Phillies, who remains the only pitcher from that team ever to win an All-Star Game. It was a bright spot in an otherwise disappointing year for Raffensberger, a six-foot-two-inch left-handed control specialist who walked only 449 hitters in 2,151 innings over fifteen major-league seasons.

He was a twenty-game loser for the Phillies in '44, the most in the league, but he continued to impress people with his control—only 45 walks in 258 innings. That was an average of only 1.57 walks per 9 innings, the best in the league.

"I remember I lost a lot of one-run games that year," he said after he retired, "including one in sixteen innings against the Cardinals. I pitched the full sixteen innings. It was the longest I ever pitched. I had struck out Whitey Kurowski three or four times that day, but in the sixteenth, I didn't get the pitch where I wanted it. He hit it up on the roof at Shibe Park, and I lost the game." He walked only one man that day.

Raffensberger never got a chance to improve on his record the following year. After pitching in only five games, he joined the Navy. The Phillies traded him to the Reds after the war, where he completed a major-league career that lasted fifteen years and produced 119 victories.

They used to say he could have driven carnival operators out of business by knocking over their milk bottles along the midway. "They tell me I had pretty good contrtol," he said in later years, "but I really didn't think too much about it. I think I went forty-five innings one time without allowing a base on balls, but to me it was just pitching."

Another popular pitcher in the National League that season was a thirty-seven-year-old transfer from the American League, Fritz Ostermueller, in his eleventh season, most of them with the Red Sox, but a Pittsburgh Pirate in '44. He was declared 4-F by his draft board because of arthritis. How he got to pitch for the Pirates was a story that Bill Benswanger, their former president, liked to tell.

Ostermueller was traded to the Browns by the Red Sox in

1941 and then went to Brooklyn in '43. During the '44 season, the old Pirate hero, Paul "Big Poison" Waner, then a Dodger, tipped off Benswanger that Ostermueller might be available. He added, "He's my roomie. I know he can help you."

On that recommendation, Benswanger made the deal, buying Ostermueller for the waiver price of $7,500. "Frankie Frisch was my manager then," Benswanger said, "and he objected when I told him about the deal. Frisch thought Ostermueller was too old at thirty-seven to help us. I told him I didn't care. I was willing to take a chance on him for $7,500."

Then, in the cold, hard world of professional sports, Benswanger treated himself to one of the enjoyable moments. He had the pleasure of calling Ostermueller's room to tell him he was buying him for the Pirates, just after the Dodgers had ordered him to report to their farm club at Syracuse. Benswanger had rescued him from the minors in the nick of time.

"I called Ostermueller at his hotel," he said, "and I can still hear his wife yelling, 'Hooray!' when I told her the Pirates had purchased her husband's contract."

They called him Old Folks, and he became a Pittsburgh folk hero until his retirement after the 1948 season at the age of forty-one. He was an immediate success in '44, winning eleven games for a second-division team. He was never an old man just hanging on. He won only five games in 1945, but he came back with thirteen, twelve, and eight wins in his last three seasons, ending his career with 114 wins stretching back to his rookie year with the Red Sox in 1934.

Old Folks injured his elbow in 1943, after which he developed a long, drawn-out windup that he thought helped him. He became known as one of the slowest-working pitchers in the majors, but that didn't bother him. "I don't care if it takes me three hours to pitch a game," he said. "I don't have anything else to do all day."

His strong years near the end of his career prompted him to say he never really learned how to pitch until he grew older, an admission made by many big-league pitchers before and since. "I lost all my stuff," he said, "and had to start thinking."

131

The Browns maintained the momentum generated by their nine-game winning streak at the opening of the season, and in early August they strengthened their hold on first place in the American League with another winning streak, this one ten games. They led the Red Sox by five and a half games on August 15. The Tigers were eight games behind and New York eight and a half.

The Brown's manager, Luke Sewell, a catcher in the American League for twenty years before retiring as a player in 1942, had a theory of why the lowly Browns were making such a serious run at the pennant while the always-powerful Yankees, pennant winners in seven of the last eight seasons, were only in fourth place. Author Bill Mead, in his book *Even the Browns* (which later appeared in paperback as *Baseball Goes to War*), quotes the St. Louis manager:

> McCarthy had a system of baseball. He just turned those big bats loose and let 'em go. Joe's theory was that if he could intimidate you early in the season, he didn't have to worry too much. But those big bats weren't there. They were in the Army. He was still playing that same kind of baseball, as if he had DiMaggio, Keller, Henrich, Dickey. Any number of games, if he had dropped some sacrifices and things of that kind, he would have won them from you."

Another wartime discovery was appearing in Chicago in the person of Gordon Maltzberger, one of 1944's best relief pitchers in the American League.

A six-foot right-hander, Maltzberger kicked around in the minor leagues for nine years beginning in 1932, pitching and playing the harmonica. When he won sixteen games for Dallas and Shreveport in the Texas League in '42, the White Sox paid $6,000 for him. He was one of the few ball players who wore glasses in those years, the result of an automobile accident in 1934 that required two stitches in an eyeball. He wore glasses during night games so he could see the catcher's signals, which presumably did nothing for the hitter's peace of mind.

He was another control specialist, like Ken Raffensberger.

Chicago sportswriter Milt Woodard wrote in the *Sporting News,* "Maltzberger represents, probably better than any other player in the majors today, that fraternity of bona fide major leaguers who might have been overlooked except for the war."

The White Sox manager, Jimmie Dykes, raved about Maltzberger's precision pitching: "In all my days of baseball," he said—a veteran of twenty-two years as a player and the White Sox manager since 1934—"I've never seen a pitcher with the control of a curve better than Maltzberger's. Some as good, maybe, but none better."

He became one of baseball's relief aces in 1944, thriving on his willingness to throw his good curveball on a count of three balls and two strikes, the kind of confidence that managers yearn for in their relief pitchers.

Maltzberger pitched in forty-six games for the Sox in '44 and tied for the league's most saves with twelve. He also had ten wins, the most in the league for relief pitchers. He was in the Army in 1945 and returned for two seasons after the war before retiring in 1947.

It wasn't only the war that gave Maltzberger the opportunity to make it in the big leagues. The weather helped, too.

A starting pitcher throughout his minor-league career, he was scheduled to start the second game of a doubleheader for the White Sox at St. Louis on the first Sunday of the '44 season. "But it started raining during the first game that day," Maltzberger said, "and we never did get to play the second game."

Two days later, Dykes brought him in to face the Indians in Cleveland in a relief role. He threw to four hitters, got them all, then allowed only one run and three hits over five innings in a second relief role against the Browns.

Thinking back, he said, "Maybe it was a break for me. If I had started, I might have gotten my ears pinned back and then been sent back to the minors."

His 1944 performance was the success he had dreamed about, but the White Sox needed more than good relief pitching. They finished next to last in the American League, eighteen games behind the Browns. The only team they beat out was our Senators.

While the Browns, Tigers, Red Sox, and Yankees competed for the pennant in the American League, the Cardinals maintained a comfortable lead in the National, eventually winning the pennant by 14½ games over the Pirates and 16 over the Reds.

Dixie Walker of the Dodgers was one of the stories worth following in the National League. "The Peepul's Cherce" was thirty-four years old, in his fifth season as a Dodger, and halfway through an eighteen-year big-league career that began with the Yankees in 1931.

He was a fixture in right field at Ebbet's Field, from a family whose baseball lineage included his father, the first Dixie Walker, a pitcher for the Senators from 1909 through 1912. His brother, Harry "The Hat" Walker, became the National League batting champion in 1947. An uncle, Ernie Walker, was an outfielder for the Browns before World War I.

The Dodgers' Dixie was born in a log cabin and was a high school dropout. He began his professional career when he was twelve years old, earning five dollars a game on a semi-pro team. After a successful minor-league career, including a .350 season for the Yankees' Newark Bears team in the International League, he was brought up to the big club amid predictions that he was the new Babe Ruth.

That expectation ended when he crashed into an outfield fence and hurt his shoulder, leaving him with a weak throwing arm, which he later aggravated on a slide into second base. With Joe DiMaggio's arrival from San Francisco in 1936, Joe McCarthy, the Yankees' manager, gave up on Walker and sold him to the Chicago White Sox on waivers.

Two years later, after one season in Chicago and another in Detroit, he was sold on waivers again, this time to the Dodgers. Tom Knight, the respected Brooklyn baseball historian, says, "Something happened when old Dix came to Brooklyn. The shoulder problems faded, and his career turned around."

Walker's rise to hero status was immediate. In his first game as a Dodger, against the Braves at Ebbets Field, he came to bat as a pinch hitter with two outs in the bottom of the eleventh inning and the bases loaded. He singled in the winning run.

He was always a reliable hitter, with averages consistently in the .290s and low .300s, finishing eighteen years in the majors with a .306 average and 2,064 hits. But it was in 1944 that he had what players call a "career year," a season when he far exceeded his performances in any other year.

He won the National League batting championship with a .357 average, ten points higher than Stan Musial, and was fourth in slugging average and total bases. He hit thirteen home runs and drove in ninety-one.

Injuries continued to bother him from time to time, and after his career was over, he said, "Sometimes I wonder how good a ball player I could've been if I hadn't gotten hurt so much. Pretty good, I guess."

When Dixie died in 1982, Harry remembered his brother's loyalty to the Dodgers over the other teams he played for. "He loved those days in Brooklyn," he said. "He didn't care much about those other teams, just the Brooklyn Dodgers."

12

THE FUN
WE NEEDED

THE TWO ST. LOUIS TEAMS CONTINUED THEIR DRIVES toward their league pennants, but only the Cardinals were able to enjoy relative peace of mind. They remained comfortably on their way to their third straight pennant, their sixth overall, but the Browns, struggling to win their first ever, were forced to endure trials and adversity to the last day. They got into a dogfight with the Tigers that gave baseball fans one of their most exciting races ever, and nobody cared that it was wartime baseball. It was baseball, period. Fun for all.

After that ten-game winning streak in early August, the Browns did an immediate about-face and lost three out of four to the second-place Tigers in Detroit, then did exactly the same thing in St. Louis. On September 4, they dropped out of first place for the first time since May 30. The Yankees, not the Tigers, took over the top spot with a doubleheader victory over the Philadelphia A's, and they accomplished it in a manner consistent with the Yankee reputation for power, in war or peace. The scores of the doubleheader were 10–0 and 14–0.

The Red Sox were still in the race too, three games back in fourth place, with the Browns and Tigers in between. Boston, however, became the latest baseball casualty of the military draft when the Sox lost one of their top pitchers, Tex Hughson, their starting catcher, Hal Wagner, and their future Hall of Famer at second base, Bobby Doerr, in the first two weeks of September.

Doerr was the American League's second leading hitter that year, finishing with a .325 average, five points behind Lou Boudreau. Wagner, a big leaguer since 1937, was hitting .332 and dividing the catcher's job with second-year man Roy Partee when he had to leave. Hughson had won eighteen games already while losing only five, giving him the best winning percentage in the league, which held up for the rest of the season while Hughson was beginning his military service.

The Red Sox, who led the league that year in runs scored, doubles, and team batting average, could not overcome such a devastating loss to the draft so late in their pennant drive. They finished fourth with an even .500 record, seventy-seven wins and seventy-seven losses, twelve games behind the Browns and six games behind the third-place team, the Yankees.

The Browns survived a king-size scare of their own. One of their best hitters, Outfielder Al Zarilla, with a .299 batting average, got his draft notice, too. But once again Bill DeWitt came to the rescue, just as he had in the case of Chet Laabs and Denny Galehouse.

Zarilla turned twenty-five during the season, and the Browns were looking to him as one of their steady hitters already and one of their stars of the future. He hit only .254 as a rookie playing in seventy games in 1943, but in '44 he raised his average fifty-five points and appeared in one hundred games for the Browns. He eventually spent ten years in the majors.

DeWitt convinced the Army brass at Jefferson Barracks, Missouri, to induct Zarilla the day after his baseball season ended. Fortunately for Zarilla, DeWitt, and the rest of the Browns organization, their season lasted six games longer than the other seven teams in the American League.

137

The Browns weren't the only traditional tail-enders in the American League who were enjoying success as the war continued and the manpower shortage worsened. The Philadelphia A's were getting better too, at least in the standings. They moved up to sixth place in 1944, dizzying heights for them, and one reason was a rookie third baseman named George Kell.

George was the pride of Swifton, Arkansas, population 526, where electricity and running water stopped at the town line. His father was the town barber and a pitcher on the local semipro team until he was almost fifty years old.

His father's love of the sport meant George grew up in a baseball atmosphere. After every ball game, the players on the Swifton semipro team would head for the Kell barber shop, where George's father owned the only public shower in town.

As he grew into his teen years, George spent more time playing baseball and less time at his part-time job picking cotton in the Arkansas fields for fifty cents a day. That was just fine with his father, who remembered his own boyhood fun playing the game and wanted his boys to be able to play as much as they liked.

The three Kell sons knew all about their father's enthusiasm for baseball, especially after hearing those stories about Dad working all week on a farm and then walking five miles on Saturday afternoon to pitch a game and then walking the five miles back.

Young George didn't dazzle every major-league authority who saw him play at the beginning of his career. The Brooklyn Dodgers invited him to their minor-league tryout camp after a career as the star of his high school team, but bad knees, caused by loose cartilages in both knees since birth, bothered him. Larry MacPhail, the Brooklyn general manager, didn't like what he saw.

The fiery, impulsive MacPhail pointed toward Kell and asked Fresco Thompson, one of his scouts, "What's he doing here?" When Thompson tried to assure MacPhail of Kell's potential, MacPhail fired back, "Get rid of him. He'll never be a ball player."

Even in his first two years with the A's he was respected more for his fielding than his hitting. His first manager in the big leagues, Connie Mack, told him, "George, you'll be a great fielder, but you'll never be a hitter."

Kell proved MacPhail, Mack, and everybody else wrong, but unfortuntely for Mack, he wasn't with the A's when he did it. Mack traded him to Detroit for outfielder Barney McCosky early in the '46 season, and Kell blossomed immediately into one of baseball's best hitters, with a .322 average in his first year as a Tiger.

He won the American League batting championship in 1949 with a .343 average and finished a fifteen-year career with a lifetime average of .306. He was one of the great "spray hitters" of his time, spraying line drives to every part of the outfield.

Kell was a classic example of a good hitter who knew his limits. He used one of the smallest bats in the majors leagues, only thirty-one ounces and thirty-four inches long. He knew he wasn't a long-ball hitter, so he didn't fool himself by swinging for the fences. He hit twelve home runs one year, three more than he hit in any other season.

One of his biggest fans through his career was another schoolboy from Arkansas who also grew up to play third base. On a summer day in 1983, the boy from Swifton and the other one, from Little Rock, sat next to each other on a red, white, and blue stand in Cooperstown, New York, where George Kell and Brooks Robinson were inducted into the Baseball Hall of Fame at the same time.

Our Senators continued to occupy last place, becoming what the writers used to call "cellar dwellers" after losing their Hispanic players in midseason. In New York, Dan Daniel had an opinion about that and its implications not only for 1944 but beyond. In early August he wrote in the *World-Telegram:*

All three were essential players. That they preferred to leave this country cannot be held against them. But the fact remains that it will be exceedingly tough for Cuban ball players to establish themselves on major league clubs in the future. The reaction of the baseball public, with emphasis on the fans of Washington, has not been a pleasant one.

In many quarters, the Washington crash is attributed to the physical and mental effects of the Cuban retirement.

A seventeen-year-old kid from Brooklyn promised to help relieve Washington's manpower shortage late in the '44 season. Eddie Yost was spotted playing on the sandlots of Queens and quickly signed to a Washington contract by Joe Cambria, the Senator's scout who had signed all of their Hispanic players.

Washington wasn't the only team that detected Yost's potential. The Red Sox saw him playing semipro ball in Ozone Park, New York, and Orange, New Jersey, and invited him to Boston for a tryout.

Yost went to Fenway Park, put on a Red Sox uniform, and promptly became disenchanted because he couldn't get more than a few swings in the batting cage and couldn't find any room at his position, third base. He went to the outfield, shagged fly balls, and then left Boston in disgust.

Cambria stepped in just in the nick of time. He signed Yost for a bonus of $500. The next day a scout for the Phillies showed up at Yost's home and offered a bonus of $1,000.

Yost appeared in only seven games in 1944 and got only two hits in fourteen trips to the plate, but the Senators were high on him and keeping their fingers crossed that he might be available to them for the new season in '45.

However, the fortunes of war caught up with them again. On January 23, 1945, Yost, who turned eighteen two weeks after the '44 season ended, sat down and wrote a letter to owner Clark Griffith in longhand:

Dear Mr. Griffith,

I just wanted to write you a few lines to let you know that I am leaving for the armed forces on the 26th of this month. I

140

didn't expect to leave quite so soon but, just as you said, they seem to be taking practically every available man.

Before closing I want to thank you for the fine opportunity you gave me in the baseball world. Please give my regards to Joe Cambria, who has been so swell to me. I hope that I can fulfill that contract before long. Best wishes.

Sincerely,
Ed Yost

Yost was only one of three teenagers in the big leagues in 1944, and he was the oldest. Tommy Brown and Joe Nuxhall were playing, too.

Brown was a sixteen-year-old shortstop from Brooklyn who realized every boy's dream of playing for his hometown major-league team. He joined the Dodgers for forty-six games that year and fifty-seven more in '45.

Duke Snider told me a few years ago that Brown's throwing arm was so wild when they started the '44 season together at Norfolk that he earned the name Buckshot. Duke said Brown's wild throws were so well known that the sailors from the Navy base who sat behind first base brought their baseball gloves with them. When a ground ball was hit to Brown, those sailors cheered—for the opportunity to catch Brown's throw themselves.

Brown never made it big—he averaged only fifty-six games a season for nine years—but he was in the big leagues until 1953, and how many players from 1944 could say the same?

But it was another high-school boy who set a record that may never be broken, appearing in a major-league game at the age of fifteen. He was Joe Nuxhall, signed to a Reds contract in 1944, but not before they received an exemption from the child-labor laws.

The scouts weren't really looking for Nuxhall. They were looking for his father. The two were playing playground ball in Hamilton, Ohio, just outside Cincinnati, with the senior Nuxhall pitching in one game and his junior-high-school son pitching in another.

Two Cincinnati scouts came to Joe's diamond and asked

141

for a player called Ox, which was his father's nickname. When told he was on another diamond, they asked about the kid pitching and were told, "That's Ox's son."

"So they stayed," Joe says today, "and watched me. Then they invited me to Cincinnati for a look. They offered my father a tryout too, but he had five kids to feed and couldn't take the gamble. He was working in a plant that made locomotives and diesel engines. But the way I always tell it is I beat my father out of a job."

Cincinnati actually gave him a tryout in 1943, when he was a fourteen-year-old in the eighth grade. The Reds took him with them for a series in St. Louis, but the schoolboy told them he wanted to finish the ninth grade so he could play another year of basketball. He did, then signed as soon as the basketball season ended in February.

Nuxhall points out today that signing a ninth grader was no stunt by the Reds. He was the second biggest player on the ball club. Frank McCormick was 6' 4" and 205 pounds. Nuxhall was 6' 3" and 195.

On June 10, his manager, Bill McKechnie, waved the junior-high kid in from the bullpen to pitch the ninth inning against the best team in baseball, the Cardinals. He gave the kid limited advice: "Just do the best you can, son."

Nuxhall said his knees were "shaking like castanets. It wasn't so much the Cardinals that scared me. It was the idea of pitching in the big leagues." He said he didn't even realize when he was pitching to Stan Musial. "He was just part of a blur."

He got the first two men out, but then "I started realizing what was going on. Here I am pitching against a junior high school two weeks before and now I'm pitching against the potential world champions."

Then he gave up five walks and two hits—by Musial and Emil Verban—plus a wild pitch. It all added up to five earned runs. Still needing the third out, McKechnie came to the mound and said, "I think you've had enough, son."

The kid answered, "Yes, sir."

The record shows Nuxhall pitched two-thirds of an inning and left with an earned run average of 67.50. He was back in school in 1945, but back in the majors in 1952, good enough and mature enough to win 135 games in the next fifteen seasons.

There is a postscript to the stories of both Yost and Nuxhall. Yost came back from the Navy in 1946, saw too many returning GIs ahead of him, and wrote a letter to the new commissioner of baseball, Happy Chandler, asking for an exemption to Chandler's rule that every returning war veteran must be retained by his former team for two years as protection for his prewar job.

That rule stood in Yost's way of developing his skills. He wanted Chandler to let the Senators send him to their farm team at Chattanooga, but Chandler refused, saying one exemption would lead to others and he was adamant about protecting the job rights of baseball's returning servicemen.

Yost was forced to stay with Washington. Then the Senators learned the unfortunate truth about their prewar star, Cecil Travis. Those frozen feet from the Battle of the Bulge, plus his age of thirty-two, cheated him out of his quickness. His reflexes wouldn't allow him to play shortstop, and he didn't have the quickness for third base either.

Travis tried 75 games at short in 1946 and 56 at third base. In '47, he played only 15 games at short and 39 at third, then was gone, a casualty of the war. Manager Ossie Bluege worked Yost into seven games at third base in '46, and in '47 he became a full-time big leaguer with 114 games at third, on his way to an eighteen-year career and the American League's leader in walks six times.

Less than halfway through Yost's career, the Red Sox, who had no room for him in the batting cage or at third base after inviting him for that tryout in 1944, offered the Senators $200,000 for him.

Concerning Nuxhall's youthful taste of big-league life, the pitcher isn't sure now it was a good idea. In fact, if his son were given the same opportunity, Nuxhall says he wouldn't let him do it. The whole episode, he remembered in later years, was "rather frightening."

Still, it didn't do him any harm. "Appearing in a major-league baseball game at age fifteen didn't have a prolonged psychological effect on me. I was awed by the whole thing, though. Johnny Vander Meer was my boyhood idol, and sitting there on the bench made me feel like I had a good seat for the game."

Nuxhall remembers one more thing about his fifteen-year-old's day in baseball history: He said the crowd for that game at Crosley Field was only a few thousand. With the passing of the years and the number of people who have told him they were there, the size of the crowd has grown to about 40,000.

The 1944 American League race developed into one of the most exciting in history. Our GIs and the civilian folks on the home front had plenty of baseball drama to take their minds off the war. On the morning of Friday, September 29, the standings showed that the Browns and Tigers were battling for first place with only four games left for each team. The Tigers led the Browns by one game as the season's last weekend began.

The Browns would have to win the pennant by beating the Yankees in a four-game series. Detroit's opposition was the Senators, also for four games. The toss of a coin decided that if there were a tie—the first in major-league history—a single play-off game would decide the pennant. It would be played in Detroit.

The Tigers were getting help from Hal Newhouser, who had never won more than nine games in four full seasons. In 1944 he blossomed into a dominating star pitcher who was later described by Joe Falls, the sports editor of the *Detroit News,* as "a man of royalty, a man of high manner and morals. He was leaner and meaner, a tremendous competitor, giving in to no man or team. They say his curveball made noise as it crackled across the plate."

With that combination, Newhouser, a slender six-foot-two-inch left-hander weighing 180 pounds, earned the nickname Prince Hal and became a local boy who made good in 1944. Detroit's native son won twenty-nine games and led both leagues in wins and strikeouts. He was still only twenty-three years old.

His twenty-ninth victory was a crucial one. It came in Detroit, on the next to last day of the season, when he beat the Senators, 7–3. Rudy York hit a home run for the Tigers, and Doc Cramer, thirty-nine years old and a major-league player since 1929, drove in two runs.

The Browns kept pace with a 2–0 win over the Yankees in St. Louis. Denny Galehouse stopped New York cold, not allowing a runner past second base. The Browns and Tigers were still tied for first place with only one day left in the 1944 season. Both teams had eighty-eight wins and sixty-five losses.

Two scenes the next morning, one in St. Louis and the other in Detroit, reflected the tension. In St. Louis, the Brown's starting pitcher, Sig Jakucki, one of baseball's best drinkers, was showing signs of wear even though he promised his teammates the night before that he would not do any drinking that night.

On the morning of the final game, Jakucki said to the Browns' trainer, Bob Bauman, "I kept my promise last night. I said I wouldn't take a drink last night—but I didn't promise I wouldn't take one this morning." He got the ball anyway, as the Browns' starting pitcher.

In Detroit, the phone rang in Dutch Leonard's room at the Book-Cadillac Hotel. He was the Senators' best pitcher, a fourteen-game winner that year, one of the four knuckleballing starters on the Washington staff. Ossie Bluege had chosen him as Washington's pitcher that day. If the Tigers were going to win the pennant, they were going to have to beat Bluege's best.

When Leonard answered his phone, a mysterious voice said, "You have a chance to make a lot of money."

Leonard didn't know what the caller was talking about, so he asked, "What do you mean?"

The caller said, "I'm authorized to offer you better than two thousand dollars if you don't have a good day."

Leonard still wasn't sure what he had on the other end of the line. He asked, "What are you talking about?"

"If you don't have a good day, you can make yourself better than two thousand dollars."

Leonard said, "You go to hell." Then he hung up.

13

HEROES. . .ALL

THE SELECTION OF LEONARD AS THE SENATORS' STARTING pitcher was bad news for the Tigers. He was the champion of that starting staff of nothing but knuckleballers, and his was the best. It was his good fortune to be pitching to a catcher with the ability to handle the tricky "butterfly" pitch and the courage to call for it.

The catcher, Rick Ferrell, made it to the Hall of Fame despite having to handle all those knuckleballs from Leonard, Roger Wolff, Johnny Niggeling, and Mickey Haefner. Ferrell knew that any of the knuckleballers meant a long afternoon for him, and he also knew that Leonard's afternoons could be especially long.

"But I liked to handle him. I know that knuckleball makes me look bad at times, but what the hell? As long as we get men out and win games, what's the difference?"

Ferrell agreed with those who called the knuckler the "butterfly pitch." He said the two acted the same way. "Did you ever try to swat a butterfly with your hand? Well, that's the way it is catching the knuckler. But what a sweetheart of a pitch it is. I'll keep calling for it as long as Dutch wants to throw it."

On the way to Detroit's Briggs Stadium (now called Tiger Stadium), Leonard told teammate George Case about his

146

telephone call. Case encouraged Leonard to tell Bluege. Instead, he told one of Bluege's coaches, Clyde Milan, who told Bluege himself in the visitors' dressing room.

After their conversation, Milan came back across the room to Leonard's locker. He handed him a new white American League baseball and said, "You're still the pitcher."

With 45,565 fans in the ballpark on Sunday, October 1, Leonard took the mound against the other half of Detroit's intimidating one-two pitching punch that year, Dizzy Trout. Trout was a six-foot-two-inch hard-throwing right-hander who won twenty-seven games in '44 and combined with Newhouser to give the Tigers fifty-six wins from two pitchers.

He was working under a heavy handicap that day—one day's rest. Manager Steve O'Neill was going with his two best pitchers in his team's last two games, even if it meant asking one of them to do it the hard way.

The Senators' outfielder, Stan Spence, whose three-run homer helped to beat Trout, 9–2, as the teams split a doubleheader on Friday night, did it to Trout again. He hit another home run, and the Senators were on their way. By the ninth inning, Washington had extended its lead to 4–0.

O'Neill sent up two pinch hitters against Leonard in the bottom of the ninth, Chuck Hostetler and Don Ross. Both of them singled, and Doc Cramer made things even more dramatic by scoring Hostetler with a long fly ball. But Leonard and his knuckleball disposed of Eddie Mayo and Mike Higgins. The Tigers lost, 4–1.

The Browns, as the sports saying goes, had their fate in their own hands, and the people of St. Louis obviously knew it. The showdown was against the defending world champions, the Yankees, and the climax of a four-game series.

The Browns had swept the Yankees in a Friday night doubleheader, beating two of the Yankees' best pitchers. Jack Kramer defeated Tiny Bonham, 4–1, and Nelson Potter beat Hank Borowy, 1–0, to tie Detroit for the league lead. On Saturday, while the Tigers were defeating the Senators, Denny Galehouse beat rookie Monk Dubiel, 2–0.

Only 6,172 fans showed up for the Friday doubleheader and only 12,982 for the Saturday afternoon game, but

37,815 jammed into Sportsman's Park for the Sunday finale. It was the largest crowd in the team's history. The fans started lining up on Dodier Street at seven in the morning. At game time, 15,000 others had to be turned away.

It was a fairy tale game for Chet Laabs, the full-time defense-plant worker and part-time Brownie. He was only five eight, but his 175-pound body gave him all the power he needed. He always could hit home runs, including his career high of twenty-seven in 1942.

On that last day in '44, he delivered the two biggest homers of his life. With the Yankees leading, 2–0, in the fourth inning, Laabs tied the score with his first homer of the day, off Mel Queen after Mike Kreevich singled. Queen became so rattled he walked two hitters before getting the Browns out.

In the next inning, history repeated itself. Kreevich singled again and Laabs homered again, a line drive to the same area in the left-field bleachers where his first one landed. Later Vern Stephens hit a solo homer. Sig Jakucki, fortified by his liquid refreshment that morning, retired Oscar Grimes for the last out of the game and beat the Yankees, 5–2, giving St. Louis a sweep of its four-game series with the defending world champions.

The Browns were the champions of the American League for the first and only time in their history, giving lie to the old expression that St. Louis, the home of so many shoe factories and breweries that it was hard to keep a count of them, was, in a paraphrase of the Washington expression, "first in shoes, first in booze, and last in the American League."

Luke Sewell, their manager, deserved some of the credit for their victory and the storybook performance by Laabs, his part-time player who had lost his regular job to Zarilla because of his commitments to his job at the defense plant.

Sewell's hitters were in a slump. He thought they might be swinging what baseball people call "a tired bat." Into that situation stepped Laabs, who had not been expected to be able to play that last weekend. Sewell noticed in batting practice before the Friday night doubleheader that Laabs looked unusually good.

The small slugger started all four games against the Yankees, got two hits in the first game of the Friday doubleheader and two walks in the second game, then had two more hits Saturday.

It was going to be an all–St. Louis World Series, a midwestern version of New York's "Subway Series" when the Yankees would meet the Dodgers or Giants. In the same year that Judy Garland sang about streetcars in St. Louis, the city was going to have a "Streetcar Series."

There was another kind of a race in 1944, and it didn't have anything to do with winning a pennant—even though baseball was drawn into it, at least by imagery. The race was the presidential campaign between President Roosevelt and the Republican candidate, Thomas Dewey, the former district attorney and governor of New York.

The Democrats were reminding the voters that FDR had steered us all through the war to the point where victory was in sight, an accomplishment even more remarkable considering that FDR was confined to a wheelchair after suffering an attack of polio as a young adult. With victory near, the Democrats adopted a campaign slogan: "Don't change horses in midstream."

The Republicans countered with a baseball illustration. They said that by the time a man pitches twelve innings he is tired and should be lifted for a relief pitcher. The Democrats trumped them by trotting out the story about the longest baseball game in history, a 1–1 tie between the Dodgers and the Braves in 1920. They pointed out that both pitchers, Leon Cadore and Joe Oeschger, pitched the entire twenty-six innings.

There was concern, even if the Democrats didn't like to admit it, that Roosevelt was at least tired and maybe worse than that. Whether in his wheelchair, standing at a podium, or waving from his familiar open car, he looked haggard, with dark circles under his eyes. On June 9, his personal physician, Vice Admiral Ross McIntire, assured reporters that the president's health was ". . . excellent in all aspects. He is in better physical condition than the average man his age."

It was revealed after the war, however, that Roosevelt had suffered a minor heart attack. The diagnosis was made in a physical examination in August of 1944 by a young Navy heart specialist, Lieutenant Commander Howard Bruenn.

Dr. Bruenn found Roosevelt to be suffering from hypertensive heart disease. He advised Admiral McIntire. Dr. McIntire, however, told reporters who were asking about the health of the president that there was "nothing organically wrong with him. He's perfectly okay." However, the president's press secretary, William Hassett, wrote in his diary: "I fear for his health despite assurances from the doctors he's okay."

Roosevelt had his own feelings about running for a fourth term in 1944. He wrote to the chairman of the Democratic National Committee, Robert Hannegan:

> For myself I do not want to run. . . . All that is within me cries out to go back to my home on the Hudson River. Reluctantly, but as a good soldier, I repeat that I will accept and serve in this office, if I am so ordered by the Commander-in-Chief of us all—the sovereign people of the United States.

FDR, always a master at turning away criticism with a chuckle and his broad smile, provided one of the highlights of the campaign while answering charges by Washington columnist Drew Pearson that FDR ordered a Navy warship to turn around and head back to the Aleutian Islands to pick up his Scotty dog, Fala, after someone forgot and left him there.

During a nationwide radio address at a labor banquet in Washington, FDR threw the controversy right back at the Republicans simply by making a joke out of the whole thing. "These Republican leaders," he said in his best shame-on-you tone, "have not been content with attacks on me, or on my wife, or on my sons. No, not content with that, they are now including—my—little—dog—Fala." Roosevelt assured the people of the United States that he would not tolerate "these libelous statements about my dog." His banquet audience roared.

After attempting to dispel concerns about his health by appearing bareheaded in the rain during long campaign parades and without a topcoat while delivering lengthy campaign speeches in bone-chilling autumn temperatures, Roosevelt won the election by three and a half million votes. In electoral votes the margin was 432–99. Roosevelt carried thirty-six of the forty-eight states.

A headline in the *Cleveland Press* on October 2 described the outlook for the World Series:

BROWNS TO BE IN FAMILIAR UNDERDOG
ROLE IN SERIES

Sports editor Franklin Lewis wrote from St. Louis that the Browns' race to the wire made "the analysis of the hectic last week of the wildest race in league history prove completely haywire. They were saying the Browns and Yankees would slug each other batty down here four times, during which the Tigers would handle the Nationals in Detroit and ease into the pennant in the process.

"But it was the Tigers who split even with the Nats and it was the Browns who mauled the Yankees and so prevented the first play-off game in major-league history."

Lewis wasn't alone in his characterization of the Browns as the year's biggest surprise team. Leo Petersen of United Press called the Browns baseball's "Cinderella Kids." The impact of the war was reflected in the listings of players in the armed forces. The Browns had twenty-six players in military uniforms.

The Browns continued to shock everyone by winning two of the first three games against the Cardinals, winners of the National League pennant for the third straight year. They beat Mort Cooper, 2–1, in the first game, on October 4, with Galehouse pitching a seven-hitter and Cooper allowing the Browns only two. But one was a home run by the Browns' first baseman, George McQuinn, with a man on in the fourth inning. Galehouse went the full nine innings.

The Cardinals tied the Series the next day in another one-run game, 3–2, this one in eleven innings. Each team got only seven hits. Max Lanier battled but Blix Donnelly was the difference. He pitched four strong innings in relief of

Lanier, striking out seven and allowing only three balls to be hit out of the infield. Ken Odea's pinch-hit single won the game for the Cards and Donnelly.

The Browns became the home team in Sportsman's Park for the next three games. The cover of their souvenir program said the World Series was "dedicated and broadcast to all members of our armed forces throughout the world." A full-page ad on the inside front cover by Alpen Brau beer, one of the many breweries in St. Louis, featured a drawing of a Japanese baseball player at bat and sweating nervously. Underneath was the message:

It's getting around to that fateful inning when our first-string fighters are going to demonstrate what is meant by *putting 'em out at home plate*. The cheering section in the bleachers and grandstand plays an important part in team morale. Today, every one of us—the crowd back home—can play a vital part in the fighting morale of our team over there. Here's something we all can do to help them put out the *last batter up:*

* Contribute to the war chest
* Buy extra bonds and stamps
* Be a regular blood donor
* Save every scrap of waste paper
* Write letters to the boys
* Conserve food and fuel

Alpen Brau beer may have been sending a message about the war to the Browns' fans, but the Browns themselves wrote about what might happen after the war. An article in the program headed "A Postwar Bid for Fans" made a pitch for continued attendance at their games.

The story said that "Brownie crowds," always smaller than those for Cardinals' games because the National League team was consistently more successful, began to grow midway through the '44 season as more fans realized the Browns had a chance to win the American League pennant. What made management even happier was that some of those new fans were coming from the rural areas of Missouri and the communities in Illinois just across the Mississippi River from St. Louis.

"There's a postwar battle in prospect," the article said, "between the Browns' and the Cardinals' management for this outside Missouri and downstate Illinois fandom, a Barnes-Breadon battle with base hits and fancy fielding for weapons."

History records that the Cardinals won the postwar battle. In 1954 the Browns left St. Louis and became the Baltimore Orioles.

The Browns jumped out in front in the World Series, two games to one, with a 6–2 victory in the third game. It came on five straight singles, a walk, and a wild pitch, all with two outs in the third inning. For the third straight game, the Cardinals got only seven hits, this time against Jack Kramer.

That turned out to be the Browns' high-water mark, and the story is that a cocky statement by the Browns' president helped to do them in.

Emil Verban, the Cards' steady but light-hitting second baseman, went to Don Barnes, president of the Browns, with a problem. The tickets given to Verban's wife by the Browns for the third, fourth, and fifth games, when they were the home team, were no good. They stuck her behind a post. She complained to her husband, "I couldn't see a thing."

Like any self-respecting husband, Verban went to the Cards' ticket staff, whose members said they were helpless to correct the situation because those were the tickets allocated to them by the Browns as the home team. Verban decided to go right to the top.

He found Barnes talking in a group of several men, introduced himself, and said, "My wife is sitting behind a post, and I'd like to have you do something about it."

Verban told reporters later that Barnes laughed at him and said, "The way you're playing, *you* ought to be sitting behind a post." He said, "Everybody joined in the laugh, but I was burned up."

The Cardinals tied the Series by winning the fourth game, 5–1, on Stan Musial's three hits and Harry Brecheen's nine-hitter. Verban got a hit in that game, his first in the Series after being lifted for a pinch hitter in each of the first three games.

The fifth game developed into a pitching battle between Mort Cooper and Denny Galehouse, with twenty-two strikeouts, twelve by Cooper. First Baseman Ray Sanders and Outfielder Danny Litwhiler accounted for all of the scoring and a Cards' win with a bases-empty home run each. Verban singled and reached base a second time when his hot drive scooted away from the Browns' shortstop, Vern Stephens. Then came the sixth game and Verban's revenge.

Playing with the fury of an infielder scorned, Verban got three straight singles, scored Sanders with one of them, and helped the Cardinals win the game and the World Series by a final score of 3–1. Ted Wilks entered the game in the sixth inning with one out and men on second and third and retired the last eleven batters to save the game for the Cards and Max Lanier.

In one final taste of sweet revenge, not only did Southworth leave Dutch in the game instead of lifting him for a pinch hitter, the Browns paid him one of the hitter's highest compliments. They gave him an intentional walk.

For the Series Verban finished as the Cardinals' top hitter with an average of .412 on seven hits in six games. Only the Browns' McQuinn outhit him, with a .438 average, and nobody topped his hit total. Only Musial, McQuinn, and Walker Cooper could tie it.

But that wasn't enough for Verban. Moments after Wilks struck out Mike Chartak to seal their triumph, Verban headed straight for Barnes in his box seat near the Browns' dugout. He told him, "Now you get behind the post, you fathead!"

When someone suggested to Verban in the dressing room that he apologize to Barnes, he refused. "I saw no reason why I should apologize," he said later. "Mr. Barnes told me I should be sitting behind a post when we were one game down, so at the first opportunity, I told him when he should sit behind a post."

Back home in Lincoln, Illinois, where his father used to work in the coal mines and later operated a grocery store, Verban became king for a day. The band from his alma mater, Lincoln High School, led a parade in his honor, followed by a celebration in the town square. Verban said his thank-you in a way that any fan would appreciate—he threw twenty baseballs into the crowd.

Verban had one lifelong ambition in baseball: to hit a home run. "Nothing burns me up more," he said, "than when outfielders come in when I come to bat. One of these days I'm going to surprise them and belt the ball a mile. Then they're going to respect me."

He got his homer in 1948 and left the major leagues two years later, still with only one home run and never hitting .300 except for his '44 World Series.

He had something more special than a home run, though. Over the years as a steady journeyman player with four teams in his seven-year career, he won the respect and fond memories of important people who thought his maximum effort every day represented the best in all of us.

That's why some high-powered baseball fans in Washington, including President Reagan, Presidential Press Secretary Jim Brady, columnist George Will, Senator Alan Dixon of Illinois, and lobbyist Bruce Ladd, formed the Emil Verban Memorial Society, so named even though Verban was still very much among the living. They were Cubs fans, a team that Dutch played 154 games for over the last half of the 1948 season and into 1949.

The group met at a dinner in Washington every two years, with Verban the guest of honor each time. Rather than considering the club a put-down of him, Verban took a different attitude. After his death in 1989, his wife, Annetta, said, "He really enjoyed the whole thing."

Three events at the end of 1944, two of them tragic and the third a tension-filled spy episode, involved familiar baseball names.

Mel Allen, the Yankees' play-by-play announcer, was recruited by his friend, band leader Glenn Miller, to join his Army Air Forces Band, but Allen declined and served in the Infantry instead.

On the evening of December 15, 1944, Major Miller stepped aboard a small single-engine liaison plane at an air base

155

west of Cambridge, England. With Flight Officer John R. S. Morgan as his pilot, Miller was headed across the English Channel for Paris to supervise arrangements personally for a Christmas show to be presented for the troops there.

The plane took off into the chilly December air and a thick fog over the English Midlands. Miller and Morgan were never seen again. Their plane was never found. Nearly half a century later, the Army can only assume the plane was either shot down or crashed because of mechanical failure.

Mel Allen spoke slowly even years later as he told ESPN's "Major League Baseball Magazine" of Glenn Miller's efforts to recruit his announcer friend: "Who knows? Only the good Lord knows—I might have been on that plane."

On December 16, the morning after Miller's plane took off, German Field Marshal Gerd von Rundstedt attacked the Allied forces of America's General Omar Bradley and England's Field Marshal Bernard Montgomery, also in a dense fog, across a seventy-mile front in the Ardennes Forest of Belgium. The attack put a bulge in the Allied lines, giving the event its name, the Battle of the Bulge.

The attack was launched at five o'clock. It was Hitler's idea, opposed by most of his generals, and in its first days, the operation was effective. More than a million men were involved. Eight thousand Americans surrendered at one time, the most since the battle for Bataan.

But it was Hitler's green, underage troops against the battle-tested American and British soldiers. Hitler lost 120,000 men, plus tanks and other equipment that he couldn't afford to lose. General Bradley wrote after the war, "Those bottom-of-the-barrel reserves that might have slowed the Russian onslaught had been squandered instead against us in the Ardennes."

Hitler's reign of terror was heading into its last hundred days.

That was the battle that stole the spring from the legs of Cecil Travis, the all-star shortstop of the Washington Senators until he was drafted at Christmas, 1941. Another man, destined to make a name for himself in baseball, remembers that battle vividly.

Lieutenant Warren Spahn, the future Hall of Fame pitcher, told "Major League Baseball Magazine" that Hitler's troops launched their attack disguised as much as possible as Americans. Spahn said, "The Germans had our equipment, our uniforms, even our dog tags." But he remembers one thing they didn't have—a knowledge of baseball.

"Our password used to be something like, 'Who's the second baseman for the Bums?' They wouldn't know who the 'Bums' were," Spahn said. "I used to pity any guy in our outfit who wasn't a baseball fan because he would be in deep trouble."

Two days after the Battle of the Bulge began, Moe Berg, a catcher in the majors for fifteen years, found himself face-to-face with Germany's most prominent nuclear physicist, with orders to be ready to assassinate him and then take his own life if necessary.

Berg was the last person you might have imagined in such a role, a scholar educated at Princeton and Columbia universities and the Sorbonne in Paris, a Ph.D., and a lawyer, conversant in anywhere from six to sixteen languages, depending on whose estimate you believed. His doctoral thesis on Sanskrit, the ancient Indian language still used in the rituals of the Northern Buddhist Church, is still on file in the Library of Congress. With his law degree from Columbia, he passed the New York State bar examination the first time he took it. He also developed a lens for color photography and was granted a patent for it.

Although people differed on how many languages he spoke, everyone agreed that he was fluent in French, Spanish, Italian, Latin, Greek, Russian, Hebrew, and Sanskrit. Presumably by the time he went to Europe during the war, he had learned German too. When he prepared to tour Japan on a baseball barnstorming tour in the 1930s, he learned that language too, and spoke with ease to the Japanese people throughout the trip.

His breadth of knowledge gained national recognition and popularity in 1939 when he appeared on one of the most popular radio shows of the time, "Information Please," with panelists Clifton Fadiman, John Kieran, and Franklin P.

157

Adams. Of thirty-two questions put to the panelists on such diverse subjects as astronomy and linguistics, Berg correctly answered eleven of them. The radio network received such a flood of letters that Berg was invited back.

Moe was interested in many things, maybe everything. One of his roommates on the Boston Red Sox at the end of his career was rookie Dom DiMaggio, who remembers that their room was always overrun with newspapers. "He had them divided into two categories," Dom was saying over drinks at his home overlooking Buzzards Bay in Massachusetts. "He called one stack, the ones he had read, 'dead.' The ones he hadn't read yet were 'alive.' They were all over the place, and you didn't dare touch one page or he'd raise hell with you."

After only a few weeks, Berg convinced the Red Sox to give him a room by himself. "He told me he realized some of our teammates liked to stop by, and he didn't want to impose on me."

Berg's teammates challenged him from time to time about the articles in all those newspapers from various cities and in different languages. They refused to believe he really read them all. But when they questioned him, Berg was able to recite the requested information as they followed the articles in the newspapers.

He was frequently invited to mingle with distinguished people at receptions, banquets, and affairs of state. Because of these social activities, he was the only player who ever kept a tuxedo in his locker at the ballpark. When he played with the Washington Senators in 1932, he lived at the fashionable Wardman Park Hotel, home of many Washington dignitaries. His teammates said he never paid for a dinner when he was in the nation's capital.

"Broadway Charlie" Wagner, a close friend of Berg's while they were teammates on the Red Sox, was taking home movies for Manager Joe Cronin on Opening Day of the 1938 season when he saw more evidence of Berg's connections with people in high places.

As we talked last summer, Charlie was remembering that the Red Sox opened that season in Washington. When Secret Service agents and others guided FDR's wheelchair up a ramp to the presidential box near the Senators' dugout on the first base side of Griffith Stadium, Wagner was close to the action to get some good films for Cronin. He saw and heard Jim Farley, Roosevelt's postmaster general and one of the most powerful political figures in the nation, turn to the president, point toward Berg, and say, "There's Moe Berg." FDR spotted Berg and called out with his trademark cheerfulness, "Hi, Moe!" The president of the United States obviously knew Moe Berg's name and face, and maybe not just from baseball.

Yet despite all of his interests and his social connections, Moe Berg's consuming passion was baseball. His brother, Dr. Sam Berg, said, "Baseball was all he lived for. He was irresponsible, and money meant nothing to him. Baseball was all he cared about."

Moe's passion caused friction with his father, who never was able to understand his son's devotion to the game considering his qualifications for brilliant success in other fields. Besides, his father told him, baseball was only a game, not the kind of thing you do professionally.

The criticism against Berg was that he was fluent in a dozen languages but couldn't hit in any of them. He played in more than seventy-six games only one season and was usually his team's bullpen catcher, warming up relief pitchers. Despite his intellectual interests, Berg could be an exhibitionist. Wagner remembers that on Ladies' Day, if the hitter sent a pop-up into foul territory, "Moe would throw his mask into the air, catch the foul ball behind the plate, and then catch the mask. The ladies loved it, and so did Moe."

Moe had a mysterious side to him. "We always suspected he was a spy for the government," Dom DiMaggio says today. "After he retired from baseball, no one could ever explain what Moe did for a living, so we began to think that maybe he had been a spy during the war and just continued to work that way after the war ended."

Officially, Berg joined the Office of Strategic Services, the forerunner of today's Central Intelligence Agency, in 1941, while he was still a bullpen catcher for the Red Sox. His first assignment was to deliver radio broadcasts in Japanese warning them of the destruction their homeland would face as

World War II dragged on and reminding them of his close friendship with them forged during eight trips to the Orient.

His fellow players remembered later that on some of those trips to Japan, Moe took movies of the Tokyo skyline. Then he went one better, convincing players like Lefty Gomez of the Yankees to let him borrow their movies, too. He did and returned them in due time. Postwar evidence indicates that the films served as aerial maps for Jimmy Doolittle's dramatic raid over Tokyo in 1942 and for the massive B-29 raids over Japanese cities in late 1944 and '45 as Americans followed a new strategy in those final months—bombing Japan into submission.

Later in the war, Berg was assigned to Europe to determine the progress of Hitler's scientists in their race to develop the atomic bomb. While most Americans, even the new vice president, Harry Truman, were unaware of our own atomic bomb project, our intelligence experts knew the Germans were working on the same thing.

His baseball reputation followed him, even in his spy work. When he was assigned his new mission, a general on the project complained, "They gave us the slowest base runner in the American League."

Berg traveled to Bisingen in Germany's Black Forest, the nerve center of the project like our own massive complex in Oak Ridge, Tennessee. On December 18, 1944, three days after Glenn Miller's plane took off and two days after Cecil Travis and Warren Spahn found themselves trapped in the Battle of the Bulge, Moe Berg sat in front of Hitler's most prominent atomic physicist.

He was Werner Heisenberg. Berg was disguised as a Swiss graduate student attending a lecture. His immediate mission was to determine, in his own judgment, if Heisenberg's remarks indicated he was trying to help Hitler develop atomic weapons. If so, Berg's orders were to kill him.

Under his coat Berg was wearing a shoulder holster that contained a Beretta revolver. He also carried a cyanide pill for his own use if he had to use the Beretta on Heisenberg. In the room with him he saw agents of Hitler's feared SS security organization.

Berg concluded that Heisenberg did not seem to be among

those involved in such work, although research since then by journalists and historians indicates the possibility that Heisenberg might in fact have been conducting scientific work on nuclear fission while attempting to keep it from the Nazis.

Later Berg was parachuted into Italy behind German lines to make contact with an Italian scientist who was to report further on Germany's progress toward production of an atomic bomb.

He continued to appear from time to time during the rest of the war. When American troops liberated the major cities of Europe, Berg had been there ahead of them. After we dropped the atomic bomb on Hiroshima, Moe's sister heard from him for the first time in five years. In his first conversation with her since before the war, he told her on the phone, "I told you not to worry."

None of this became known until years after the war. Berg remained on the fringes of the baseball world he loved so dearly, but not employed in it. That's what led to speculation that he might be a spy—nobody could tell you what he did for a living. They just knew that he never wore anything but a black suit, showed up at the All-Star Game and the World Series, and never would discuss his work. Only after he died did the real Moe Berg story come out. It even became the subject of a television movie.

As he lay dying at Clara Maas Hospital in Newark, New Jersey, on May 30, 1972, eighty years old and suffering from injuries received in a fall at his home, Moe Berg turned to his nurse and asked, "How did the Mets do today?" Then he died.

Optimism was spreading by the close of 1944. Some 750,000 people, almost as many as in prewar years, disregarded rain and fog and jammed into Times Square just like old times to ring out the old year and ring in 1945. Many other people attended church services.

All around town the end-of-the year movie hits were playing at Radio City Musical Hall, the Astor, Roxy, Rivoli, Broadway, and the Fifth Avenue Playhouse, films like *National Velvet, Winged Victory, To Have and Have Not, The Keys of the Kingdom,* and *Naughty Marietta.* At the Winter Garden,

161

Olsen and Johnson were breaking up the place with their vaudeville one-liners and sight gags. At the Capitol, Margaret O'Brien, Jimmy Durante, June Allyson, and pianist Jose Iturbi were starring in *Music for Millions,* but the biggest star of all was the man appearing in person on stage, Tommy Dorsey and his orchestra.

A page one headline in the *New York Times* on January 1, 1945, said:

NEW YEAR GREETED WITH HOPE AND
JOY BY CITY'S MILLIONS

"As if anxious to speed the departing memory of another year of war, New York's millions saw 1944 out last night with few backward looks. . . ."

The *Times* reported that singer Lucy Monroe, who often sang the national anthem at Yankee Stadium before World Series games and other major events, "was scarcely audible" above the roar of human voices as she performed "The Star-Spangled Banner" from a platform in front of a reproduction of the Statue of Liberty.

The lighted globe was dropped slowly from the Times Tower to street level in the tradition that began in 1908 but was suspended with the start of the war. The *Times* said the ball was "relighted this year as a measure of confidence that it would remain lighted from now on through victory and peace."

An electronic message snaked its away around the Times Building on the sign usually reserved for the day's headlines:

Work for victory. It is now twelve o'clock. The New Year is here. Let us make it a year of victory. Let us each pledge ourselves to get on with the job so that those we love may soon be home with us again.

Part Five

1945

14

IN GOOD TIMES AND
BAD, PLAY BALL!

AS THE FIRST DAY OF 1945 DAWNED, OUR BOMBERS WERE
blasting the Japanese-held island of Iwo Jima for the twenty-
fourth straight day. On the other side of the globe, Hitler
issued a New Year's message to the world saying his Nazis
would never give up.

The beginning of the war's fourth year brought different
kinds of news to different people. The daily casualty totals on
the front page of the *Washington Post* on January 1 showed
three more area men killed in action, making the region's
total 602. For Beulah Taylor, the news was far better. A
twenty-year-old nursing assistant in the Washington suburb
of Alexandria, Virginia, she landed a leading role in a movie
based on the writings of Ernie Pyle called *G. I. Joe.*

Twenty days later, President Roosevelt was inaugurated
for the fourth time, in a muted atmosphere. There was no
star-spangled ceremony on the steps of the Capitol Building,
no formal dress, no lengthy inaugural address, no long parade down Pennsylvania Avenue.

Instead, FDR, with his son Marine Colonel Jimmy Roosevelt at his side, stood on the south portico of the White House
in a blue business suit and recited the oath of office as

administered by Chief Justice Harlan Stone. Then, with snow on the ground and under what the *Post*'s Robert Albright called a "gray and unsmiling" sky, Roosevelt delivered the shortest inaugural address in presidential history—551 words, 6 minutes long.

Standing bareheaded, he called for God's help "to see the way that leads to a better life for ourselves, and all our fellow men—to the achievement of His will and peace on earth."

A crowd of 7,800 people applauded with gloves on in the January cold, adding to the day's subdued tone. One person in the crowd was Marion Hargrove, author of the best-selling book about life in the Army *See Here, Private Hargrove*. By the day of FDR's fourth inauguration, Hargrove's book had sold three million copies and had been made into a movie. Of almost equal importance, Hargrove wasn't a private anymore. By then he was a sergeant.

The entire inaugural ceremony, during which FDR twice shed his trademark cape, lasted fifteen minutes.

Reporter Albright said, "You thought not so much of Lincoln and the only other wartime inaugural. You thought of Woodrow Wilson and his fight for the League of Nations." When it was over, Dr. McIntyre said, "Everything is fine . . . he's carrying a thunder of a lot of work and getting away with it in grand style."

Ten days after Roosevelt's inauguration, one of the annual highlights of the Washington social season took place, FDR's birthday. As the nation's most prominent polio victim, the president used his birthday each year to raise funds for the March of Dimes to combat the disease.

On his sixty-third birthday, eight balls were held in Washington. Mrs. Roosevelt made the rounds. The main ball was at the Statler Hotel on K Street, now the Capitol Hilton, where she read a message from her husband. Some of the biggest names in show business appeared—Kay Kyser and his band, Margaret O'Brien, George Murphy, Myrna Loy, Charles Bickford, Victor Borge, Joe E. Brown, Alan Ladd, and Seaman Second Class Gene Kelly.

At another Washington location, Walter Reed Army Hospital, the New Year was dawning with promise in the always optimistic attitude of Bert Shepard. He was being fitted for a new artificial leg to replace a homemade wooden stump from prison camp. He was determined that he would resume his baseball career. What he didn't know was that powerful new help was only a few miles away from the hospital's grounds in the tree-filled northwest section of Washington.

Shepard was liberated from Stalag IX-C at Meiningen, Germany, in late October, 1944. At Meiningen, he was the "P.M.C.," president of the Messing Committee, a British term for the head of his dining table of eighteen English, Canadian, Australian, and American prisoners. To him fell the mealtime responsibility of doling out two thin slices of black bread and a bowl of stew, plus tidbits from the Red Cross on rare occasions.

When he wasn't serving as P.M.C. or performing his other prison camp duties, he was, of all things, practicing baseball, thanks to the genius of a fellow prisoner, Dan Errey of Canada, who used his mechanical know-how to manufacture a makeshift artificial leg. It wasn't what we would call state-of-the-art, but it was good enough for Bert. On it, the former left-handed pitcher and first baseman for Bisbee in the Arizona-Texas League began to run himself into baseball shape and practice pitching.

He recruited other prisoners to work out with him so he could practice the one skill where he might be vulnerable—fielding bunts. Shepard knew that baseball players weren't going to feel sorry for him. If they found out he couldn't handle a bunt, then that's what he'd get—all game long.

Besides, baseball players all over America in those years knew the sad experience of Monty Stratton, a right-handed pitcher who won thirty-six games for the Chicago White Sox from 1934 through 1938. Stratton, who stood six feet five inches tall, lost his leg in a hunting accident but might have made it back to the major leagues on an artificial leg except for that one failing—he couldn't come off the mound fast enough to field a bunt.

When the Allies captured Shepard's part of Germany and the prisoners became free men, Bert strolled out of the gate after eight months in Stalag IX-C. One of his fellow prisoners, Wright Bryan, said Bert was "wisecracking at every step."

167

He told Bryan, "I'll be playing ball again when you get home, Wright."

Bryan said sarcastically, "Sure you will." He said he "felt sick inside for the disappointment I thought Shep was going to face."

The under secretary of war, Robert Patterson, arranged for a group of former POWs being treated at Walter Reed to be brought to his office so he could learn how they were treated by the Germans while in captivity. Patterson wanted to use the information for publicity in the government's campaign of wartime propaganda.

He went around the room asking each former prisoner what he wanted to do after the war. When he got to Lieutenant Shepard, Bert surprised him by saying, "I'm going to be a professional baseball player."

Secretary Patterson told him candidly but sympathetically, "But you can't do that."

Bert said, "Oh yes I can. I did it before the war, and I'm going to do it after the war."

Patterson continued his skepticism. "But now you have an artificial leg."

Shepard was as determined as Patterson was skeptical. "That doesn't make any difference," he responded. "I've been practicing in prison camp, and I know I can do it."

His attitude impressed Patterson so much that the under secretary, who was promoted to secretary later in the year, picked up the telephone and called Clark Griffith and asked him to take a look at this young man during the Senators' spring-training camp at Maryland University. Griffith, the patriotic owner who did so much for servicemen and -women during two world wars, agreed instantly.

Shepard arrived at the Maryland University campus in College Park on March 14. He quickly found work as the only left-handed batting-practice pitcher for the Senators' hitters, worked out at first base, and lined some shots to the outfield from the batting cage.

I was in that camp too, having offered my services as a batboy and been accepted on the spot. The experience lasted long enough for me to get a close-up look at my heroes and call most of them by their first names, including Shepard and

168

a local boy who made good in the 1930s with the Yankees, Jake Powell, and others.

Being a batboy wasn't always easy, though. It was bad enough that three of us had to shine the shoes of every player and coach, more than thirty of them, every day, had to spend the whole day running errands, didn't get paid and scraped up whatever money we could only through our ingenuity in selling foul balls and cracked bats without getting caught.

But when they made us ride into Washington and scrub the scum off Griffith Stadium's shower room walls, left over from the end of the Redskins' season six months before, and faced with the prospect of getting home from every game some time after one A.M. following a late-night ride on the streetcar and another on the bus while still in the eighth grade, I quit.

Every afternoon before then, however, I saw Bert come into the locker room after the day's workout, always smiling and in high spirits, unstrap his artificial right leg, place it in his locker, and then hobble into the showers on one leg.

Then there was the day when Frankie Baxter, the gruff but kind hunchbacked equipment manager and the supreme boss of us batboys, hid Shepard's artificial leg while he was in the shower.

Bert came hopping out of the shower, and when he saw that his leg was missing from his locker, he started looking, knowing that it must be some kind of a gag. The more he looked, the more he knew somebody was putting him on.

Finally he settled on Frankie. "All right, Baxter," he said, "where is it? I know damn well you did something with my leg." Then it occurred to Bert to check the garbage can. There it was.

Baxter told Bert his reason for putting it there: "Well, I felt it, and there was no pulse. It was cold, and I thought it was dead. So I just threw the damn thing away."

Shepard's timetable was about average for a rookie trying to win a job on a big-league team. Even with almost three years of a world war behind him, he was still only twenty-four years old.

169

On his first day in camp, when he walked onto the field in his Senators' uniform, a reporter said, "There's a helluva story." Shepard says today, "In about two hours the newsreels were out there along with twenty-five reporters." The photographers asked him to go back into the clubhouse and put his Army uniform on again so they could get pictures of him as he changed from one uniform into the other.

Bert did this and everything else cheerfully. Walter Haight, one of America's most respected writers on horse racing, who was pressed into service covering the baseball team while Shirley Povich covered the war in the Pacific, wrote, "Seldom has any athlete received so much publicity in so short a time. Reporters, photographers, feature writers, magazine writers, movie cameramen have kept him covered, and yesterday radio discovered him. He will be on several programs within the next few days." Shepard was also signed up quickly to be the guest speaker at the next weekly luncheon of Washington's famous Touchdown Club.

To this day he considers himself lucky: "I could have lost my left leg," he told me not long ago when we were reliving that 1945 spring training that was such a thrill for both of us. "You need the back leg for balance and since I'm a southpaw, I would drive off my left leg." He said coming down on an artificial front leg "doesn't hurt a thing. There's very little handicap as far as thowing is concerned."

A cameraman from Paramount Pictures was filming Shepard's first day on the diamond when he asked the key question: "Lieutenant, can you field a bunt?"

Shepard told the cameraman, "I think I can." Al Evans, one of the Senators' catchers, was in the batting cage. While the other players stopped their practice work to watch, Evans dropped a bunt six feet in front of home plate,

Haight reported, "Shepard came in catlike, gathered in the ball, pivoted as left-handers must, and then heaved the ball on a line to Joe Kuhel at first." Manager Ossie Bluege called out, "Atta boy, Shep."

The cameraman said, "Let's try it again." Evans did the same thing, and so did Shepard.

He reached another dream-come-true level on March 29 when the Senators signed him as a coach. Griffith told reporters, "We'll let him do anything he thinks he can." Meanwhile, his pal from prisoner camp, Wright Bryan, read the news in an American magazine at an Army hospital near Paris. The story said Shep would be coaching base runners, but it also said that Shepard insisted he was going to pitch.

And Bryan remembered Shep's prediction.

During the spring-training period in 1945, another left-handed pitcher found himself otherwise occupied. Lieutenant Warren Spahn was a member of the American units who captured the strategically important Remagen Bridge over the Rhine River in Germany. They arrived on March 7, just before a team of German demolition experts could finish its work and blow up the structure, an old railroad bridge.

American troops and vehicles then poured across to establish a beachhead on the other side, continuing their sweep through Germany and their now-certain defeat of the German army. The prediction was heard everywhere: the capture of the bridge would shorten the war in Europe by several months and save thousands of casualties.

Like everyone else, Spahn, who was twenty-three years old, had his own reason to hope the prediction was true. The sooner the war ended, the sooner he could get back to the Boston Braves. He'd made it up to the big leagues briefly in 1942, appearing in four games for the Braves without a won-lost record.

On the afternoon of March 17, Spahn was talking to another officer as they prepared to change guard units; Lieutenant Spahn and his men were due to take over the guard duty. Spahn would be walking onto the bridge at four o'clock to supervise his men as they took up their positions. The time was 3:59.

Suddenly, the bridge collapsed. The Allies had poured so many men and so much equipment over it in the ten days since its capture that the structure simply caved in under the weight of its twenty-four-hour-a-day burden. Spahn remembers the sound as well as the sight. "The rivets just popped out of that bridge. They sounded like machine-gun fire."

If the collapse had occurred one minute later, Spahn would have been on it. "I felt like a pretty lucky guy," he said,

171

"and I guess that luck followed me through my baseball career."

The 4-F baseball players faced a new worry as they limbered up in spring training. By 1945, in spite of optimism about the war, the manpower shortage was becoming critical. Jimmy Byrnes, the director of War Mobilization and Reconstruction, ordered that all draft deferments for professional athletes be reexamined, saying, "It is difficult for the public to understand, and certainly it is difficult for me to understand, how these men can be physically unfit for military service and yet be able to compete with the greatest athletes of the nation in games demanding physical fitness."

Byrnes pointed out that athletes could serve in noncombat positions in the military or work in war plants. He was apparently unaware that many of them were working in war plants already and had been doing so for a year or two.

The director of the F.B.I., J. Edgar Hoover, always one of America's strongest patriots, disagreed emphatically. "If any ball players, or other athletes, were attempting to dodge service," he said, "it would be our job to look into such cases. But our records show there are few, if any, such cases among the thousands of ball players."

Others said Byrnes was off base, so to speak, because his logic didn't allow for the extra treatment many athletes required before and after playing their sport. Those defending the athletes pointed out that many baseball players had to undergo special treatment such as massages, whirlpool baths, and heavily taped ankles. They said some players continued to reinjure key parts such as knees. Lou Boudreau, playing all through the war on bad ankles, broke the same ankle three times. George Kell's bad knees made him unqualified for Army basic training from birth, hardly a reason not to play baseball.

Senator William "Wild Bill" Langer of North Dakota sided with Byrnes and introduced legislation requiring that 10 percent of the players on every major-league team be men who had lost one "or more" arms, legs, or hands.

Langer was consistent if nothing else. Five years later he took to the floor of the Senate to accuse Clark Griffith of

172

being a "wartime profiteer" for scheduling a "day-night" doubleheader, requiring separate admissions, at the request of the Yankees in the first months of the Korean War. I interviewed Griffith at his ballpark that night in 1950 to get his reaction. Baseball's most patriotic American told me bluntly, "Mr. Langer doesn't know what he's talking about."

Whether Byrnes and Langer knew what they were talking about or not in 1945, the War Department complied with the Byrnes directive. The result was blatant discrimination against an entire group of young men who were being reexamined, and in some cases drafted, simply because they were professional athletes. Ron Northey was Exhibit A.

Northey, a twenty-four-year-old outfielder for the Philadelphia Phillies, was classified 4-F on January 2 for no fewer than three reasons—a punctured eardrum, a heart condition, and high blood pressure. It was the second time he had been classified 4-F. He was looking forward to the 1945 season after enjoying the best of his three years in the majors in '44 with a .288 batting average, 22 home runs, and 104 runs batted in.

Two weeks after being notified of his deferment for physical reasons, Northey was ordered to report for his third examination. Before that became necessary, he tried to enlist in the Navy. He was turned down, physically unqualified because of his ear.

On January 29, in the midst of the new pressure from Byrnes, Langer, and others, he was examined again in Philadelphia and sworn into the Army on the same day. By nightfall he was in a contingent of recruits who were en route to the Army induction center at New Cumberland, Pennsylvania.

Congressional opposition to the Byrnes edict built quickly. One of the staunchest opponents was a senator, Happy Chandler of Kentucky, who spoke out on behalf of the baseball players. A freshman congressman from Illinois, Melvin Price, whose district bordered the Mississippi River in East St. Louis, directly across from St. Louis, received a request for help from the Browns.

The Browns were in a bind. On March 1, with spring training scheduled to start in twelve days, they had announced the signing of only four players, two of them rookies. "The club's big problem," the Associated Press reported, "is the national manpower muddle centering around the controversial 'work-or-fight-or-jail' legislation in Congress."

The A.P. said, "Many of the players are 4-F, but have been working in essential jobs. Some draft boards have warned men in essential industries if they quit they will be drafted regardless of physical condition or Congressional action."

Thanks to the pressure generated by Chandler, Price, and others, the War Department suspended the regulation in May, the same month that it began to look as if the manpower problem might be on the road to solution anyhow because of the Allies' victory in Europe and Germany's surrender. In the meantime, Senator Chandler was appointed commissioner of baseball, succeeding the late Judge Landis.

In *Even the Browns*, Bill Mead reports that cancellation of the regulation came just in time to spare Dutch Leonard and Mickey Haefner of the Senators, Wally Moses of the White Sox, and Allie Reynolds of the Yankees.

Haefner's teammate on the last-place '44 Senators, Center Fielder Stan Spence, wasn't so lucky. He was inducted and missed all of 1945. But the reversal in policy was especially devastating to the defending world champions, the Cardinals. Two of their starters, Catcher Walker Cooper and Left Fielder Danny Litwhiler, were also called back and then inducted. Cooper missed all but four games, and Litwhiler missed the entire season.

The Cards, with Ken O'Dea substituting behind the plate and a future Hall of Famer, rookie Red Schoendienst, starting in the outfield for the only season of his career, were unable to repeat as champions.

15

WHEN WE LOST
A LEADER
AND A FAN

ON APRIL 12, FIVE DAYS BEFORE THE MAJOR-LEAGUE SEASON
was scheduled to start, President Roosevelt was posing for an
oil portrait at the "Little White House" in Warm Springs,
Georgia, where he went as often as possible to rest and enjoy
the therapeutic effects of the warm spring water on his
polio-weakened legs.

Just before his latest trip down South, FDR welcomed
Clark Griffith into the Oval Office, where the Senators' owner went through his annual ritual of presenting the nation's
chief executive with his season's pass to major-league games.
As the two old friends chatted and went through the manda-
tory poses for photographers, President Roosevelt turned to
his favorite baseball owner and said, "You've got to give me
credit for night baseball."

Griffith was always willing to give Roosevelt credit for the
large increase in night baseball. He scheduled more night
games than any other owner after FDR's "green light letter"
in 1942. Even with blackouts and dimouts, night games enjoyed a priority status of their own.

By the afternoon of the twelfth, President Roosevelt had
been in Warm Springs for twelve days, gained eight pounds,

and was looking forward to more good eating at a barbecue that afternoon. He was sitting in a chair for a watercolor painting by Elizabeth Shoumatoff when he put his hand to his head and said, "I have a terrific headache."

A moment later, at 3:35 P.M., Eastern War Time, he died.

Despite FDR's worsening appearance in newspaper pictures and the movie newsreels, his death shocked the world. After all, there were those reassuring statements from his physician, and the White House reporters never seemed to disagree or question those reassurances.

We found out in later years that FDR's health in the last year or so of his life—the critical years of World War II—was never as good as we had been led to believe. One of the most prominent radio commentators of the day, H. R. Baukhage, called it "the greatest conspiracy of silence in the history of journalism."

Maybe Roosevelt's death shocked us kids more than any other group. He was the only president we ever knew. As I walked down the street from school that afternoon, I saw one of the older mothers in the neighborhood sitting in her rocking chair on her front porch and crying. She said the United States was in for a terrible time because our leader was dead.

When I got home, I said, "Mom, Mrs. Timmons says she doesn't know what's going to happen to us because President Roosevelt was such a great man."

My mother, a staunch Roosevelt supporter, saw the situation with a simple confidence that made me feel better: "No one is indispensable, not even the president."

In Berlin, the news was greeted with fanatic enthusiasm by Adolf Hitler's propaganda minister, Joseph Goebbels. With the "fatherland" almost on its knees as Eisenhower's Allied armies stormed across Germany, Goebbels nevertheless telephoned Hitler and said gleefully, "My Führer, I congratulate you! Roosevelt is dead! It is written in the stars that the second half of April will be a turning point for us!"

Hitler answered that FDR was "the greatest war criminal of all times." Twenty-five days later, Germany surrendered and Hitler was dead, by his own hand.

Newscaster John Daly of CBS Radio broke into an afternoon kids' program, "Wilderness Road," to broadcast the bulletin that Roosevelt was dead, the victim of a cerebral hemorrhage. The death certificate signed by Dr. Howard Bruenn listed arteriosclerosis as a "contributing cause."

In the first hours after his death, the switchboard at Vice President Truman's apartment building on Connecticut Avenue was jammed with calls from people in housing-scarce Washington asking if his apartment would be available now that he was moving into the White House.

In more respectful responses, 10,000 people turned out in Charlotte, North Carolina, to watch the funeral train roll through town, and knots of folks in smaller towns all along the East Coast to Washington did the same. For three days of national mourning, movie theaters were closed and radio stations played nothing but the somber tones of chamber music.

In the nation's capital city, the funeral procession wound its way up Pennsylvania Avenue under a flyover of twenty-four B-24 bombers. The casket rested under an American flag on a caisson drawn by six white horses as Arthur Godfrey, still a Washington disc jockey, broadcast his description over CBS Radio from the roof of the Riggs Bank at Fifteenth Street and Pennsylvania Avenue.

Godfrey saw people standing fifteen and twenty deep in some places, thirty and forty deep in others in an outpouring of sentiment that lined Pennsylvania Avenue and Fifteenth Street for as far as the eye could see. Americans came, in his words, "to pay their last respects to . . . the man who was their leader, the commander-in-chief, and their friend."

Troops in combat uniforms and helmets stood with their rifles at parade rest on both sides of the entire route. Others marched by the thousands or rode in Jeeps and other machines produced for the war in the same factories that once manufactured new cars. Men and women both dabbed at their eyes with their handkerchiefs. Executives in white shirts, ties, and business suits cried openly. Boy scouts in uniform rendered their three-fingered salutes. Servicemen and -women dotted the crowd with their uniforms.

The mood was one of overpowering grief and solemn silence as Godfrey, in those days before television, described the scene for his nationwide radio audience in an account

177

that has become a part of broadcasting history. His deep voice was appropriately subdued and solemn. As the procession neared his vantage point a short block from the White House, Godfrey's emotions were clearly detectable. Toward the end, his voice began to break, and he was forced to switch his listeners back to the CBS studio hurriedly to avoid breaking down completely on the air:

> It is fitting that this procession should be as—what shall I say?—magnificent is the word. It's so hard to find adjectives to describe the funeral procession of your idol. And these crowds and crowds of people standing mutely . . . quietly . . . dazed expressions on their faces, still unable to believe, and I know that lots of them feel, just as I do . . . we just won't believe until the caisson itself passes us.
>
> May God give me the strength to do this.
>
> And behind is the car bearing the successor to the late President Roosevelt, the man on whose shoulders now fall the terrific burdens and responsibilities that were handled so well by the man to whose body we're paying our last respects now.
>
> God bless him, President Truman. We return you now to the studio.

The CBS Washington studios were flooded immediately with phone calls and telegrams from listeners expressing their admiration for Godfrey's human description of what he saw and felt because it reflected so accurately what they felt, too.

A world war in its fourth year and the death of our leader, the man who wanted baseball to continue, couldn't stop the baseball season from opening on schedule, but rain could. The Opening Game, scheduled for April 16 against the Yankees, was washed out. Instead of Opening Day, the biggest story in Washington that day was an address to Congress by President Truman. The *Washington Post* called it a "humble, homespun talk."

The next day another big story hit Washington and the world. It was about a local boy who had made good and was

178

as loved and admired everywhere else as he had always been in Washington. Ernie Pyle was dead.

The war correspondent who humanized the war in Europe better than any other newspaper reporter and then answered the urgings of the Pentagon brass by going to the Pacific because they told him his presence would help the morale of our men there was killed by a Japanese sniper's bullet. It happened on a speck of land called Ie Shima, an island of only ten square miles just west of Okinawa.

Shirley Povich still remembers the tragic day with a personal sadness. He told me years ago that he ran into Pyle while they were both covering the fighting on Okinawa. Povich wasn't the only former sportswriter reporting on the war in the Pacific. There were so many of them they could have formed their own chapter of the Baseball Writers' Association of America.

Gordon Cobbledick of the Cleveland *Plain Dealer* was there with Povich, as well as Don Donaghee of the *Philadelphia Bulletin,* John Lardner of *Newsweek* magazine, Bob Sherrod of the *Saturday Evening Post,* and Bob Ruark of the Scripps-Howard newspaper chain.

Povich and Pyle were old newspaper pals from Washington, where Pyle wrote for the *Washington Daily News,* a Scripps-Howard tabloid, and Povich for the *Post.*

Pyle told Povich he really hadn't wanted to go to the Pacific. He was convinced he would never live through it, and he told Povich so many times. He said he had pressed his luck too many times in Italy, where he won world fame, respect, and affection not only among the fighting GIs but among the folks on the home front, too. He moved among the rank-and-file troops and shared their foxholes and their mess kits as well as their gripes and fears and homesickness more compassionately than any other correspondent and wrote of them the same way.

He told people that what he saw in war made him a changed man. "I believe I have a new patience with humanity that I've never had before," he said. "I don't see how any survivor of war can ever be cruel to anything, ever again."

Pyle told Povich he was exhausted after the war in Europe and ached to stay home with his family and friends. He said

179

he felt he had given enough of himself to the war, but pressure from the Pentagon persuaded him to pick up his portable typewriter and shaving kit and head off to war for the second time.

By the time the two ran into each other on Okinawa, Pyle had another complaint. He felt he was being used for publicity purposes. "I'm here because the damn brass wanted me here," he told Povich, "but I can't get to the real war because of them, with their lousy receptions and cocktail parties. Hell, I have more fun with the GIs. This social whirl ain't my kind of war."

Povich and Pyle were stationed on the *El Dorado,* one of 1,300 ships engaged in the Okinawa campaign, when Pyle suggested they look for a different kind of story the next day. "Tomorrow we head for Ie Shima," he announced. "There aren't many people there, but maybe we should take a look at it for a feature as one of the unknown islands involved in this campaign. Let's go together."

Povich loved the idea, but the ship's doctor didn't. He immediately vetoed Povich's half of the excursion because he was being treated for back injuries after three incidents: he was bounced to the ceiling of a C-47 cargo plane in foul-weather turbulence; two days later he was thrown to the floor of a B-24 bomber when its door flew open and a blast of wind whooshed through the plane; and as if that weren't enough, a half-track vehicle tipped over on him on Okinawa.

The doctor informed Povich that X-rays showed he had two fractured vertebrae. He was being moved to a hospital ship for transfer to Pearl Harbor. The war was over for Povich, and Pyle headed off to Ie Shima by himself the next day.

He was riding in a Jeep with Lieutenant Colonel Joseph Coolidge and rounding a corner when a Japanese sniper opened up on them with machine-gun fire. They immediately dived into a ditch along the road. Pyle, in his eagerness to see what was going on so he could write about it for the folks back home, peered over the edge of the ditch. He was hit three times in the temple.

The killing of the beloved correspondent was received with almost as much shock and sadness as FDR's death six

180

days before. Sergeant John Chiodo of Johnstown, Pennsylvania, was still stationed with the Fifth Army in Italy when he heard the news. "Poor old Ernie," he said sadly. "He felt he was going to get it sooner or later."

Another GI in Europe, Sergeant George Bentley of Belmont, North Carolina, compared the loss of the two leaders, the president and the reporter. "First Roosevelt and now Ernie, " he said. "The GI has lost two of his best friends in less than a week."

At the scene of his death, his GI pals erected a simple grave marker:

At This Spot the 77th Infantry Lost a Buddy.

Ernie Pyle. 18 April 1945.

By the time the weather allowed the Senators to open their home season four days late, after playing a road series against the A's in Philadelphia, the number of former major-league players in the armed forces was approaching five hundred, and the number of minor leaguers was four thousand. Only 24,494 fans, nearly 10,000 below Griffith Stadium's capacity, turned out as the Senators met the Yankees.

President Truman was busy with his new job and the war, so Speaker of the House Sam Rayburn of Texas threw out the first ball, flanked by Clark Griffith and the immortal Senators' pitcher of earlier years, Walter Johnson. In a touch of irony, Rayburn's toss was caught by one of Griffith's Cuban players who decided to play baseball in the States and take his chances with the draft. He was Carlos Santiago Castello Ullrich, a twenty-three-year-old pitcher.

Ullrich seemed appropriate for fate's choice to catch the first ball. He joined the Senators in 1944, won three games for them—all in '45—and was never seen in the majors again.

Reporter Al Costello wrote in the *Washington Post* that the atmosphere was "almost eerie" at Griffith Stadium in those first days following the death of President Roosevelt. The weather was cold and gray.

In FDR's memory, the crowd observed a minute of silence which Costello said was "absolute." Then a bugler played taps, followed by the national anthem, performed, as it was every year, by Goldman's Band.

The Yankees won, which also seemed to happen every year. Costello wrote with a sense of awareness that baseball and the war, and their effect on each other, were clear to see. "The color of other years was missing . . . but it was baseball and Opening Day despite the lack of pomp and splendor that usually goes with openers. It was baseball despite the lack of the game's big names who are playing a bigger and more important game."

Team rosters were still being knocked cockeyed from one day to the next by the military draft. The first casualties in 1945 were the Philadelphia Phillies and the St. Louis Cardinals. The Phillies unexpectedly lost their ace pitcher, Ken Raffensberger, on April 30, when the season was less than two weeks old.

Raffensberger was the twenty-seven-year-old left-hander who won thirteen games for the last-place Phillies in 1944 and was being counted on as the anchor man of their staff in '45.

The Phillies were in a state of shock. Their secretary-treasurer, George Fletcher, said, "Whew! We didn't expect it to happen so soon. It's a severe loss to the team. He was, perhaps, our number-one pitcher."

The Cardinals lost their star catcher, .317 hitter and leader Walker Cooper, the next day. In reporting his induction into the Navy, the Associated Press gave him much of the credit for the success of his team's pitchers. AP said there was "little doubt that Walker was a major factor in guiding wartime pitchers past the 100-victory mark in all three years" of the war to date. Under his behind-the-plate leadership, the Cardinals won 106 games in 1942 and 105 in both 1943 and '44.

The Dodgers lost Mickey Owen, who enlisted in the Navy early in the season. He was buying some real estate at the time but had to sell part of his property because he wasn't sure he'd be able to keep up his mortgage payments given his loss in income.

"You had to pay for it, and you didn't know how long

182

you'd be gone," he said. "Most others had to do the same thing."

Still, Owen remembers that most folks weren't discouraged about the present or afraid of the future. "People were a little bit different then," he said. "We had just come out of the Depression and been through some hard knocks, so as far as anything scaring them was concerned, it didn't. Their whole attitude was toughened up by the Depression."

Another player who filled in a wartime vacancy was Jimmie Foxx, the illustrious Hall of Famer whose big-league career, which began in 1925, was considered virtually finished following the 1942 season after eighteen years as a power-hitting star.

During his all-star career, first with the Philadelphia A's and then the Boston Red Sox, he won the American League batting championship twice and the home run title three times, tied for tops in homers once, and was voted the American League's Most Valuable Player three times. His major-league days appeared to be over when "Double-X" dropped out of the big leagues in 1943, but he was back in '44 for one season with the Chicago Cubs, appearing in only fifteen games, eleven as a pinch hitter. In twenty times at bat, he got only one hit, a double.

In 1945, Foxx, then thirty-seven years old, saw a new opportunity to prolong his career. With the manpower drain worse than ever, he decided to become a pitcher. It wasn't going to be an entirely new experience for him. He appeared in one game as a pitcher for the Red Sox in 1939, pitching one inning, striking out one hitter, and giving up no hits or walks.

In fact, playing another position wasn't a new experience for Foxx at all. He may have been baseball's most versatile star. He played in 1,919 major-league games as a first baseman, but he was also good enough to play 135 games as a third baseman, 109 as a catcher, 21 as an outfielder, and 1 as a shortstop, plus that game in 1939 as a pitcher. In 1945, he pitched in nine more games for the Phillies, won one game without losing any and showed a sparkling average of only 1.59 earned runs per nine innings.

Foxx didn't limit his contributions in 1945 to pitching. He continued his versatility by playing forty games at first base and fourteen at third, while also hitting .268, including seven home runs. When the war ended near the close of the '45 season, Foxx left the majors. At the time, he was second only to his fellow Marylander, Babe Ruth, in home runs and third behind only Ruth and Lou Gehrig in runs batted in.

A certified character in 1945 was a rookie with the Washington Senators named George Binks. They called him "Bingo," but by the end of the season, when he played a decisive but bizarre role during a day-to-day, to-the-wire dogfight with the Detroit Tigers for the pennant, his teammates may have called him something else.

He confessed that he began playing baseball for a practical reason—"to get out of hard work." He began playing at a camp of the Civilian Conservation Corps in Skokie Valley, Illinois, during the Depression.

After six years in the minor leagues, including stops at towns like Monessen, Pennsylvania, and Owensboro, Kentucky, and Tyler, Texas, Binks moved up the ladder to Cedar Rapids, Iowa, and Green Bay and Milwaukee, Wisconsin. With the start of the war, however, Binks dropped out of baseball to work as an expert machinist in a converted automobile factory in South Bend, Indiana, turning out war materials in 1942 and '43.

He returned to baseball and Milwaukee with a bang in 1944, playing in one hundred games as an outfielder-first baseman and hitting .374. Then his dream came true when the Senators bought his contract from Milwaukee and he made it to the majors for five games at the end of the '44 season.

He was twenty-seven years old by then and had already made one decision to improve his chances of making it as a major leaguer. He changed his name from George Binkowski, a product of Chicago's Polish neighborhoods, to Bingo Binks, a name easier for the writers and others to remember. Without knowing it, he improved his chances for newspaper publicity even more because headline writers love anyone whose name will fit into a one-column headline.

Blessed with a smooth left-handed batting stroke, Binks opened his first full year in the big leagues by getting four hits off Buck Newsom and a parade of A's pitchers in Philadelphia, then followed that performance with three more hits in his next two games. As an outfielder he quickly showed grace and sure hands, prompting his manager, Ossie Bluege, to remark, "Binks has the greatest gloved hand I've ever seen on an outfielder. I've never seen him drop a ball that he got his glove on."

Binks was fine where natural ability was involved, but in the thinking end of the sport, he drove Bluege crazy. Bluege was a product of the old school, an outstanding third baseman who spent his entire eighteen-year career with the Washington Senators beginning in 1922, playing with them in three World Series. He placed a premium on fundamentals and the mental part of baseball.

With Binks that could be a problem. He threw to the wrong bases, he hit when he got the bunt sign, he bunted when he got the hit sign, and sometimes he just ignored the signs altogether and made his own decisions on what to do.

"He's an enigma to me," Bluege said in frustration. "I've felt like benching him a dozen times for some of the things he does wrong and some of the things he doesn't do at all, but I'm scared to keep him on the bench. It could be the wrong thing to do, because he has a lot of ability."

His teammates were equally aware of Bingo's problems, and like baseball players everywhere, they showed no mercy in kidding him about them. After he hit a home run off Jim Tobin in Detroit, the next hitter, Joe Kuhel, greeted him at home plate with a handshake but told him, "You missed the bunt sign."

Kuhel was kidding, but Binks was in no position to make that assumption. Instead, he played it safe and stayed away from Bluege for the rest of the day.

In spite of this, Bingo became one of the Senators' most valuable players almost immediately because he could play both the outfield and first base. He was listed on the Washington roster as an outfielder, but he took over the first base job on the team's second western swing of the year when Kuhel was injured. With Binks on the bag and swinging a

185

productive bat, the Senators won sixteen of their next twenty-two games and became pennant contenders.

Back in the outfield later in the season, Binks received hand instructions from Bluege in the dugout on where to play the hitters. "I move him over to the left or right as the case may be," Bluege said, "and then between pitches he starts strolling around out there with his head down and is back where he shouldn't be playing. I've always been afraid he's going to walk out of the park some day."

Binks was 4-F because he was deaf in his left ear as a result of a childhood mastoid operation. Sometimes that condition hurt his team, like the time in Chicago he was caught off second base as he rounded the bag in a game against the White Sox because he couldn't hear the warnings from the dugout that the second baseman was creeping in behind him.

Every time Binks played in the outfield, George Case, the base-stealing champion who was able to cover the outfield with a sprinter's speed, feared a collision because Binks couldn't hear him coming or yelling.

Bluege saw a certain convenience in Bingo's deafness. "After I bawl him out," the manager said, "he says to me, 'I haven't heard a word you said.' "

Dave "Boo" Ferriss was another rookie success story in 1945, a right-handed pitcher from Shaw, Mississippi, who stood the American League's hitters on their ears with twenty-one wins for the Boston Red Sox.

After serving in the Army Air Forces for twenty-six months, he was discharged because of an asthma condition that hospitalized him for four months. The doctors advised him to move to Arizona for its dry climate and change from baseball to another profession. "But I had a ball in my hands as long as I can remember," he said, "and I like baseball. All I ever wanted to be was a ball player. I never wanted to be a fireman or engineer, just a ball player."

On the way to his twenty-one victories, Ferriss won eight games in a row early in the season, four of them shutouts, then reeled off another eight-game winning streak. In 1946, when the stars came home, he won twenty-five games.

Through all of his success, Ferriss charmed Red Sox

followers with his innocence and modesty. When he joined the team from Boston's farm club at Louisville, Trainer Win Green assigned him a rusty nail in the dressing room instead of a locker. "Lockers," the trainer explained, "are for the regulars."

As Ferriss piled one pitching success on top of another, reporters suggested that now he was entitled to a locker, but Ferriss didn't receive the upgrading in his accommodations. "No one will dare move me while I'm winning," he said. "I guess I'm the only one on the team who isn't superstitious."

Columnist Red Smith of the *New York Times* used to tell a story to prove Ferriss was "the only pitcher in baseball history who had Earle Mack, Connie's son, to thank for a career in the majors."

Against the A's in his first start of the season, his first twelve pitches in the major leagues missed the strike zone. Having seen the opposing pitcher load the bases on walks, Earle Mack, then the first-base coach for his father's team, called the next hitter, Bobby Estalella, up the line to the coach's box.

Presumably Mack wanted to remind his cleanup hitter of one of the cardinal rules of hitting: if the pitcher hasn't thrown a strike in a long time, take the first pitch and as many more as necessary until he does throw one. In other words, make the pitcher prove he can still throw a strike, especially a rookie who was off to that kind of a start.

But Mack didn't say that. According to Smith, Mack shocked Estalella by telling him, "Hit the first good pitch."

Estalella swung at the first pitch and popped it up. Ferriss got the next two batters and got out of the inning without any runs being scored. Ferriss won the game and was off to a memorable year that could have ended before it started—except for that help from an opposing coach.

Billy Jurges, like Jimmie Foxx and others, was another veteran who was still playing in the big leagues in the last year of the war. He was an all-star shortstop for the Cubs and Giants in a career that began in 1931. By 1945 he was playing in his fifteenth season and was thirty-seven years old, but he could still play the game. He hit .324 in sixty-one games and filled in at shortstop and third base.

Even though he wasn't playing full-time, his presence and his skills were enough to gain the appreciation of New York sportswriter Joe King. While Jurges was filling in for Nap Reyes at third base because Reyes was in a batting slump, King offered a renewed admiration for the ability of the prewar stars and a growing longing for their return:

> Jurges stands out like a stake horse who has by some mistake been entered in the eighth race at Oriental Park. The fielding style, the finesse which the new lads cannot copy, is a treat to see. The strong arm that levels the ball across the infield is there. He knows where to be—automatically—when the play must be cut off or backed up. He breaks up a double play with artistry and employs the bat as a subtle weapon and not only as a bludgeon.
>
> Those are the graces of yesteryear, and when in fleeting glimpses the fan of today is reminded of them, he is entitled for once to a full pardon when he pines for the good old days.

16

MORE WITH LESS

AS THE WAR CONTINUED, SO DID BASEBALL'S POPULARITY. Despite the occasional grumblings by a minority who complained about the drop-off in skills while also commenting about supposedly physically fit specimens playing a game instead of fighting a war, both leagues reported increases in attendance. Even with a lopsided race in the National League, attendance in 1944 grew by 178,000. With the race in the American League undecided until the final day, its totals were more than a million fans above the 1943 number.

In *The New York Times Book of Baseball History*, Arthur Daley offers an explanation, one that would have brought a smile of pride to President Roosevelt's face: " . . . new fans, with high wages in their pockets, have been able to attend more games than the old fans, and a flood of night baseball has brought in people never before able to attend."

Daley agreed with Joe King on the fans' continuing love of their sport despite the decline in the ability of the players. "It's not easy," Daley wrote, "to discern that the current center fielder missed catching the ball by the extra step a Joe DiMaggio would have taken or that the batter missed making a hit by the fraction of an inch which would not have eluded a Ted Williams or a Stan Musial. The spectator takes what he gets, asks no questions, and seems eminently satisfied with it."

The national enthusiasm for the sport even after three seasons of the wartime level of playing performance proved to Daley that baseball would endure forever: "If the war couldn't kill it, nothing will."

The sport had someone new presiding over it, only the second commissioner in its history. Judge Landis, after guiding baseball out of the notorious Chicago "Black Sox" scandal following the 1919 World Series, through the prosperity of the post-World War I booming economy, the depths of the Great Depression, and the challenges of the Second World War, died in Chicago in November, 1944.

As his successor, the club owners elected Senator Chandler, the man who defended their players so eloquently in the Senate against the pressures for recalling, reclassifying, and then drafting the 4-F athletes.

Chandler, a graduate of the University of Kentucky and Harvard Law School who was also a former governor of Kentucky, was chosen unanimously at an owners' meeting in Cleveland on April 24. At age forty-six, he was elected for a seven-year term at an annual salary of $50,000.

If the fans and the members of the news media thought baseball was leaning toward the world of politics in considering a new commissioner, it was understandable. The word was that the short list of candidates included Senator Chandler, Governor Frank Lausche of Ohio, Democratic National Committee Chairman Bob Hannegan, and the former postmaster general, Jim Farley. In the names being speculated about, only Ford Frick, a former New York sportswriter and then the president of the National League, had a baseball background.

Chandler turned the job down at first, but later decided that the improved outlook in the war in Europe made him feel better about leaving the Senate. "Now that the war with Germany is virtually over," he said, "I can conscientiously leave my other duties," which may have prompted General Eisenhower to wonder just who was running the war in Europe anyway.

His election was another political exercise, baseball style, for the lifelong politician. One group of owners preferred to continue operating for the rest of the war under a three-man ruling body set up after Landis died. The group was composed of Frick, American League President Will Harridge, and Leslie O'Connor, secretary to Landis. An opposing group argued for choosing a new commissioner quickly.

The latter group won out, thanks to the combined forces of a New York one-two punch: Yankees President Larry MacPhail and Giants President Horace Stoneham.

Commissioner Chandler said that when MacPhail called him in Washington to tell him of his election, "Larry told me that the decision finally was made on the basis of who among all the candidates loved baseball the best."

That may or may not have implied something about the amount of love for the sport felt by Frick as president of the National League, but then Chandler, who became famous for saying in his Kentucky drawl, "Ah love baseball," never took a backseat to anyone on that subject.

Just as Commissioner Landis took office in the first days of the excitement stirred by Babe Ruth's home runs, Commissioner Chandler took office during a stir of excitement about a man being billed as the second Ruth.

He was an outfielder for the Yankees, Russ Derry, six feet one inch tall and 180 pounds, twenty-eight years old, and a Princeton man—born in Princeton, Missouri. Before April was out, he had hit four home runs, including two with the bases loaded. In a 13–4 win over the Senators at Yankee Stadium on April 29, before the largest crowd of the season—35,308 fans—Derry hit two homers.

His fast start inspired Dan Daniel to write in the *World-Telegram,* "In the Yankee clubhouse now they call him Babe." Fortunately, Daniel also made sure to report, "Derry scoffs it off."

Maybe it's just as well. Derry hit thirteen home runs that year, after connecting for four in his rookie season the year before. But he never hit another and was gone after part-time service with the Philadelphia A's in 1946 and two times at bat, with no hits, for the Cardinals in '49.

The real story at the start of the season was being written across the East River in the Polo Grounds, where Mel Ott's Giants were the hottest thing in either league. They won

191

twenty-five of their first thirty-two games, the best start in the National League in twenty-five years.

Ott, one of the most popular of all Giants, was leading by example. It was well known that Ott took his mangerial responsibilities extra seriously. He was confined to bed for two weeks in 1943 with stomach problems when his team dropped to last place, but in 1945 he met with success after taking matters into his own hands.

He was hitting .341 early in the season, his thirty-six-year-old thighs responding each day to an olive-oil rubdown to avoid his long-time nemesis, charley horses. *Time* magazine called him "clearly the best of the returning big leaguers."

The Giants were getting help from, of all things, an ex-Dodger. He was a gifted pitcher who was also the proud possessor of baseball's most original name—Van Lingle Mungo, the pride of Pageland, South Carolina.

Mungo threw hard, played hard, and lived hard, a six-foot-two-inch right-hander who tried to overpower every hitter, whether he was a muscular home-run hitter or a "Punch and Judy" type who couldn't overpower any pitcher.

He won 102 games for the Dodgers from 1931 until joining the Giants for the '42 season, and missing 1944 because of Army service. As a rookie, he caught everyone's eye immediately by winning his first start and pitching a shutout against the Braves, a two-hitter with twelve strikeouts.

He was good enough to strike out seven hitters in a row, but he was also bad enough to lead the league in walks three times. And his temper did him in too many times, so often that by his own estimate he paid $15,000 in fines, which just happened to match his highest salary with the Dodgers.

His fiery temper may have been expressed best by his reaction after he lost a game when one of his outfielders, Tom Winsett, messed up a fly ball in the ninth inning. Mungo left the field in a fury, trashed various parts of the clubhouse, and then sent a telegram to his wife that quickly became a part of Dodgers lore:

Pack up your bags and come to Brooklyn, honey. If Winsett can play in the big leagues, it's a cinch you can, too.

His drinking was as legendary as his temper, and one of his favorite companions in that department was Ernest Hemingway. They used to tell the story of the time when the two kept throwing down the booze during one of the Dodgers' trips in the thirties to Havana, Hemingway's base of operations at that point in his writing career.

Hemingway always loved to fight when he got drunk, and he often challenged the visiting baseball players, whose companionship he enjoyed with such zest, to put on the gloves and box him. One such encounter appeared to be headed toward a possible double fatality when Hemingway and Mungo drunkenly took each other on in a duel, Hemingway waving a sword and Mungo defending himself nobly with a baseball bat.

Cooler heads jumped in, presumably with precision timing, and Hemingway and Mungo were spared to write and pitch again.

The man with the musical name still had enough smarts to win fourteen games for the Giants in 1945. Then he walked away. He had every reason to believe he could continue to win when the boys came home again, but he decided to become a manager in the minor leagues instead. He was the skipper of the Clinton, North Carolina, team in 1946.

The folks in Pageland named a stretch of highway for him in 1983, but his biggest return to fame came in the 1970s with the publication of a song whose lyrics were solely the names of baseball players from Mungo's era.

Lingle was his mother's maiden name, and the song, called simply "Van Lingle Mungo," became a hit on an album called "Oklahoma Toad."

One thing more about Van Lingle Mungo and his terrible temper: when he took that minor-league manager's job in '46, he was suspended during the season—for his part in a riot.

The Browns were in the running throughout 1945, trying to prove that their pennant the year before was no oddity, at least no more than some of the other things happening in wartime baseball.

In fact, the Browns had something unusual themselves, an

outfielder with only one arm. He was Pete Gray, a player who was good enough to be a star with the Memphis Chicks of the Southern Association in '44, hitting .333 and stealing sixty-eight bases. He was voted the league's Most Valuable Player and even came to the attention of the War Department, which made movies of him and showed them to wounded GIs in military hospitals.

For Pete Gray, playing in the major leagues was more than a dream because so many people said it was an *impossible* dream. But there he was, his right arm severed in a childhood accident, yet playing in seventy-seven games for the Browns, thrilled most of all at being able to play in the very symbol of baseball excellence—Yankee Stadium.

His real name was Pete Wyshner. When he was six years old, his arm was mangled in the spokes of a moving grocery wagon and had to be amputated above the elbow. As a six-foot-one-inch, 160-pound left-handed hitter, he batted .381 for Three Rivers in the Canadian-American League, leading the league, and then put together two excellent seasons at Memphis. One of his most remarkable statistics was that in his two years there, he struck out only fifteen times.

The Browns paid Memphis $20,000 for Gray, and his search ended. "I've been turned down by more big-league managers than any other man in history," he said at the start of the 1945 season. "I spent more money trying to get into baseball than I've earned in the game."

In one of the meanest responses to Gray's requests to try out with a team, one manager told him to come out the next afternoon and perform and the team would pass the hat through the crowd for donations. Owner Don Barnes of the Browns was determined to avoid that kind of attitude and treatment. He had a clause written into Gray's contract specifying that his one-armed player was not to be exploited as a freak. Barnes also ordered his manager, Luke Sewell, to treat Gray like any other player and view him on his merits.

When the '45 major-league season opened, there Pete Gray was, starting in left field for the Browns in Sportsman's Park and hitting second behind Don Gutteridge.

The Detroit Tigers were the opposition, and several players expressed skepticism about Gray's chances, wondering if he could get his bat around fast enough to hit big-league pitching and how he would handle fly balls and grounders in the outfield.

The umpires would be watching Gray closely, too. Using a special technique he developed, Gray caught fly balls with a glove that had no padding, one made especially for him by a shoemaker. Then he rolled the ball across his chest, took the ball in his left hand, and threw it back to the infield.

On ground balls, his routine was different. To speed up his throw back to the infield so the hitter couldn't take advantage of him, Pete would flip the ball a couple of feet into the air, toss the glove to one side, catch the ball, and then make his throw to the infield.

"I could field the ball in the air with any of them," he told me, and the pride was still in his voice.

Will Harridge, president of the American League, told his umpires to enforce the rules the same way the umpires in the Southern Association did. If Gray dropped the ball after flipping it into the air following his catch, it was to be ruled a catch.

Was he uncertain of his chances, fearful that he might be cut from the Browns during spring training? "I felt pretty good about my chances in 'forty-five," he said. "I played in 77 games—hey, that wasn't bad for a guy with a handicap like that."

Swinging his thirty-five-ounce bat, he singled sharply off Hal Newhouser in his first game as the Browns beat the Tigers. He would have had a double on another trip to the plate except for a sensational catch in the outfield by Doc Cramer.

In the outfield, only two balls were hit his way, a home run by Paul Richards and a drive by Eddie Mayo. Gray slipped and fell coming in to pick up Mayo's bouncing hit. He recovered and held Mayo to a double.

When the Browns made their first eastern swing, Pete got to play in Yankee Stadium, an experience with extra meaning for him. As a kid growing up in Nanticoke, Pennsylvania, he became a Yankee fan as he listened to the radio broadcasts from New York 120 miles away and thrilled to the home runs of Babe Ruth.

Pete played for the Brooklyn Bushwicks, one of the most outstanding amateur teams in the country, in nearby Dexter Park, and in other leagues in the New York area. "That's all I talked about with my brothers when we were kids," he said. "Playing in Yankee Stadium was everyone's dream."

On a rainy afternoon, 38,328 fans showed up to see the Browns, especially Pete, in a doubleheader against the Yankees, and they weren't all New Yorkers. His parents, immigrants from Lithuania, came from Nanticoke, where his father was a coal miner, and several hundred others came from nearby Scranton and Wilkes-Barre and gave him a war bond worth fifty dollars.

It was the only time his parents saw him play in the big leagues. Pete lined out to Johnny Lindell, walked, and hit another liner, this one to Bud Metheny. In the second game, his luck was better. He entered the game as a pinch hitter and pulled a line drive single into right field.

What Gray accomplished in 1945 was phenomenal, but the harsh truth is that he did not help the Browns in their hopes to repeat as American League champions. Some of his own teammates have been quoted as saying they thought he cost them the pennant.

Center Fielder Mike Kreevich and Shortstop Mark Christman were among Gray's critics, even though they liked him personally. "Pete did great with what he had," Christman told Bill Mead in *Even the Browns*. "But he cost us the pennant in 1945. We finished third, only six games out."

Christman continued, "There were an awful lot of ground balls hit to center field. When the kids who hit those grounders were pretty good runners, they could keep on going and wind up at second base. I know that cost us eight or ten ball games. . . . That took away the double play, or somebody would single and the runner would score. . . ."

Christman claimed the experience prompted Kreevich to quit. Gray was playing center field instead of Kreevich, a .301 hitter for the Browns the year before. On August 8, the Browns sold Kreevich to the Senators for the waiver price. Kreevich had a point. A .283 career hitter in twelve big-league seasons, he hit .252 in 1945, thirty-four points higher than Gray's .218.

While the fans and players were wondering at the start of the year whether Gray could hit major-league fastballs swinging with only one arm, the real question was whether he could hit anything else.

Gray could whip the bat around quickly enough to handle the fastballs. It was the off-speed pitch that got him out. One of the fundamentals of hitting is to be ready for the fastball and adjust your swing by delaying it slightly if you see the pitch is a curveball or some other pitch.

The reason is simple: you can't speed up your swing if you're set for a curveball and it's a fastball, but you can do the reverse—unless you have only one arm.

Gray found he was way out in front on curves and other off-speed pitches because he could not delay his swing after seeing that the pitch wasn't a fastball. The word flashed around the American League, as it always does when a hitter's weakness is discovered, and he got nothing but curves and other slow stuff.

The major-league infielders also took away his other offensive tool, the bunt. The third basemen began to play shallow against him because they knew he wasn't as much of a threat to smoke the ball past them to the opposite field as other hitters would be against a shallow defense.

Pete never really got going against big-league pitching, even the wartime quality. His average at the end of April was .188, and in May he hit only one point higher. By the end of June he was still hitting only .224. He reached his peak with a .235 average for the season by the end of July but slumped to .218 by the end of the year because September was his worst month of the season.

When Sewell benched him and inserted him into games only in pinch-hitting roles, the results were even worse. In twelve appearances as a pinch hitter, Gray got only one hit, a single, and hit .083.

Other teammates, including Don Gutteridge and Ellis Clary, felt Gray developed an attitude problem. "Pete always thought people were feeling sorry for him, even when they weren't," Gutteridge once said. "He always seemed to have a chip on his shoulder and would resent it if you tried to help him in any way. . . . The only thing he'd let anyone do was to tie his shoes. It was about the only thing he had trouble doing himself."

Clary remembers Gray's personality. "If Gray was playing today," Ellis was saying over the phone from Valdosta, "he'd make four million a year. He could run like a scalded dog. But he had a complex about the arm. He didn't want anybody to feel sorry for him. If he could see that you felt sorry for him, he resented that. But I liked him."

The Browns farmed Gray out to Toledo in 1946. He sat out the '47 season, played for the Browns' team in Elmira, New York, in '48, and at Dallas in 1949. There his career ended at the age of thirty-two.

I asked him if he felt bitter or resentful about being farmed out after his one season in the bigs. "No, not at all," he answered, and his response was quick. "I figured they were going to send me to Toledo, and that's the way it worked out. All I wanted to do was play one game in the big leagues, and that was it."

Everyone who saw him play has a favorite memory of him. Mine is the night at Griffith Stadium in 1945 when he drove the Senators' right fielder up against the outfield wall to haul in his long fly ball in right center field. In later years I learned the significance of that obscure play: Gray lacked the power to reach the fences. Balls that others hit would clear the wall for home runs. Gray's would be caught just in front of it for outs.

In Memphis some fans still remember the time the Chicks received a touching letter from a Los Angeles fan whose six-year-old son had just lost his right arm. Pete Gray became the kid's idol, so arrangements were made for a trip to Memphis.

Gray gave the father blunt advice: "If the kid falls down, don't pick him up. Don't let him ever feel sorry for himself. That's the way my father treated me."

Then, with the little boy and his father in the stands that night, Pete hit a home run, a double, and a single, stole two bases, and won the game for his team.

Pete Gray, like Bert Shepard, can always say he was good enough to play in the major leagues. That was enough for his friends and neighbors around Nanticoke. The folks there honored him with "a monster banquet" in Wilkes-Barre attended by five hundred fans including David Vaughan, the sheriff. Lou Boudreau and Roger Peckinpaugh of the Indians, Chief Bender of the Athletics, and Jimmie Foxx, then of the Cubs, were there, too.

Recognition of his accomplishments came from across the country. The Spokane Athletic Round Table presented Gray with its annual award for sportsmanship. Sportswriter Bob Ritter of the *Pomona Progress Bulletin* said Gray "must be the symbol of returning wounded veterans who have lost the services of a limb. His inspiration will no doubt speed many of them on their way to useful lives once again, despite handicaps."

In later years, the TV folks made a movie about him. He liked the title because he agreed with it: *A Winner Never Quits.*

When he's asked how well he might have done with two arms, Pete answers, "Who knows? Maybe I wouldn't have done as well. I probably wouldn't have tried as hard and practiced as much as I did. And I probably wouldn't have been as determined."

Today Pete's glove is in the Hall of Fame, but he's never been there to see it. What he accomplished earned the admiration of thousands, maybe millions. Of all the praise, maybe the briefest was also the highest. It came from the Philadelphia Sports Writers Association, which honored him with a plaque saying simply:

With less, he achieved more.

17

A FAN COMES HOME

ON HARRY TRUMAN'S SIXTY-FIRST BIRTHDAY, AND THE twenty-sixth day of his presidency—May 8—Germany surrendered. The war in Europe was over. It was "V-E Day," victory in Europe.

Adolf Hitler wasn't around for the finish. He took his own life eight days earlier, shooting himself in his underground bunker after ordering his staff members to cremate his body in the Reichschancellery gardens, along with the body of his long-time mistress, Eva Braun, whom he married at the end.

Churchill and Truman announced the European victory simultaneously in London and Washington. Crowds formed from out of nowhere to cheer the news wildly in the downtown streets of those two cities and in Moscow, as well as in other cities and small towns all over the United States and Europe.

General Eisenhower signed the surrender treaty at his headquarters in Reims, France, telling observers the victory meant "one war down, one to go." In Washington, the *Post's* Shirley Povich was speaking at the Touchdown Club and proposing the Medal of Honor for every Marine fighting on Iwo Jima and elsewhere in the Pacific war he had just left.

On that day, the Chicago White Sox were leading the American League by a margin of half a game over the New

York Yankees. In the National League, Mel Ott's still-hot Giants were leading the Brooklyn Dodgers by two and a half games.

That information was always of interest to General Eisenhower, one of America's most enthusiastic baseball fans. He was a frequent visitor to Griffith Stadium before the war during his Army assignments and after the war too when he served as chief of staff of the Army and later as our thirty-fourth president.

Eisenhower—Ike—wasted no time getting to see another baseball game after the war in Europe ended.

He came home to the United States as a conquering hero, arriving at Washington's National Airport on June 18. A million people greeted him in a gigantic parade. The throng—it was too big to be called simply a crowd—included my mother and me, two of the lucky ones who got to stand on the curb in the front row on K Street, Washington's "Little Wall Street," at its intersection with Fifteenth Street.

The *Washington Post*'s respected White House correspondent, Eddie Folliard, wrote, "Nothing quite like it had ever been seen in Washington." Americans couldn't get enough of Ike in this moment of triumph, and Washingtonians were no exception. We were out there standing and waiting for what seemed like hours, in ninety-two-degree temperatures. Some of those around us passed out from the heat.

Eisenhower's day included a visit to the White House, where President Truman awarded him an oak-leaf cluster to add to his Distinguished Service Medal; a trip to Walter Reed Army Hospital to pay a courtesy call on the hero of World War I, General John J. Pershing; an address to Congress; and a luncheon at the Statler Hotel, where those lucky enough to get tickets paid five dollars each. Luncheon officials said they had to turn down 23,000 requests.

Then it was on to New York—and a baseball game. In New York City, the acclaim was overwhelming. Seven million New Yorkers turned out to proclaim him, two million of them at City Hall. They made him an honorary citizen of their city.

One of the highlights of his New York visit for Eisenhower was his trip to the Polo Grounds for a game between the Giants and the Boston Braves. Mel Ott and the Braves' manager, Bob Coleman, gave Ike baseballs autographed by their teams, and Ott added an autographed bat.

It was billed as the "Eisenhower Day Game," and 27,026 fans of either the Giants or Eisenhower or both turned out that afternoon, even though it was raining from the start.

The Giants had fallen on hard times since their early-season lead over the rest of the National League, and the outcome of the Eisenhower game wasn't any better than most of their other games in recent weeks. The Braves won, 9–2, on an eight-hitter by Jim Tobin, who also hit a home run over the left-field roof with two on in the sixth inning. It was the fourth straight loss for the Giants and the eighteenth in their last twenty-three games.

Ike had a box seat with the owner of the Giants, Horace Stoneham, but they left it after three innings of sitting in the rain and took shelter in Stoneham's office, where they were able to continue watching the game until Eisenhower had to leave in the eighth inning.

Tommy Holmes of the Braves singled off Bill Voiselle of the Giants in the ninth inning to keep his hitting streak alive at sixteen straight games, which was to become significant in the days immediately ahead. No one knew it, but Tommy was on his way to a record.

Something else happened during Ike's visit. He told the two managers before the game that he, too, had played professional baseball. It was back in the Kansas State League, and Ike played under an assumed name—Wilson.

When Ott and Coleman asked the future president what position he played, he answered mysteriously, "That's one of the secrets of my life."

Ott could remember that part of his pregame conversation with America's newest war hero, but he couldn't remember what he said in response. "I was too nervous," he said to reporters trying to get their stories from him. "Boy, my hands were shaking."

What Ott didn't know was that Eisenhower's hands might have been shaking, too. He was a lifelong baseball fan, and later during his presidential years he made no attempt at impartiality when it came to having a favorite player. It was

Mickey Vernon, and Vernon obliged our new chief executive by winning his second batting championship in Ike's first year in the White House.

Ike envied major-league players, and surely a star of Ott's status, a certain future Hall of Famer even then, drew even more envy from our war hero. There is proof of this in an eloquent story told by President Eisenhower in later years:

> When I was a boy growing up in Kansas, a friend of mine and I went fishing, and as we sat there in the warmth of a summer afternoon on a riverbank, we talked about what we wanted to do when we grew up.
>
> I told him I wanted to be a real major-league baseball player, a genuine professional like Honus Wagner. My friend said that he'd like to be president of the United States.
>
> Neither of us got our wish.

That visit from Ike may have been the last highlight of the season for Ott. His team never recovered from its midseason swan dive. *Time* magazine suggested, "The only thing left untried: hiring a hackman to drive a wagonload of barrels (a traditional omen of good luck) around the Polo Grounds. But there was a shortage of barrels."

Ott was thirty-six years old at that point, playing his twentieth season. He finished tied for fourth in the National League in home runs with twenty-one and drove in seventy-nine runs with a .308 batting average. He was still using his patented batting stroke, in which *Time* said, he squared away "as if to beat a rug" and raised his front leg "like a dog leaning into a hydrant."

That technique may have amused the people at *Time,* but it, plus a short right-field wall at the Polo Grounds, helped Ott, at only five feet nine inches and 170 pounds, to hit 511 home runs, the eleventh most in history—more than Lou Gehrig and a long list of others.

He hit only one more homer in his career after 1945 and retired in 1947. At one point in his career he might have been the subject of speculation concerning Babe Ruth's lifetime record of 714 home runs, which stood until Hank Aaron hit 755, but Ott said he didn't want to think about it.

"Somehow," Ott said, "I wouldn't want to see anybody break the Babe's record."

Another prominent war hero returned that month—Hank Greenberg. And he was destined to become the kind of hero he preferred to be now—a baseball hero.

Greenberg, a captain in the Army by then, received his honorable discharge on June 15 after serving in the China-Burma-India theater of operations with the 20th Bomber Command. He was awarded the Presidential Unit Citation and four battle stars.

His return to Detroit and the Tigers came not a day too soon. His old team, with all the new faces, was in first place, but its margin over the second-place Yankees was only half a game. The Red Sox were in third, four games behind, a half-game ahead of the Browns and White Sox. The Senators were in fifth place, five and a half back with a record of twenty-one wins and twenty-three losses.

In the National League, as the Giants grew colder, the Chicago Cubs grew hotter. In one midseason stretch, they reeled off twenty-six victories in thirty games.

The Tigers' star was the first major leaguer to return from the war. Whitney Martin of the Associated Press said, "He will be watched as a symbol of hope to all the other ball players in the service who fear their absence from the game might impair their effectiveness and money-earning capacity. He is in the nature of a test case, the answer to the question: can the major-league stars in the service come back?"

Greenberg, a prewar star and thirty-four years old, answered the question in his first game. On July 1, he made his return in the first game of a doubleheader against the Philadelphia A's. The A's were dead last that year, but the fans flocked out to the ballpark to see their returning hero. They formed the largest crowd of the year at Briggs Stadium—47,729.

After going hitless in his first three postwar trips to the plate, Greenberg came to bat in the eighth inning to face a wartime left-hander, Charlie Gassaway, who won four games that year, none the year before and one the year after, the extent of his career in the big leagues.

Greenberg hit a home run over the left-field wall.

His return was the first sign that things would get back to normal after all, especially when we finished off the Japanese in the Pacific. Another signal that baseball was beginning to return to normal came two months after Greenberg's discharge. Bob Feller was discharged from the Navy after missing the entire 1942, '43, and '44 seasons and most of '45.

For Feller, the return was as immediate as it was dramatic. He was discharged from the Navy in mid-August, after being rotated off the U.S.S. *Alabama* and assigned to the Great Lakes Naval Training Center near Chicago, where he was able to pitch for the base team.

Lou Boudreau didn't have to ask anyone if Feller was in playing shape because he always was, one of the first physical-fitness enthusiasts in any sport, lifting weights and doing stretching exercises and other routines before most professional athletes even knew about that side of team sports.

Boudreau was also convinced that Feller's arm, strong enough to lead the league in innings pitched for his last three years in a row before the war, would be ready after pitching half a season for Great Lakes. He named the returning all-star as his starting pitcher for a game against the Tigers in Cleveland's huge Municipal Stadium two nights later.

The Indians' fans went nuts, and 47,000 of them showed up. The Indians' telephone operator, Ada Ireland, was flooded with so many calls about Feller's start that the switchboard broke down.

The adoring folks of Cleveland gave their hero, then twenty-six years old, a Jeep for his farm in Iowa before the game. The governor of Ohio, Frank Lausche, was there, and so were Cy Young, the winningest pitcher in baseball history, and Tris Speaker, the Indians' Hall of Fame outfielder.

Feller's first major-league opponent in three years and eleven months was Detroit's left fielder, Jimmy Outlaw. Bob's first pitch was a fastball for a called strike—and the fans went

205

crazy. Outlaw and Feller battled to a 3–2 count, and then Bob struck him out. The fans went crazy all over again.

The strikeout king of the big leagues had returned from the war with eight battle stars to his credit and struck out the first man he faced. Hollywood couldn't write a better script, and Norman Rockwell couldn't paint a better picture.

The story got better as the game progressed. Feller pitched a four-hitter, not allowing the Tigers a hit after the third inning. He struck out twelve hitters, including Greenberg and Rudy York twice each. Then he ended the game the same way he started it—by striking out Jimmy Outlaw.

"I was back," Bob told me in later years. "Nothing seemed different, even after that long absence. Everything still seemed natural to me—the velocity on my fastball, my pitching rhythm and coordination, the feel for the game at key points—everything seemed the same."

Feller received verification from a reliable and impartial source, George "Snuffy" Stirnweiss, the second baseman for the New York Yankees. Stirnweiss was in a heated battle with Tony Cuccinello, the third baseman of the White Sox, for the batting championship. After Feller struck him out for the final out in a win over New York at Yankee Stadium, Stirnweiss told reporters that Feller was the fastest pitcher he'd ever seen.

As the Senators continued to chase the Tigers, there was evidence again of the unpredictability of the wartime pennant races. With their players coming and going because of the military draft, the fortunes of every team could change drastically in any season, any month, any week, or even any day. The plight of the Senators was even worse as their Cuban players seemed to take turns deciding to return to Cuba and then changing their minds.

The Senators finished in second place in 1943, last in '44, and were in the thick of the race throughout 1945. In the National League, the Cubs were another case in point. They finished thirty games behind the first-place Cardinals in 1944 but beat them out for the pennant in '45. The Tigers had the same experience—thirty games back in 1942, only one game out of it by '44, and in first place during most of 1945.

It was crazy, but it was still baseball, and in their own way, the fortunes of war were helping to keep the pennant races exciting.

The Senators weren't exactly doing it with mirrors in 1945. They were doing it with their all-knuckleball starting pitching staff—Dutch Leonard, Johnny Niggeling, Roger Wolff, and Mickey Haefner.

Niggeling was a special story. By 1945 he was forty-two years old, and he had a genuine appreciation for life in the big leagues after spending six years in the minor leagues because he was known to be a knuckleballer. In the early 1930s, that scared off the big-league scouts. The knuckleball was viewed with disrespect and skepticism, with its critics charging that no knuckleball pitcher won consistently in the major leagues.

By 1945, Niggeling had two heroes, Dutch Leonard and Rick Ferrell, Washington's aging catcher, by then a veteran of seventeen seasons in the big leagues dating back to 1929, who was approaching his fortieth birthday.

In the heat of the '45 pennant race, during which he won seven games for Washington, Niggeling viewed Leonard and Ferrell with gratitude.

"Dutch Leonard and Rick Ferrell are the guys who made the big leagues change their minds about the knuckleball," he said. "Leonard showed a pitcher could throw the knuckleball and win. He was lucky to have a catcher like Ferrell who wasn't afraid to call for it. There were other catchers in the big leagues, supposed to be good catchers, who wouldn't risk their reputations by calling for the knuckler because it was so hard to handle."

When Leonard came up from Atlanta to the Dodgers in 1933, the Brooklyn catchers wouldn't call for the knuckler, according to Niggeling. But when Leonard joined the Senators, Johnny said, "he found out he could pitch to Ferrell and win, and the whole league got knuckleball conscious."

That was 1938. The next year, with Ferrell calling for the knuckler, Leonard was a twenty-game winner on a team that finished in sixth place and won only sixty-five games.

Then along came Niggeling, Wolff, and Haefner, and Ferrell suddenly found himself called upon to serve the

Senators above and beyond the call of duty. But he kept flashing the sign for the knuckler, they kept throwing it, and the Senators—at least in 1945—kept winning.

The knuckleball was enjoying a respectability it never had since pitchers started throwing it in the 1920s after the spitball was declared illegal. The screwball became the off-speed pitch of choice, thrown by some pitchers as a change of pace. Some, like Carl Hubbell, used it as their "out pitch," but the strain that the "scroogie" puts on a pitcher's elbow proved too great even for King Carl himself. Hubbell eventually splintered his elbow and almost ended his Hall of Fame career prematurely.

The knuckler was just the opposite, placing no strain at all on the arm or elbow. But no one except Leonard was willing to throw it as his out pitch until Niggeling came along, the beneficiary of Leonard's eradicating the prejudice against the knuckler. Then Haefner and Wolff joined the Senators' starting staff, and all of a sudden Ferrell had his mitt full.

Clark Griffith was smart enough or lucky enough—or both—to have the right man in the right job at the right time. Ferrell was one of the best catchers in baseball during his career, good enough to play the entire first All-Star Game in 1933 while the manager of the American League team, Connie Mack, was content to leave Bill Dickey and Mickey Cochrane on the bench.

With the Senators, Rick wasn't just handling four knuckleballers. He was also handling four men who threw the pitch with three different grips. Ferrell said Wolff's darting pitches were the most difficult to catch because they broke the widest. "They were almost impossible to catch," he said recently as we went down the list of the knuckleballers.

Leonard was the second most difficult. Niggeling was the easiest for him because his pitches broke the least and were thus easiest to control—and for Ferrell to follow.

Mickey Owen testifies to the difficulties in catching any knuckleball pitcher, specifically Leonard. They were teammates on the Chicago Cubs after the war. Owen developed a healthy respect for the "butterfly pitch" and its erratic path to the plate after one of Leonard's pitches hit him in the face

208

during warm-ups. From that day on, Owen wore his catcher's mask even when warming up Leonard.

"Dutch's pitch would break twice sometimes," he said. "That's what makes those pitches so hard to catch. The pitch would start off one way and then reverse its field like a football runner and go the other way. You have your glove over here and the ball's over there."

As we talked, Owen recalled a conversation with Leonard in which he said, "I sure am glad you don't throw that pitch any harder."

Leonard told him, "I can throw it harder, but you'd never catch it and I wouldn't have any control of it."

Wolff, like Niggeling, was stuck in the minors far too long—ten years—because of the early prejudice against the knuckler, and thus had reason to rejoice at Ferrell's ability and courage in calling for the pitch.

With the Senators in '45, pitching to Ferrell, Wolff became a twenty-game winner. Leonard won seventeen games, and Haefner sixteen. With Niggeling's seven wins, the four knuckleballers accounted for sixty of Washington's eighty-seven victories.

For Ferrell, there was satisfaction beyond the knowledge that he was making a major contribution to his team's success. He broke the American League record that year for the most games caught in a career—1,805, a mark that lasted until Carlton Fisk broke it.

Thirty-nine years later, Rick Ferrell, superb catcher and team player, was elected to the Baseball Hall of Fame.

Bert Shepard, whose dream seemed as impossible as Pete Gray's, came within one step of a happy ending for his Cinderella story on July 10. There was no All-Star Game in 1945, the only year since its start in 1933 that it hasn't been played, because of tighter restrictions on wartime travel. If your trip didn't have something to do with the war effort and you didn't have priority papers to prove it, you couldn't get on a train or a bus, and forget about an airplane. There weren't that many airline flights yet, anyhow.

Instead of the All-Star Game, the major-league teams

played each other in exhibition games for war-related charities. In Washington, it was the Nats against the Brooklyn Dodgers at Griffith Stadium, with the proceeds going to the War Relief Fund for the families of servicemen who were killed in action.

Washington won the game, 4–3, but nobody really cared that much about the final score. What they did care about was that Bert, after spending the first half of the season as a batting-practice pitcher and coach, got to start the game for the Senators—and became the winning pitcher.

Bert was something of a folk hero by now, and an inspiration to others who had two legs. Joe Kuhel was one of them. He was a veteran, playing his sixteenth American League season and destined to play only two more, and the dog days of summer were taking their toll.

At that point in the 1945 season, Kuhel, one of the most graceful performers ever seen around first base, said, "Bert, I'm thirty-nine years old and some days I feel as if I can't make it. But then I see you with one leg and taking infield at first base and pitching batting practice, I feel that I can't quit and I think to myself, 'I have to give it another good try today.'"

Bluege told Bert two days before the Brooklyn game that he would be his starting pitcher. As we were reliving his experience last winter, Bert told how he felt the night before:

Having not started a game in almost four years, I knew I felt the pressure, and I knew there were an awful lot of people who thought I couldn't do it. And there were things that could happen out on the field—if I messed up a bunt or slipped like any other pitcher fielding a ground ball, they'd say it was because of the leg. If that happened to me, it would be lights out. Mr. Griffith gave me a chance, but there was much more pressure on me because everybody else was afraid I'd fail.

Was Bert afraid of that, too?

"I was willing to give it a good try and see what the hell happened. Like your first mission in combat. It's what you've trained for. There's the enemy. Let's go over and see what happens."

210

He tossed and turned the night before, but he expected to. "I don't think anybody sleeps good in situations like that," he said. "If you sleep good, you're in trouble. I don't think anybody going into an important game has ever felt really good. You don't sleep too good, you warm up very carefully, you can't wait for the game to get started, and then you settle down."

His first inning against the Dodgers proved he was right. The once-wild left-hander became somewhat of a control artist in 1945 and threw twenty-seven straight strikes in batting practice that season, but he walked the first two Dodgers on eight pitches.

The pressure was even greater at that point. He said to himself, "Oh, my God. You've got a house full of people here, and you'd better get this straightened out pretty soon." He was on the brink, knowing that another walk or two could spell disaster for him. He admitted, "I was pretty concerned."

Rick Ferrell was his catcher, and he resisted the temptation to go to the mound and talk to Shepard, which might have made the returning veteran even more nervous. "My pitches were close," he said. He told himself, "Damnit! I *know* I can get it over the plate."

He was right. His control came to him on the third hitter and he escaped the inning without giving up a run.

Bert pitched the first four innings, and it's hard to imagine any pitcher performing better after a layoff of three years and pitching on an artificial right leg. He held the Dodgers to five singles. He walked one hitter, struck out one, and turned a 3–2 lead over to Roger Wolff.

How did Bert feel in the Senators' dressing room after his game? "I was just happy as hell that it turned out that way."

Bluege was enthusiastic. He told the Washington reporters covering the team, "The kid looked good, didn't he? . . . Looks as if I'll have to put him on the active player list."

Bluege wasn't just saying that to be nice. He did ask Clark Griffith to activate Shepard, and the owner, an old pitcher himself who won 240 games in his career, readily agreed.

That decision made it possible for the one-legged pitcher to reach the top of his mountain.

211

The Senators were Detroit's chief threat by late summer, and on August 4, Bert made a contribution to their chances of winning the pennant. In the second game of a doubleheader, those days that can exhaust your pitching supply and seriously complicate your pennant hopes, Bluege found himself in a game beyond reach. Rather than using one of his other pitchers on this afternoon during the dog days of baseball, he brought in Shepard, walking on a new artificial leg, from the Senators' bullpen.

It wasn't the first time we'd seen Shepard on a game day. Those of us who came out to Griffith Stadium as early as possible to watch batting practice and everything else we could treat ourselves to saw Shepard pitch batting practice and work out around first base. The people in Boston got to see even more.

"I had been doing some running in the outfield in Yankee Stadium in the series before Boston, and I heard a little crack," he remembered. "But the leg still felt solid and we moved on to Boston. I was pitching batting practice, and after a few pitches I came down on it and it cracked a little bit."

Shepard didn't want to heed the warning, so he kept on pitching. "I made another pitch, and the leg turned sideways. So I straightened it up and threw another pitch, and by now the leg is almost at a ninety-degree angle. So I straightened it up again and made another pitch, and this time the foot broke completely off inside my sock."

The fans in Fenway Park saw Shepard's foot, still in its sock and shoe, dangling loose as the batting practice pitcher went into his next windup, brought his leg up, kicked back toward center field to get his momentum, and began his pivot toward the hitter—only to have the shoe and the foot fly off and head toward center field.

"I just turned around casually and made another pitch," Bert was saying, "and the players were lying around on the ground laughing," which is what I was doing as he was telling me the story. "Think of the fans! They didn't know I had an artificial foot."

Rick Ferrell told me the story, too. "The crowd gasped," he said, laughing. "They thought it was his real foot."

Before 13,035 applauding fans in Washington, Bert Shepard got his longed-for chance against the Red Sox. He walked from the bullpen in foul territory down the right-field line, across the foul line, and to the mound in the fourth inning. Unlike his exhibition game against the Dodgers, he didn't have the night before to get nervous this time. He suspected from the way the game was going that he might get the call. "They were fighting for the pennant," he said, "and they had used up all their pitchers." One more unmistakable sign: as the Red Sox continued to pound the Senators' pitchers before him, Bert was the only one warming up.

Once again he was displaying his courage, because the Red Sox had just scored twelve runs in the inning. It takes a brave man to walk into a game like that.

There were two outs, and the bases were loaded. The hitter was George "Catfish" Metkovich, Boston's center fielder while Dom DiMaggio was in the Navy, who was in the third season of a ten-year big-league career.

After almost being put to sleep by Boston's marathon inning, the fans stirred awake as Shepard took his warm-up pitches, throwing to the Senators' Cuban catcher, Mike Guerra. When Bert was ready, Guerra didn't come out from behind the plate to talk to him, and none of the infielders came over to help him relax with a few reassuring words. "I guess they figured I could handle it," he said. "Besides, there's not a helluva lot you can say in a situation like that."

After Shepard told the home-plate umpire, Art Passarella, that he was ready, the pitcher and the hitter battled their way to a full count, adding still more drama to the moment, which hardly seemed possible.

In that situation, the three runners take off as soon as the pitcher begins the first motion of his delivery, because there is no risk to them. One of three things will happen: a walk, a strikeout, or the batter will hit the ball.

If it's a walk, the runners move up anyway. If it's a strikeout, the inning is over, so the runners won't be thrown out. And if the batter hits a line drive right at somebody, the runners can't be doubled up because there are two outs.

With the Red Sox runners already in full flight toward the next base, Shepard continued his left-handed windup and

213

threw to Metkovich. Catfish, a left-handed hitter, swung at Shepard's fastball, above the waist and on the inside half of the plate, and missed.

Bert Shepard, the only man in the history of baseball to pitch in the major leagues on an artificial leg, had struck out the first man he faced. With the inning over, Shepard walked briskly to the Washington dugout on Griffith Stadium's first-base side. The fans gave him a standing ovation.

The former prisoner of war wasn't finished. Bluege, with no more pitching help available for that day, sent him back out for the fifth inning, and the sixth, seventh, eighth, and ninth. Bert wasn't surprised. He was well aware that the game was his to finish.

He pitched five and one-third innings. He was five eleven and 185 pounds, and he was standing tall as he held the Red Sox to one run on three hits and struck out three men against a batting order that included veteran hitters like Pete Fox, Leon Culberson, Dolf Camilli, Eddie Lake, and Tom McBride.

He threw out two hitters on ground balls back to the mound. The twenty-five-year-old kid from Clinton, Indiana, who had trouble with his control when he was pitching in the low minors before the war, walked only one hitter.

"I was enjoying it," he said. "I felt that I could get them out."

The unrelenting demands of the pennant race forced Bluege to stay with his veteran pitchers in the Senators' stretch drive to overtake the Tigers. Bert never pitched in another major-league game.

The outlook for his career seemed bright as he sat in the dressing room after the game. He had every reason to believe he would pitch in the big leagues again, if not in 1945 then again in '46. But it never happened.

The Senators invited him to spring training, and against the returning stars of the prewar era, Bert got to pitch in two exhibition games, three innings each. In each game, he held the opposition to one run.

"But there were so many good pitchers in that camp," he told me a few months ago, "that the handwriting was on the wall for me. There was no way I was going to make that staff, with Dutch Leonard, Sid Hudson, Walter Masterson, Bobo

Newsom, Mickey Haefner, Roger Wolff, and Ray Scarborough. They even had a future Hall of Famer, Early Wynn."

At Shepard's request so he could get to pitch regularly, Griffith assigned him to the Senators' top farm team, the Chattanooga Lookouts in the Southern Association, but new troubles were beginning for Bert.

He needed corrective surgery on his stump to clean up the emergency surgery performed by the German doctors in the POW camp. The American doctors, however, botched the job. Bert was in Army hospitals for five operations over the next three years. As a major-league pitcher, he was finished.

He wasn't finished in Washington, though. He was a favorite among the writers and broadcasters and the general public, too. After the war, they paid tribute to him with a "roast" at the Touchdown Club. The emcee was Arch McDonald, Washington's radio play-by-play announcer.

McDonald, with his most serious deadpan expression, told the audience, "I don't know why we're honoring this guy, when you think of how much money he's cost us taxpayers. First we bought him one of those expensive P-38s. We spent even more money teaching him how to fly it. We paid for him to take a trip to Europe. Then he cracks up his airplane. As if all this isn't enough money, he gets his leg shot off so we have to pay his medical bills. After all this, what does the government do? They give him a bunch of medals! And now we're having this fancy occasion for him. And for what? For costing us all this money?"

Arch went on, "Well, ladies and gentlemen, I want to tell you this: I was the air-raid warden in my neighborhood through the whole war. Not one person on my block had his house bombed at any time—but nobody ever gave me a damn thing."

During the three years after his game in the big leagues, Bert visited children's hospitals around the country and made appearances for President Truman's Committee for the Employment of the Handicapped, with Harold Russell, the man who lost both hands in the war and starred in the Oscar-winning movie *The Best Years of Our Lives*.

In addition to promoting the cause of amputees and other

215

"handicapped" persons, the former pilot found time to give help on a one-on-one basis, too. One such case involved a baseball Hall of Famer, Joe Tinker of the immortal Tinker-to-Evers-to Chance double-play combination of the Chicago Cubs just after the turn of the century.

Tinker was sixty-six years old and recovering from a leg amputation of his own in January, 1947, in Orlando, Florida, the spring-training headquarters for the Senators. His long-time friend Clark Griffith wrote to Shepard in Ward 10B at Walter Reed Hospital, where Bert was recovering from his latest leg surgery.

Griffith needed Shepard's help. He told Bert that Tinker "was a great old-time ball player and had that same courage that you possess, but when I visited him the other day, I saw that his dobbers were down a little, so I told him about you and what you had gone through and finally accomplished."

Tinker asked Griffith to find out from Shepard what kind of an artificial leg to get "so he could walk again." The Senators' owner asked Bert to drop Tinker a line at Orange Memorial Hospital.

Ever willing, Shepard put his own concerns aside and wrote to the Hall of Famer with advice and encouragement. In return, he received a letter from Tinker saying, "Your fine letter was received, and I don't know how to thank you, as it is just what I wanted to know about my leg."

Tinker told his fellow amputee, "Now I feel fine and I do not worry about my loss. I can carry on just the same as you boys that went over. I will be grateful to you for everything you may tell me about a new leg. . . . I know you will let me know through your friend in Washington. . . . It is great for you to help me out."

The shortstop who became a legend and the pitcher who got into only one big-league game continued to write to each other. Eighteen months later, Joe Tinker died.

Bert still wasn't finished as a professional baseball player. Playing on only one real leg never made any difference to Bert. Dividing his playing time between the pitcher's mound and first base, he played two seasons in the minor leagues. He stole five bases one season. He pitched for a team of American League all-stars on postseason "barnstorming"

216

trips and got to pitch against the most famous barnstorming team of them all, Bob Feller's All-Stars, twice. In one of those games, he struck out Stan Musial.

In one game as a pitcher in the minor leagues, the other team's hitters became so frustrated at being unable to hit Shepard that they resorted to bunting, fully aware that the man out there had only one real leg.

The laid down nine bunts against Bert. He threw them all out.

He chuckles when he tells that story today. "If they had done that all game long," he told me, "I would have had a perfect game."

After baseball, Shepard became a safety engineer with IBM and Hughes Aircraft, working in the United States, Saudi Arabia, and Venezuela, and now enjoys retirement in Hesperia, California. Along the way he's won the National Amputee Golf Championship twice.

He achieves another distinction in that annual tournament every time he plays in it. He's the only leg amputee in the tournament who walks every round.

18

PEACE AND BASEBALL

VICTORY IN THE PACIFIC NOW WAS CLEARLY ONLY A MATTER of time, and the excitement was building with the news every day, but there was one tragic interruption when the war wasn't the biggest news of the day.

On the morning of Saturday, July 28, a B-25 bomber crashed into the seventy-eighth and seventy-ninth stories of the Empire State Building. Thirteen people were killed, including the pilot, and twenty were injured. The shock spread across the nation in a flash.

Lieutenant Colonel William Smith, twenty-seven years old from Watertown, Massachusetts, a West Point man, recently returned from one hundred combat missions over Germany, was flying his plane, *Old Feather Merchant*—the GI's nickname for civilians—from Bedford Field near Boston to New York's LaGuardia Airport.

It was a foggy morning. The LaGuardia tower put Smith on hold, then cleared him to land at Newark instead. When Smith asked for a description of the weather, the control-tower operator told him, "At the present time, I cannot see the top of the Empire State Building."

The crash set off a four-alarm fire. Burning gasoline covered ten stories. Smoke engulfed the two floors where the plane struck. Fuel, metal, and concrete poured down outside the building and through its elevator shafts onto Thirty-fourth Street, nine hundred feet below, for a half-hour. The impact tore a hole in the landmark skyscraper eighteen by twenty feet.

The fog was so dense that the people below had trouble seeing the scene or the falling debris, but a crowd formed on Fifth Avenue anyhow and grew to ten blocks long, stretching from Thirty-second Street to Forty-second.

Ten of the victims were employees on the War Relief Services staff of the National Catholic Welfare Conference, who were working overtime on the seventy-eighth floor. One of them, the conference's publicity director, Paul Deering, jumped to his death, willing to take a chance instead of facing certain death in the flames that engulfed the two floors.

One of the plane's two propellers was embedded in the side of the building. An engine tore through the building and landed on the roof of the Waldorf Building, adjacent to the Empire State Building, on Thirty-third Street. The other engine plunged into an elevator, killing the operator and dropping the car to the street.

Like so many tragedies, this one could have been far worse. On a weekday during the war years, the Empire State Building was occupied by 5,500 workers. On that Saturday, there were 1,500.

For those who sought escape from this grim news bulletin on the radio, there was the day's baseball news. The Tigers defeated the Chicago White Sox, 8–3, and the Nats lost to the Red Sox, 6–2, on Jim Wilson's three-hitter. The Tigers increased their lead to four games behind the pitching of Dizzy Trout, and his teammates made this one easy for him. They got seventeen hits, and every man in the lineup got at least one.

The Cubs were leading the National League by five games over the Cardinals after an 8–3 win over the Reds at Wrigley Field. That game was a story within a story.

Paul Derringer was the winner for the Cubs, but Hod Lisenbee, who appeared in relief for the Reds, was the real pitching story that day. Lisenbee was a relief pitcher in exactly 100 games of his 207-game career. But he hadn't been either kind of pitcher—starter or reliever—in the major leagues for nine years.

Lisenbee was forty-seven years old that season. He pitched in thirty-one games for the Reds, accepting their signing bonus of three thousand dollars, won one, lost three, and saved another. As hard as it was to believe, the manpower shortage was still getting worse.

By necessity, the war set in motion profound forces of change in American society. Blacks were distinguishing themselves by their combat performances in all-black units in the Army and Air Force. Women were leaving their homes for the armed forces and war plants because in many cases they needed jobs and their country needed them. American society was on the threshold of thunderous change and one of the most powerful catalysts was professional baseball.

The armed forces were still segregated. So were our schools, restaurants, movie theaters, and even many ballparks. But major-league baseball was more than that. It wasn't just segregated. There were no black players, period.

The war was about to change that.

The question of permitting black men to play in the big leagues was nothing new. It had been talked about and rumored about for decades. In 1938, the subject was even on the agenda for a meeting of the big-league owners, at the request of "a delegation of American Negroes."

After the delegation's leader made his presentation supporting the admission of black players into the big leagues, Commissioner Landis asked them, "Is that all, gentlemen?"

They said yes, thanked the commissioner for hearing them, and then left. Landis then asked, "What's next on the agenda?"

When one owner protested that they should discuss the matter, Landis asked, "What is there to discuss? The gentlemen asked us for an opportunity to address this joint meeting. They were given the opportunity. What is next on the agenda?"

Shirley Povich once told me that Bill Veeck, who was elected to the Hall of Fame as these words were being written, said he wanted to integrate the major leagues by buying the Philadelphia Phillies with Abe Saperstein, the man who originated the Harlem Globetrotters. Povich said Veeck told him, "Landis stopped me, I think."

Veeck said he went to Landis with his idea at a time when the Phillies were being operated by the National League after their owner, Gerry Nugent, gave up. The league took the team over to keep it going until a new owner could be found.

Veeck's idea was to buy the Philadelphia franchise and field a team of stars from the Negro National League, an "all-Negro team." Veeck said he pointed out to Landis that the move would relieve some of the sport's racial problems.

Landis referred Veeck to the president of the National League, Ford Frick. "I always will believe Landis leaked our plans to Frick," he told Povich. "Frick wouldn't talk business with us. Instead, he sold the Phillies to William Cox, whom Landis later had the pleasure of kicking out of baseball on charges of betting on games."

Veeck almost drooled at what might have been. He told Povich he could have fielded a team with Satchel Paige as its star pitcher, Josh Gibson and Roy Campanella as catchers, Monte Irvin and Oscar Charleston in the outfield, and Buck Leonard at first base.

Then Veeck added, "I don't blame the other club owners. We'd have walked away with the pennant."

Other approaches were attempted by other groups, some with heavy hitters. One such delegation was headed by Paul Robeson, an internationally distinguished opera star and actor and a former all-American football player. He and his group were ignored, too.

However, while the wartime manpower shortage created new problems it also created a new opportunity. As a result, another visionary almost beat Branch Rickey to the historic role of breaking down big-league baseball's color barrier.

In 1945, a Boston city councilman, Isadore Muchnick, said he would move to revoke the law permitting Sunday baseball in Boston unless the Red Sox gave a tryout to black players. He asked Wendell Smith, a respected sportswriter for one of America's most prominent black papers, the *Pittsburgh*

221

Courier, to recruit the strongest prospects he could find to impress the Red Sox and make it difficult for them to turn down every one of the players.

Smith produced three outstanding players. Two of them were veterans of the Negro leagues, a second baseman for the Philadelphia Stars named Marvin Williams, and Sam Jethroe, then with the Cleveland Buckeyes. The third player was a rookie with the Kansas City Monarchs, just recently discharged from the Army as a lieutenant. He was Jackie Robinson.

The Red Sox gave the three players a tryout on April 16—hitting, fielding, running, and throwing. The men were then told to fill out the appropriate application cards. They never heard from the Red Sox again.

Robinson wasn't the only one of the three to play in the big leagues. Five years after getting the cold shoulder from the Red Sox, Jethroe was playing in Boston anyhow—for the Braves. He played with them for three years before being traded to the Pittsburgh Pirates with five other players for one of the young stars in the National League, Danny O'Connell. In his first two seasons, Jethroe led the league in stolen bases.

The Red Sox? They didn't sign their first black player until Pumpsie Green joined them as a second baseman fourteen years after that 1945 workout at Fenway Park.

In 1945 the Red Sox were unwittingly playing into the hands of Branch Rickey, in his third year as general manager of the Brooklyn Dodgers. Unknown to the Red Sox, or to any other team, Rickey had three of his best scouts—George Sisler, Wid Matthews, and Clyde Sukeforth—looking for talented "Negro" players.

Other owners were also becoming anxious to sign blacks, although not pursuing them as eagerly as Rickey. The subject was on the agenda at a joint meeting of the two leagues in Cleveland early in 1945.

Meanwhile, the Dodgers had settled on Robinson as the black player with the leadership and the athletic, educational, and social credentials they wanted. He was a twenty-six-year-old former UCLA football, basketball, baseball, and track star from Pasadena, California, who was playing shortstop for the Kansas City Monarchs, one of the nation's best-known and most successful black teams.

Robinson was invited to meet Rickey in Brooklyn on August 29. When he left three hours later, after having had racial taunts hurled at him by Rickey as a test of his ability to hold up under the pressure that Rickey knew would come his way, Jackie agreed to sign with the Brooklyn organization for a bonus of $3,500 and a salary of $600 a month. It was a raise of $100 a month over his salary with the Monarchs.

Mayor Fiorello LaGuardia of New York got word that the Dodgers were about to sign a "colored" player. He asked Rickey to let him report over his radio program that big-league teams would soon break down baseball's color barrier by signing Negro players. LaGuardia wanted to be able to say the historic development was the work of his committee on antidiscrimination.

Rickey asked LaGuardia to wait a week, then sent a telegram to Robinson to meet him in Montreal. There, the first black man to play professional baseball signed a contract with the Montreal Royals, and the Dodgers made the announcement. The date was October 23. LaGuardia was still in New York, unaware that Rickey was scooping him.

In a world where shocking news was hardly a shock at all anymore, the greatest one since Pearl Harbor occurred on August 6. President Truman delivered an announcement to the world by radio:

> Sixteen hours ago, an American airplane dropped one bomb on Hiroshima, an important Japanese army base. That bomb had more power than twenty thousand tons of TNT. . . . It is an atomic bomb, harnessing the basic power of the universe. . . . What has been done is the greatest achievement of organized science in history. . . . If they do not now accept our terms, they can expect a rain of ruin from the air the like of which has never been seen on this earth.

The newspapers and radio networks reacted to the news in awe. The headline on the top of the *Washington Post* the next morning spread all across the page and ran three lines deep:

SINGLE ATOMIC BOMB ROCKS JAPANESE ARMY BASE
WITH MIGHTIER FORCE THAN 20,000 TONS OF TNT
TO OPEN NEW ERA OF POWER FOR BENEFIT OF MAN

Not everyone made it to the sports page that day, but those who did learned that the Tigers, after splitting a doubleheader with the White Sox the day before, now led Washington by only a half-game. In the National League, the Cardinals were rained out in Pittsburgh, the idle Cubs still leading them by six full games.

One other item: Howie Schultz, Brooklyn's 6' 6½" first baseman, was farmed out to Montreal. He was hitting .239.

After a second atomic bomb was dropped on another Japanese city, Nagasaki, a seaport on the west coast of Kyushu, on August 14, the Japanese surrendered. It was "V-J Day," victory over Japan.

President Truman announced the victory from the White House at 7:02 P.M., Eastern War Time, and Americans once again went crazy with joy. A crowd of 1,500 people in Lafayette Park across Pennsylvania Avenue from the White House, waiting there since late afternoon because of reports that something big was in the works, heard the announcement over a special public-address system. Moviegoers at the Earle Theater on Thirteenth Street had their movie interrupted by the announcement.

A half-block up the hill from the Earle, automobiles were prohibited from using F Street between Twelfth and Fourteenth streets to allow everyone to celebrate. People waved bottles of champagne and stronger spirits, hugged strangers, and kissed them too. Some never made it home that night, in the unrestrained jubilation that was sweeping the world, especially the United States.

At a Coast Guard base in Michigan, Tommy "Old Reliable" Henrich, the Yankees' star right fielder in the prewar years, broke out a bottle of old Irish whiskey that he was saving for exactly that occasion. In the Pacific, other familiar baseball names—Warren Spahn, Bobby Doerr, Pee Wee Reese, and more—had an additional reason to celebrate. They were

224

training for the invasion of Japan, scheduled for October, when the bulletin came that they wouldn't have to worry about being in an invasion after all.

The next day, reporter Bus Ham of the Associated Press wrote that Commissioner Chandler convened a special two-day meeting of major-league and minor-league officials at the Mayflower Hotel in Washington. The purpose was to plan for baseball's first postwar season.

The surrender of the Japanese was made official on September 2, on the decks of one of the most famous of all American battleships, the U.S.S. *Missouri*—the Mighty Mo—in Tokyo Bay. General MacArthur and Premier Suzuki of Japan signed the documents for their countries. MacArthur, with his characteristically strong voice and oratorical eloquence, told a worldwide radio audience:

> It is my earnest hope . . . that from this solemn occasion a better world shall emerge . . . a world dedicated to the dignity of man. . . . Let us pray that peace be now restored to the world, and that God will preserve it always. These proceedings are closed.

As MacArthur, dressed in khakis and with his shirt collar open, signed the treaty, his photographer, Billy Rowe, sat perched on a gun turret. By the following spring, Rowe was helping Jackie Robinson make his way through the South during spring training as baseball's first black player.

Six days later, President Truman did something he'd wanted to do since April. He threw out the first ball at a game between the Senators and Browns. Truman, whose wife Bess used to keep score when they went to Griffith Stadium, was accompanied by Admiral William Leahy, Press Secretary Charlie Ross, Attorney General Tom Clark, Secretary of the Treasury Fred Vinson, and three U.S. senators: Alben Barkley of Kentucky, Robert LaFollette of Wisconsin, and Arthur Vandenberg of Michigan.

Three years later Barkley, the senate majority leader as he sat with the nation's new chief executive in Griffith Stadium's presidential box on the home plate side of the Washington dugout, was elected vice president in Truman's upset victory over Tom Dewey.

225

The Senators beat the Browns, 4–1, continuing their presidential good luck begun by FDR. Truman, up to his old tricks, fooled the crowd—and the photographers—by throwing left-handed.

The president of the United States knew he couldn't take all of the credit for the size of the crowd—20,310 screaming fans who were as happy as he was to be enjoying baseball in a world at peace again.

There was another reason for the crowd. Cecil Travis, one of the "battling bastards of Bastogne" in the Battle of the Bulge with the Army's 76th Division nine months before, was back in a Senators uniform for the first time since getting his draft notice on Christmas Eve, 1941.

Only eight months earlier, Travis was snowbound with the rest of the U.S. troops around Bastogne. They were stuck in the snow for a month, with no dry socks and no relief from the subzero temperatures. Cecil described the life for me: "You slept where you could, in a barn, anyplace, but there was no heat. You were so cold you'd just shake and freeze. It was just terrible. At nights you just couldn't get warm."

He came home after V-E Day, but only because he volunteered to fight in the Pacific. There was an incentive that appealed to him—a thirty-day furlough for him back home in Georgia with his wife and child. After that, he'd be headed for the Pacific to train for the invasion of Japan in October.

"While I was home," he said, "they dropped the atomic bomb. That's one time when I hit it lucky."

The Cardinals never could quite close the gap on the Cubs in the National League. Chicago was sustaining its success despite a disappointing drop-off from the year before by Bill Nicholson. "Swish" started 1945 off on the right note by hitting the first home run of the major-league season, a bases-empty shot at Wrigley Field off Ted Wilks of the Cardinals on Opening Day. The rest of the season was a struggle for him.

The same hitter whose power swing produced league-leading totals in each of the previous two years with a total of 62 homers and 250 runs batted in fell to 13 home runs, 20 below his 1944 figure, and 88 RBIs, a drop of 34 from the year before.

In June he was reclassified 1-A by his draft board in Chestertown, Maryland. Just before the season started he quit his job in a war plant to prepare for the '45 season, so now he was vulnerable to being called to active duty with the Pacific war still very much underway.

He took his big gamble, and it worked as far as playing baseball was concerned. He was able to play the entire season, and the war with Japan ended in the meantime. His survival was one thing, but his performance was another.

By mid-August his batting slump was so prolonged that New York sportswriter Joe King called him "the mystery man of the National League." Before a series with the Giants at the Polo Grounds, King reported that the New York pitchers "view Nick as an atomic bomb." King said he was "like a time bomb in the Cub lineup, and when he'll explode nobody knows."

The Giants, and King, were remembering Swish's performance in a doubleheader the year before, when he hit four home runs on four different kinds of pitches from three pitchers. Since the 1890s, only Lou Gehrig and Jimmie Foxx had hit homers in four straight at-bats.

Mel Ott marveled at Nicholson's day at the plate, saying, "He was hitting every kind of pitch—outside, inside, curve, screwball."

There were no days like that for Nicholson in 1945. The Cubs manager, Charlie Grimm, benched Nicholson on August 28, when the Cubs opened a series in Pittsburgh. Swish's figures showed only ten home runs, seventy-five runs batted in, and a .253 batting average.

It was the first game he missed since 1942, replaced in right field by Phil Cavarretta, whose first-base job was filled by Heinz Becker, a native of Berlin. Becker was in only his second major-league season, and he was no long-ball threat—two home runs and twenty-seven RBIs—but his .286 average at season's end was forty-three points higher than Nicholson's.

Then, on September 11, the unthinkable for any Cubs fan

happened: Bill Nicholson was lifted for a pinch hitter, for the first time since his first full season in the big leagues with the Cubs in 1939.

Frank Secory hit for Nicholson in the ninth inning against the Braves in Wrigley Field, even though Swish had hit his thirteenth homer of the season in the second inning. Grimm removed him when Del Bissonette, who succeeded Bob Coleman as the Braves' manager two-thirds of the way through the season, sent in Bob Logan, a left-hander, to pitch.

Grimm's strategy worked. Secory walked to load the bases, and the Cubs eventually won the game, 5–4, but the development was such a shock that the Associated Press made a separate story out of Grimm's decision. One newspaper headline, alluding to Lefty Gomez's reputation as a weak hitter during his Hall of Fame pitching career with the Yankees, said:

ALMOST LIKE GOMEZ BATTING FOR RUTH

Despite Nicholson's decline from the year before, which he was able to reverse in eight postwar seasons en route to a 235-homer career, the Cubs maintained their grip on first place. One reason was their uncanny ability to sweep doubleheaders.

The Cubs were two games ahead of the Cardinals on September 14. They split a doubleheader with the Phillies that day, but the Cardinals lost both games of a doubleheader to the Dodgers and fell three full games behind the Cubs.

Ten days later, with the Cubs a game and a half ahead and six games to play, the Cards and Cubs met head-to-head in a two-game series at Wrigley Field.

The Cubs, with their new ace righthander, Hank Borowy, acquired from the Yankees on July 27 for $97,000, beat the Cardinals in the first game, 6-5. It was Borowy's twentieth victory of the season, ten for the Yankees and ten for the Cubs, after winning forty-six games for the Yankees in the first three years of his career.

The Cardinals came back to win the next day, but then the Cubs won doubleheaders from the Reds and Pirates, giving them twenty doubleheader sweeps for the year. That's forty wins right there. When you're chasing a team that wins four games in two days in the final days of the pennant race, the percentages may be too much to overcome.

The Cards gave the Cubs fits in late August and September. Harry Brecheen, the stylish lefty who was called "The Cat" because of his quickness coming off the mound to field ground balls, faced the Cubs in five games that year and beat them four times, prompting Phil Cavarretta to remark later, "That Brecheen almost killed us."

With Brecheen's help, the Cardinals beat the Cubs nine times out of twelve games in the stretch drive for the pennant. But those forty victories in doubleheader sweeps provided a safety net for the Cubs. They won the pennant by three games.

The National League was a runaway compared to what was going on in the American. The Senators kept nipping at the Tiger's heels, with George Case hitting .294 and stealing thirty bases, a prewar fringe second baseman named George Myatt providing enough hustle and holler for ten men while hitting .296, the flaky Bingo Binks helping with a .278 season and some sensational catches in center field, the aging Joe Kuhel hitting .285 while still showing his characteristic grace around first base, and Rick Ferrell guiding his knuckleballers to their sixty victories.

Returning veterans were beginning to make a difference on the few teams lucky enough to get one or two of their prewar stars back during the '45 season, the Senators and Tigers for instance.

Cecil Travis got into fifteen games for the Nats, the full effect of his war damage not yet apparent. Gil Torres, one of the returned Cubans, was holding down the shortstop job to Ossie Bluege's satisfaction and leading the league in putouts at that position, so Travis shifted over to third base. At bat, he managed to get thirteen hits.

Washington received far more offensive help than it could possibly have expected from Buddy Lewis. Always a tough out—with three years above .300 and three more above .290 in his six prewar seasons—Lewis was a left-handed threat every time he came up.

He returned from 300-plus missions and over 2,000 hours of flying time as a pilot in the China-Burma-India theater of operations in time to play in sixty-nine games. And he wasn't just appearing as a pinch hitter: he played right field in all of those games and came to bat 258 times for his old team. He made a significant contribution to his team's success by hitting .333.

Lewis had a persistent cold in his back when he returned to the Senators and wasn't able to shake it right away. Eventually, with rubdowns by the team's trainer, who used his own patented Mike Martin's liniment which Clark Griffith kindly allowed to be advertised on the right-field wall of his ballpark, Lewis began to respond.

His first time at bat came in Chicago, and he received some unusual treatment from the home-plate umpire, Bill McGowan. Talking about it in 1991, Buddy showed that his amusement has lasted to this day.

Earl Caldwell was the pitcher, and suddenly, with Lewis at the plate, he developed problems with McGowan's calls. On the first two pitches to Lewis, McGowan called them both balls even though they were in the strike zone. "So Caldwell comes down off the mound," Lewis remembers, "and walks halfway to the plate, and says, 'What in the hell is going on?'

"McGowan tells him, 'This is Buddy's first time at bat after being in the war, and there ain't no way you're going to throw a strike.' "

Caldwell told McGowan, "Well, if that's the damn case. . . ." Then he motioned to his catcher to step away from the plate, threw two more pitches wide, and walked Lewis.

In addition to Lewis and Travis's important second-half help, the Senators picked up last-minute assistance from a third returning veteran. Right-handed pitcher Walter Masterson was discharged from the Navy and defeated Bob Feller on September 13, at a time when every win was taking on gigantic importance. Ten days later, in the last game of the season, he was a central figure in one of the most dramatic and bizarre finishes of any pennant race in the history of either league.

The Tigers were getting help from a combination of

sources: their own returning veteran, Hank Greenberg, and two 4-F pitchers, Hal Newhouser and Dizzy Trout.

Greenberg was experiencing the same kind of success for Detroit that Buddy Lewis was for Washington. He hit .311 in seventy-eight games, including thirteen home runs and sixty runs batted in. Like Lewis, he wasn't just making pinch-hitting appearances. He played in the outfield in seventy-two of his games.

The determination to make up for lost time wasn't Greenberg's only incentive in 1945. Being in a pennant race against the Senators suited him just fine.

"I hated Washington," he wrote in his autobiography, which Ira Berkow edited after Hank died in 1986. "They had played a lot of dirty tricks on me over the years, like Jake Powell running into me for no reason at all and breaking my wrist, and that catcher telling Jimmie Foxx the pitches so he could tie me for the league home-run title in 1935. And Joe Kuhel, the former White Sox player with whom I once had a fight, was now the Senators' first baseman."

The year before, Newhouser and Trout were the only two pitchers to win twenty games. Between them, they won fifty six. For Newhouser, 1945 was an extension of a success that began in 1944 after taking five years to arrive.

He was the American League's Most Valuable Player in 1944, with his twenty-nine wins as the Tigers went down to the last day of the season before losing to the Browns when Dutch Leonard defeated them after getting that phone call about taking a bribe. In '45 he won MVP honors again, the only time a pitcher has won the award two consecutive seasons.

It was a new life for a local boy who was making good after winning thirty-four games in five seasons before 1944. His success was no wartime fluke, either. Newhouser led the league in wins with those twenty-nine victories in '44 and with twenty-five in '45, and in the years after the boys came home in '46, he won another 119 games.

The war brought out Newhouser's greatness, but his potential was detected long before that. A Tiger scout, Wish Egan, spotted the six-two left-hander pitching on the Detroit

231

sandlots in 1937. The first time Egan saw him, Newhouser struck out twenty-four hitters in a junior American Legion game.

That was enough for Egan. He seldom let Newhouser out of his sight for the next three years, the rest of the boy's sandlot and high school careers, and invited him to start working out with the Tigers at Briggs Stadium. After Newhouser graduated from Wilbur Wright High School, he put aside his ambition to become a draftsman and turned down scholarship offers from Duke and Yale. Egan signed his seventeen-year-old friend to a contract for $150 a month, plus a bonus of $400.

Pitching baseballs wasn't what Newhouser had in mind when the war started. He volunteered for the Army. He wanted to become a pilot, and the Air Corps wanted to swear him into the service at Briggs Stadium's home plate before a Tigers' game.

But he flunked his physical when the doctors discovered a leaking heart. That's when he got that one-word letter saying "Bastard" on yellow paper. If Newhouser wasn't able to enlist, it wasn't his fault. He was examined four times, and the doctor rejected him every time.

His own physician even advised him to quit playing baseball after the discovery of his heart problem. When Newhouser wouldn't hear of it, the doctor gave him strict orders: get plenty of sleep, eat often but not heavily, and don't get tired.

The future star followed orders. He ate steaks, got eleven hours of sleep a night, and took six iron pills a day. He changed his eating routine for pitching days, dropping his practice of pitching on an empty stomach.

"The doctor told me to take something just before starting to work," he said, "preferably a meat sandwich, because bread and meat give more sustaining energy than a chocolate bar that a lot of guys eat before game time."

H. G. Salsinger, the sports editor of the *Detroit News*, noticed another difference in the spring of 1944. He remembered that rap on the immortal Lefty Grove—"He arrived in the big leagues with a very fast ball and a very bad disposition." Salsinger said, "The same applies to Newhouser. He,

232

too, arrived with a blazing fastball and a bad disposition. There is an improvement in control all around—control over his fastball and curve, and control over himself. The combined improvement should produce one of the best, if not the best, pitching records of the coming season."

Newhouser received help from the Tigers' respected catcher and leader, Paul Richards. After losing seventeen games in 1943, Newhouser asked Richards why he wasn't winning big in the major leagues.

Richards gave it to him straight. He said Newhouser was "acting like a kid." He said his teammates were upset with his temper and his habit of blaming them for his defeats.

That advice and Newhouser's own determination to change his attitude help explain his leap from a record of 8–17 in 1943 to 29–9 and his first MVP year in only one season.

Newhouser and Trout formed a lefty-righty one-two punch for the Tigers that was the pitching class of baseball in 1944 and '45. Before Newhouser went on a tear and led the league in wins for three straight years, Trout led it in 1943 with twenty. He won twenty-seven in '44 and failed to lead the league only because Newhouser won two more than he did, and in '45 he contributed eighteen more wins en route to 170 victories in fifteen seasons.

Trout was the extrovert. They said he gave himself the nickname of Dizzy over his given Paul because he wanted to duplicate the success of Dizzy Dean. "I figured," he said, "if that guy can get thirty or forty thousand a year for being a screwball, that's for me."

As might be expected, Trout had more than one version of how he got his nickname. "I was pitching in the minors and all of a sudden it started to pour. I saw this awning in center field and started to run under it. The only trouble was the awning was painted on the wall. From then on I was Dizzy."

His sense of humor didn't always contribute to his career advancement. As a minor leaguer trying to make the Tigers in spring training, he suffered a couple of shellings in exhibition games but found relief from the pressure by grabbing a policeman's motorcycle and driving it around the field.

As if that weren't enough, Trout had the nerve to call out

happily to his manager, Mickey Cochrane, "How am I doing?"

"Just fine," the skipper told him. "You can keep riding that thing to Toledo, because that's where you'll be this year." He was, too.

For Trout, 1945 was an eventful year even before the season started. He was called before a board of the Office of Price Administration to face charges that he violated gasoline rationing regulations on a trip to northern Michigan to go deer hunting.

Trout said he was in Marquette to make a banquet speech and made legal use of the class B ration coupons to buy his gas. He argued that under OPA guidelines, Marquette was within the legal driving distance of Big Trout Lake, where he shot a four-point buck on the same trip.

Then, of all things, his car broke down and he was towed home by no less than the chairman of the OPA's own ration board.

Case dismissed.

19

THE DRAMATIC, THE BIZARRE

WHAT MAY STILL BE THE STRANGEST ENDING TO A MAJOR-league season occurred on September 23—and on the 30th.

Detroit was hanging on to a slim lead over Washington in the American League pennant race. The Senators, we found out much to our shock, had to end their season a full week ahead of every other team in either league. Clark Griffith had rented his stadium to the Washington Redskins for the 1945 football season, as he did every year, but to accommodate his tenant, he made a radical adjustment to his team's schedule by agreeing to end its season in time for the Redskins' opener on September 30.

Whatever their situation was by nightfall on Sunday, September 23, the Senators wouldn't be able to do anything more about it. They would play the same number of games—154—as all the other teams, but they would finish their schedule a full week early and then have to sit for a week and hope the Tigers would lose.

As if that weren't enough, their last day of the season was a far greater shock than Griffith's scheduling.

The Senators were in Philadelphia for a doubleheader at

Shibe Park against the A's. The tension that had surrounded them all year long was at its peak. They knew they needed to win both games to put as much pressure as possible on Detroit as the Tigers played the last week of their season with the Senators idle.

The tension had been building within the Washington team for several weeks and became a serious problem for manager Ossie Bluege. On September 11, Bluege got into a heated argument with one of his substitute infielders, Fred Vaughn, over a messed-up play by Vaughn which enabled the White Sox to beat the Senators, 2–1.

The upshot of the shouting match was a $100 fine for Vaughn, and Clark Griffith had to talk him out of quitting the team. But the extension of Vaughn's career was only temporary. Never more than a wartime player, he played only in 1944 and '45, appeared in only 110 games, and was gone from the major leagues twelve days later when the last wartime season ended.

Two nights after the Bluege-Vaughn confrontation, two pitchers, Marino Pieretti and Alex Carrasquel, got into a fight over who owned a certain bat. Carrasquel suffered a cut over his left eye, but he got revenge of a sort—he broke the bat over a locker.

Then the Senators headed into a murderous stretch of five games in three days against Detroit at Griffith Stadium in the next-to-last weekend of the season. They won four of the five and were still neck-and-neck with the Tigers when they took the field in Philadelphia on the twenty-third for the final day of their season.

The A's were in last place, but they made themselves a part of the pennant story as they took the Senators into extra innings in the first game of the doubleheader. Now it was the twelfth inning.

Walter Masterson was cruising along for the Senators, pitching no-hit ball after entering the game in relief of Dutch Leonard in the eighth, when the A's scored three runs with the help of errors by Washington's two returning stars, Buddy Lewis and Cecil Travis.

The twelfth inning wasn't any problem for Masterson so far. The A's had two outs and nobody on base. Walter's chances of another hitless inning looked good, because the next hitter was Ernie Kish, a Washington native, who experienced his only big league season. He was destined even then to play in only 43 games, hit .245 with no home runs, and drive in only ten runs.

It was a mostly cloudy afternoon, but the sun was playing peek-a-boo from time to time. In the Senators' half of the same inning, Philadelphia's center fielder, Sam Chapman, asked for time out and sent to the A's dugout for his sunglasses.

With Kish up, the sun made another brief appearance overhead. Joe Judge, a longtime Washington favorite as the Senators' first baseman during the Walter Johnson era, was a coach that season. When Kish stepped into the left-handed side of the batter's box, matching his five-foot-nine-inch frame against Masterson's six feet two inches, Judge was the acting manager.

Bluege had been ejected in the eighth inning for protesting a call by umpire Eddie Rommel. He was in civilian clothes and popping in and out of the Washington dugout, undetected by Rommel. Judge ran the team between Bluege's secret visits. As he stood in the dugout, Judge wondered aloud to no one in particular if Binks had remembered to take his glasses with him to center field, especially after seeing Chapman put his on during the same inning.

Then Kish, obviously no threat, lofted an easy fly ball to straightaway center field, where Binks cruised into position to make the catch. It was what the players call "a can of corn," a routine fly ball requiring only a routine play.

Suddenly Binks, the flaky one, began to stagger uncertainly. Judge, to his horror, saw that Binks did not have his sunglasses. The ball dropped safely ten feet away from him. Kish reached second base, one of only five doubles for him in his one-year career.

Masterson was ordered to walk First Baseman Dick Siebert intentionally to set up a force play at any base except home plate. Siebert was a far greater threat with the bat than on the bases. He was in his eleventh and last season in the big leagues, a .300 hitter twice, and a man who finished his

237

career with a .282 average. Besides, his run wouldn't mean anything. If Kish scored, the game would be over anyhow.

The next hitter, George Kell, singled to right field. The game was over.

The Senators came back to win the second game, 4–3, behind Marino Pieretti. It was called after eight innings because of darkness, but the damage was already done, and everyone knew it—especially in the Washington dressing room.

Between games, Shirley Povich said, "The dead stillness reeked of a morgue." He heard one player say of Binks, "They ought to fine him $4,000," a reference to what might have been a World Series share for each player.

Nobody talked to Binks. He was left alone, maybe remembering to himself that he didn't commit either of those errors in the eighth inning. Maybe he also remembered that he was one of the main reasons for his team's success with his .278 average and eighty-one runs batted in.

He could have remembered, too, that he made all those outstanding catches in center field and filled in at first base for twenty games in an emergency while Joe Kuhel was injured. In his hip pocket as he sat on the stool in front of his locker were the sunglasses that he got from the bench in the twelfth inning—after Kish's "double."

For the Tigers, the fly ball that fell safely to the Shibe Park turf was something from heaven. They had not been playing well and had already lost their game that day to the Browns. A doubleheader sweep by Washington would have cut the Detroit lead to a half-game, adding to the pressure for the Tigers.

As it was, Washington's final record was eighty-seven wins and sixty-seven losses. Now all the Senators could do was hope that they hadn't lost a pennant in the sun.

"Today," Povich wrote in his column from Philadelphia, "surely was the blackest day for a Washington team in history. . . . September 23, 1945, is a date to remember, or forget. You can take your choice."

By the Tigers' last day of the season, history was repeating itself. It was the Tigers-Senators-Browns triangle from the year before, when the Browns won the pennant on the last day of the season as the Senators knocked Detroit out of it.

This year the Browns and Senators were switching roles, with St. Louis instead of Washington as the potential spoiler.

If St. Louis defeated Detroit twice in their doubleheader on Sunday, September 30, the American League race would end in a tie. Representatives of the two teams had already tossed a coin to see where the first play-off game in the history of major-league baseball would be played. Detroit won the toss and would be the scene for a one-game play-off. No four out of seven or three out of five. Not even two out of three. One game, winner take all.

On Saturday, four Washington pitchers—Masterson, Leonard, Haefner, and Niggeling—boarded a train for Detroit. Bluege wanted them there and rested in case of a play-off game. They arrived at the Book-Cadillac Hotel just as the Tigers and Browns were taking the field at Sportsman's Park in St. Louis.

The four pitchers had two adjoining rooms, two to a room. They turned on the radio to listen to the broadcast from St. Louis.

Virgil "Fire" Trucks, a fastballing right-hander who was just out of the Navy, started the first game for Detroit, and everyone felt an immediate sense of relief just to be playing the game. Steady rain in St. Louis had caused rain-outs for three days and, in fact, it was still raining, delaying the start of the first game for fifty minutes. The games probably wouldn't have been played at all if it wasn't for their importance. Only 6,613 fans were in the stands for the showdown.

In the sixth inning, Trucks got into a jam and Steve O'Neill brought in Newhouser as a relief pitcher, one of four appearances out of the bullpen that year for the best starting pitcher in baseball. The Tigers were leading, 2–1, when Newhouser entered the game. By the ninth inning, it was still a one-run game, 3–2, but now the Browns were leading.

O'Neill sent Hub Walker to the plate to pinch hit for Newhouser as Detroit's leadoff hitter in the inning. Walker was a man with enough experience to handle the pressure of the moment. He broke in as an outfielder with the Tigers in 1931 and played parts of four seasons with Detroit and Cincinnati. He hadn't played in the majors since 1937, but he

239

was back in the war's last year to play in twenty-eight games, mostly as a pinch hitter.

Walker singled. Skeeter Webb, the shortstop, bunted so Walker, representing the trying run, could advance to second base and be in scoring position with Doc Cramer and Hank Greenberg coming up. The bunt went down the first-base line. George McQuinn, the veteran all-star first baseman for the Browns, fielded the ball cleanly but his throw to second base was late.

O'Neill was pushing a lot of buttons now. He flashed the bunt sign again, this time to Eddie Mayo, his veteran second baseman, who got a second chance at the big leagues in 1943 after a five-year absence and made good after the war for three more seasons.

Mayo laid down a successful sacrifice bunt. Now the Tigers had two runners in scoring position instead of just one—the potential tying run on third and the go-ahead run on second. There was still only one out.

Luke Sewell told Nelson Potter, the Browns' fifteen-game winner, to walk Cramer, Detroit's forty-year-old center fielder. His strategy was to set up a force play at the plate on a ground ball or, better yet, a double play anywhere that would end the game with a St. Louis win and place enormous pressure on Detroit to win the second game to avoid a play-off.

It was getting dark in St. Louis, and it was still raining. Potter's first pitch to Greenberg was ball one. The next was a strike.

Then Hank, one of the most intelligent hitters in the sport, detected something. Just before the third pitch, he spotted Potter's screwball grip on the baseball. Knowing in advance what pitch he was getting, Greenberg was able to hit a line drive into the left-field bleachers, a few feet inside the foul pole. Third-Base Umpire Cal Hubbard, dashing down the foul line, signaled it was a fair ball—a home run.

For the entire team and all of the Detroit fans, it was a grand slam, in more ways than one. As Greenberg crossed the plate in St. Louis on the hit that won the pennant for the Tigers, Eddie Borom, whose major-league career consisted

240

of two wartime seasons as a utility infielder for Detroit, kissed him.

On the train back to Detroit, the players and the writers covering them enjoyed a marathon party, a wild scene that lasted all night. When it was over, there was no check. Dizzy Trout had picked it up beforehand.

At the ballpark the next day, as the Tigers prepared for the World Series, Trout walked up to Lyall Smith, the sports editor of the *Detroit Free Press,* and whispered, "Let me have fifty, will you? I blew all my roll last night."

In Washington, the Senators were at Griffith Stadium, packing for one of two trips and listening to the Tigers-Browns doubleheader on a Washington radio station. They were going either to Detroit for the play-off game or home for the off-season.

Rick Ferrell remembers the reaction when they heard Greenberg's home run over the radio. "We just kept packing," he told me. "We told each other, 'Well, guess I'll see you next year.'"

In Detroit, the four Washington pitchers left their hotel rooms and checked out of the Book-Cadillac three hours after checking in, their beds still made.

The batting races were as exciting as the pennant races, and if there was one sentimental favorite in either league it had to be Tony Cuccinello.

"Cooch" was playing on borrowed time. Everyone in baseball knew it, and so did the fans. His knees were shot by 1945, the target of too many runners sliding into him to break up double plays when he was a second baseman with the Cincinnati Reds and Boston Braves during the first ten years of his career.

While he was with the Braves, Dick Bartell of the Giants took him out on a play at second base, and surgery was necessary. He was out for two months with torn cartileges and chipped bones. When the doctors operated to repair the damage and remove the bone chips, one of them told him, "You're loaded with arthritis." It was in his back too, even though he was still only in his thirties.

241

The doctors for his draft board found all of that and more in classifying him 4-F. They discovered fallen arches and chronic problems with his throat from his days as a kid on Long Island when he mysteriously lost his voice for two years. It came back just as mysteriously and suddenly as it disappeared.

"I was home one day after school and all of a sudden I let out a holler," he said. "I scared the hell out of the whole house."

He was thirty-seven in 1945, but the White Sox needed players badly because of the manpower shortage, and Tony felt a loyalty to the White Sox. They signed him during the 1943 season and enabled him to extend his career, so in '45 he promised Mrs. Grace Comiskey, the team's owner, that he would play one more season, even though his body was telling him to hang up his spikes.

As the season rolled on, Tony was threatening to stage something of a miracle that would compare with that time when his voice came back.

Cuccinello, who moved over to third base in 1940 because he couldn't cover the ground around second anymore, could still hit. The man who already had four .300 seasons led the American League hitters throughout 1945, right from the first day. At one stage late in the season he was ahead by twenty points. Then September came.

His manager, Jimmy Dykes, rested his aging, aching veteran when possible. "Jimmy was wonderful to me," Tony remembers. "He tried to pace me. He rested me in the second game of doubleheaders, and if I got on base in the late innings of a game, he'd send in Joe Orengo to run for me."

In September, "My body just gave out on me. That twenty-point lead kept dropping every day, until it was almost a dead heat on the morning of the last day of the season, a battle between the aging veteran, always a popular player, and another popular infielder, George "Snuffy" Stirnweiss.

Stirnweiss was another local boy making good, the son of a New York cop, born in a house near the corner of Fifty-fourth Street and Fifth Avenue. His family moved when he was small, and he grew up in the East Bronx, just a baseball's throw from Yankee Stadium.

242

Cooch remembers he was hitting .308, two points ahead of Snuffy, going into the last day of the season. The White Sox were going to play a doubleheader against the Indians in Comiskey Park while the Yankees were playing a single game against the Red Sox in Yankee Stadium.

"The old body was really aching," Cuccinello said, so Dykes asked him which game of the doubleheader he wanted to play.

"He gave me the choice of facing Allie Reynolds or Steve Gromek," Cooch says, "and I told him, 'Jim, I'll play the first game and see what happens. If I get enough hits, I'll quit.' "

But then nature took over. The doubleheader was rained out.

Meanwhile, Sitrnweiss, New York's leadoff hitter, doubled in the first inning. In the third he hit a slow roller to the Red Sox third baseman, Jack Tobin, who fumbled the ball and Stirnweiss was safe. He went hitless in his next two trips and then singled sharply to right field in the eighth inning in his last time at bat for the season.

The totals showed Snuffy had three hits for the day, but one of them was on the suspicious side. Cuccinello was told later by several of the Boston writers covering the Braves, men he knew from his years of playing for the Braves, that the official scorer was Bert Gumpert of the *Bronx Home News* and that he originally charged Tobin with an error on the ground ball in the third inning.

Tony says the Boston reporters wrote to him after the season and told him about the change and the timing of it. "They were so damn mad," he told me in 1990.

They said Gumpert reversed his ruling only after word came over the Western Union ticker that Cuccinello's games were rained out. The doubleheader wasn't going to be made up because neither team was in contention for the pennant.

That meant Stirnweiss had a chance to win the batting championship without worrying about what Cuccinello might do. That's when Gumpert changed his ruling on Snuffy's third-inning ground ball, according to Cuccinello's sources.

The statisticians had to carry the two averages out to four places before they could determine the batting champion.

Cuccinello finished with an average of .3076, which comes to .308 when rounded off. Stirnweiss finished with .3088, which rounds off to .309. Stirnweiss was the batting champion.

His average is the third lowest for any batting king in the history of the American League, better only than Elmer Flick's .308 in 1905 and Carl Yastrzemski's .301 in 1968, but Snuffy joined elite company. He accomplished something that only the mightiest of Yankees—Ruth, Gehrig, and Di-Maggio—had done before him.

His manager, Joe McCarthy, found consolation in Snuffy's championship. The Yankees' domination was another casualty of the war. They finished third in 1944 and fourth in '45.

"Well, we got something out of the race anyway," he told reporters. "Snuffy deserved his victory over Cuccinello. Snuffy, for the good part of the war, was the best all-around player in the majors and certainly in our league. It's a distinction when a leadoff batter makes off with the hitting crown."

As one of his awards, Stirnweiss received a certificate for a new car. They couldn't give him the car itself. There weren't any yet.

The timing of the scorer's reversal wasn't the only thing questionable about the play that gave Stirnweiss the batting title. "When the season was over," Cooch told me, "I got a letter from Jack Tobin, Boston's third baseman. He said the play was an error all the way."

From talking to Tony today, you can still detect the disappointment in his voice. "That was my last year as a player," he told me. "I had my release in my pocket. I told Mrs. Comiskey two weeks before the season ended that I would have to retire after '45. I just couldn't play anymore."

Cuccinello also knew that Don Kolloway was already in Chicago after being discharged from the service, waiting in the wings to become the White Sox second baseman in '46. Luke Appling and others were coming back, too. The team wasn't going to need him anymore.

"She called me into her office on Saturday of that weekend," he said, "and thanked me for what I had done for the team. She gave me my release, and it was going to be announced after our doubleheader."

244

Cooch remembers the missed batting championship today, saying with disappointment, "I would have gotten a five-hundred-dollar plaque and my name in the record book." Then he adds in a soft voice that is without bitterness, "It would have been nice to go out with the title. Gee, it was a damn shame."

Tommy Holmes was another New York product who was trying to do in the National League what Cuccinello was trying to do in the American. He was in the fourth year of a bright career that produced a lifetime batting average of .302 over eleven years. In 1944 he had the first of his five .300 seasons with a .309 average, and in '45 he was far ahead of that pace.

He was a Brooklyn kid who grew up on Fifty-eighth street and was blessed with a sweet left-handed swing. He wasn't a power hitter—except for 1945—but he could beat you with singles and doubles all season long.

He got his first taste of playing baseball for money when he went out for a semipro team in Brooklyn as a teenager. The team's promoter, knowing Holmes was still in school, suggested using a different name to protect his high school eligibility. Tommy came up with Kelly, remembering his nickname: Slide, Kelly, Slide. His fans called him that as a throwback to a popular turn-of-the-century player named Kelly whose sliding prompted fans to cheer him on with shouts for him to slide.

The promoter asked, "Can you play left field?" Holmes said simply, "Sure." The promoter had one more caution.

"You'll be facing Satchel Paige."

"Who's Satchel Paige?"

The kid from Brooklyn got two hits off Paige. As Tommy Kelly, he was paid five dollars, which was welcome in the Holmes household, where Tommy was one of eight kids.

Two weeks later, Paul Krichell, the Yankee scout who discovered Lou Gehrig, approached Holmes. Tommy's real intention was to become an engineer, and Krichell said he could get Tommy into Duke University to play baseball.

But the Holmes family was still feeling the effects of the Depression. "I didn't have the money for clothes and things,"

Holmes says. "I had to go to work." That being the case, the Yankees signed him and sent him to Newark, which had one of the best teams in baseball, better than most major-league teams. There he played center field, until fate intervened.

The general manager of the Yankees, George Weiss, told Holmes his career opportunities were limited with the Yankees, and the reason was summed up in two words—Joe DiMaggio. No center fielder, at Newark or anywhere else, was going to beat DiMag out of that spot with the Yankees.

Weiss promised to make a deal to send Holmes to the Braves, where he would have a good chance to make the big leagues. "I'll sell you where you'll stay ten years," he said. "I'll sell you to Casey Stengel."

Holmes asked why Weiss couldn't trade or sell him to the Dodgers or Giants so he could play close to home. Weiss explained that those teams had so much talent, a rookie had to make an immediate impression or he would be sent down to one of their farm teams. The Braves, with less material, would be more patient if Holmes got off to a slow start. There would be less pressure on him.

After reporting to the Braves, Holmes asked Stengel, his new manager, how he knew about his performance at Newark while he was busy managing the Braves. "We played the Giants and the Dodgers in daytime," Stengel explained. "At night I went over to Newark."

Weiss knew what he was talking about. Holmes, after a slow start in his first season, hit for averages in the .270s in his first two years and improved to .309 in 1944. Then 1945 arrived, and it became Tommy's "career year." And it never would've happened except for the severe sinus problem that had made him physically unfit for Army duty. A medic examined him at his draft board and told him, "We can't take you. You'd be a pension case."

But when they found out during the examination that he was a professional athlete, six doctors flocked to him to look more closely. The original finding stuck, especially after one of the doctors told him, "If you go to England, you'll die."

Besides getting a longer look with the Braves than he might have with the Giants or Dodgers, there was a second plus in Holmes's sale to Boston. He got to play with Paul

Waner, the Hall of Fame hitter who achieved a lifetime batting average of .333 for twenty big-league seasons, mostly with the Pirates. The man they called Big Poison—his brother and teammate, Lloyd, was Little Poison with a .316 average in eighteen seasons—was the National League batting champion three times with averages of .362, .373 and .380. He hit over .300 fourteen times.

For Holmes, there was a particular advantage to playing on the same team as Paul Waner. Not only could the man hit, he could teach, too. And Holmes was the same kind of hitter as Waner—an exceptional "wrist hitter," able to generate outstanding speed with his bat because of strong, quick wrists.

Waner had a pet theory about hitting, something he called "zoning." Holmes explains it this way: "If you look in just one area, ninety times out of a hundred you're going to get your pitch. I checked with the umpires, Augie Donatelli and Bill Stewart and the others, and they agreed with that."

Waner told his protégé, "Tommy, the first time up, zone. Later on, if you get more proficient, you can zone twice." The logic was simple: No pitcher can make the perfect pitch every time. "That's the way the master taught me," Tommy says now. "I hit that way for eleven years."

"Zoning" worked for him. But besides an excellent career average, he accomplished something else that's more than just excellent—it's remarkable. He struck out only 122 times in his life. As the Braves' leadoff hitter, the most times he ever struck out in one season was twenty. This was while he was going to bat 550 and 600 times a year. In 1945, with 636 at bats, he struck out only nine times.

No wonder Stengel gave him an autographed baseball in later years with the message, "To Tommy Holmes—My best leadoff hitter."

In '45 Holmes set the modern National League record for the longest hitting streak by hitting safely in thirty-seven straight games, a record that stood until Pete Rose broke it with forty-four straight in 1978. He led the National League in doubles with 47 and hits with 224 and finished second to Dixie Walker in runs batted in with 117.

Something else happened, too, and it shocked everyone.

He became a power hitter for the only season in his career, thanks to a desire by management.

Left-handed power hitters at Braves Field faced a strong wind blowing in from the right-field wall, 345 feet from home plate. When we talked about it, Tommy said, "Up there the wind blew in thirty days out of thirty-one."

Tommy managed to hit a home run into the teeth of that wind off the Charles River one afternoon, prompting the Braves' general manager, Bob Quinn, to call him to his office the next day and tell him, "Son, you can reach those seats. We'd like to have you pull the ball more."

Holmes had a simple solution: "Move the fence in."

"They brought the fence in to something like three hundred twenty feet," he remembers. After leading the league with twenty-eight homers in '45, the Braves recognized his performance in his paycheck. "They doubled my pay," he said.

How come he didn't keep hitting twenty-eight or thirty home runs every year after that? Holmes gives a convincing answer: "They moved the fence back."

Why?

"Maybe they didn't want to pay me more, or maybe the enemy was hitting more homers than we were."

His sizzling bat cooled off just enough to lose the batting title to another popular player of the day, First Baseman Phil Cavarretta of the Cubs, who got two hits against Pittsburgh on the last day of the season and finished with a .355 average, three points higher than Holmes. For that and his other contributions to his team's pennant, Cavarretta was voted the National League's Most Valuable Player.

Cavarretta, deferred from military service because of a perforated eardrum suffered during an attack of spinal meningitis as a child, disputes the notion that success was easier to achieve in 1945.

"That wasn't an easy season," he says today. "Even though it was during the war, there were a lot of good players still around, and more were coming home from the war."

Something else was making 1945 more difficult than the previous wartime seasons—travel. "The travel was harder," Phil says, "but we weren't complaining. We thought of the guys who were overseas."

Cavarretta says the Cubs took buses to certain cities, such as from New York to Philadelphia, then to Brooklyn. He remembers sitting up all night on coach cars "quite a few times" because Pullman cars were unavailable. "It was the least we could do as far as I was concerned," he told me, "and a lot of other players felt the same way."

Holmes laughs now at another reason he lost out to Cavarretta in their photo finish. Sal Maglie, the pitcher they called The Barber because he "shaved" hitters by pitching close to them to keep them from taking over the plate, was a rookie that year. He won five games for the Giants.

Maglie knocked Holmes down repeatedly that season, as he did so many hitters throughout his career, to move him off the plate. He confessed there was another reason he was so hard on Holmes, one that favored the Italian Cavarretta. "If you were Italian," Maglie said in later years, "I wouldn't have decked you so many times."

The Holmes hitting streak was a story in itself. One of the most serious challenges to its extension came halfway through the streak, when Holmes broke his best bat.

The Braves' manager, Del Bissonette, came to the rescue. He told Tommy, "I'll bring you one from my attic that's a piece of concrete. It's a Johnny Frederick model," referring to a Brooklyn outfielder from ten and fifteen seasons before who was a lifetime .300 hitter and had the ability to hit the long ball, too.

True to his word, the manager went to his home in Maine on an open date, looked around his attic, and found the old bat. "He brought it down, and it was just what I like," Holmes says. He was only five feet ten and 180 pounds, but Holmes favored big bats, thirty-six ounces and thirty-six inches. "I swung a telephone pole," he said, but he could get away with it because of those wrists. He added to his wrist power by choking up slightly on the bat, his bottom hand an inch or so above the knob.

The Frederick bat was a perfect substitute for his own: "I hit like hell with it right through my streak."

Holmes had help from another source as well, his loyal supporters in the "Jury Box." The right-field bleachers at

249

Braves Field jutted out almost to the foul line. Boston right fielders in those years were on speaking terms with the fans who sat in those 1,573 seats. The section became known as the Jury Box.

The star and the fans established a relationship. "Nobody ever got as close to the people as I did to those fans," Tommy said. "They were responsible for at least ten percent of that streak."

They gave him encouragement and advice, reminded him to relax at the plate, and told him when they thought he was trying too hard to pull the ball to right. Holmes always accepted their comments in a positive manner.

"When I was in the batter's box," he said, "they were in there with me."

Holmes started his streak in the first game of a double-header on June 6 and ended it sixty-six hits later in the second game of a doubleheader on July 8. During that stretch he hit .423, compared to Joe DiMaggio's .408 during his fifty-six-game streak in 1941 and Rose's .385 during his streak. Holmes hit nine home runs, drove in forty-four, and struck out only twice in 156 times at bat.

When he broke the previous modern record of thirty-three straight games held by Rogers Hornsby, he had to do it the hard way, against two good left-handers, Preacher Roe and Fritz Ostermueller. He got three hits in each game.

When he was finally stopped, by right-hander Hank Wyse of the Cubs, he had no excuses, just a simple explanation: "I batted four times, and if you put all four together they wouldn't reach the outfield."

But for those thirty-seven games in a row, Tommy Holmes was unstoppable. As we talked about it, Tommy's memory of his hot bat was still clear and unmistakable. He remembers that his bat was sizzling—and he also remembers that there were no official scorer's rulings or lucky bounces or slow rollers. "I was hot," he said. "All of my hits reached the outfield. There wasn't one where there might have been a doubt. No bunts. Every one of mine was clean."

Appropriately enough, when Pete Rose broke Tommy's record in 1978, he did it at Shea Stadium, and Tommy was there in connection with his responsibilities as the Mets' community relations director. As we talked, he described his responses when reporters asked him if he was pulling for Rose to break his record. "Of course I'm pulling for the guy," he told them. "I had it for thirty-three years." But Tommy made one request to Rose: "Don't tie me. Beat me or not, but don't tie me."

He expressed no resentment or disappointment. On the contrary, he said he was grateful.

Reporters asked him why he felt grateful, and Tommy told them, "It's great talking about it. I feel like a major leaguer again."

20

STAGGERING HOME

WITH THE WARTIME CAST STILL MAKING UP THE BULK OF THE team rosters, the Tigers and Cubs prepared to meet in Detroit for the first peacetime World Series in four years, but one that had all the markings of the war just ended.

The quality of all teams was still at its lowest point. Men like Feller, Greenberg, Travis, and Lewis, those in the service the longest, were among those discharged first because they had accumulated the most points required under the system for determining discharge dates, but they were the exceptions. Maybe the world was finally at peace again, but the rosters of the major-league teams, including the Tigers and Cubs, still had that wartime look.

Painfully aware of this, Jerry Liska of the Associated Press asked Warren Brown, a prominent Chicago baseball writer, for a prediction on who could win the World Series. Brown told him, "I can't conceive of either team winning a single game."

The first signs for which President Warren Harding popularized a word, *normalcy*, after World War I, began to appear again. In Detroit, the Tigers weren't the only cause for joy that autumn. The War Production Board ruled that the city's automobile factories could resume the manufacture of automobiles after four years of turning out war bombers and fighter planes, warships and tanks.

The Labor Department prohibited the war plants from hiring girls sixteen and seventeen years old anymore. Instead, the girls had to go back to school. On September 1, penicillin, the World War II miracle drug developed by Sir Alexander Fleming that saved so many lives, became available to the public.

Maybe the happiest news of all except President Truman's announcement of the war's end on V-J Day was the word from the government that rationing was being discontinued. Now you could go into the grocery store and buy anything there without having to produce a book of ration stamps.

And when you went to a baseball game, you didn't need to keep your fingers crossed hoping that the P.A. announcer wouldn't scare the living daylights out of you with some shocking bulletin.

What mattered most to Americans everywhere wasn't what cities the World Series was going to be played in—just that it was going to be played in peace.

The Series opened in Detroit on October 3, with the Cubs favored. Their team batting average was fifteen points better than Detroit's, the result of solid performances by Cavarretta, supported by their third-year center fielder, Andy Pafko, and their thirty-five-year-old third baseman, Stan Hack. They also had a reliable pitching staff in Hank Borowy, Claude Passeau, Hank Wyse, and thirty-eight-year-old Ray "Pop" Prim.

The Tigers, in almost a preview of the Boston Braves of three years later with a pitching rotation of "Spahn and Sain and two days of rain," won mainly behind the one-two punch of Newhouser and Trout, aided by Al Benton and Frank "Stubby" Overmire.

When someone asked Steve O'Neill how he could account for Newhouser's second straight outstanding season, he explained it was due to "control, a happy married life, a baby, control, an amazing change in disposition, the tremendous influence of Paul Richards, and control."

On offense the Tigers scored runs from three home-run bats, swung by Greenberg plus the veteran first baseman Rudy York, and their right fielder, obtained in April from Cleveland, Roy Cullenbine. York and Cullenbine tied for second place in the American League in home runs and Cullenbine was second in runs batted in.

O'Neill, a big-league catcher for seventeen years and a manager for another fourteen, detected another factor in the success of his team—the weather throughout the season.

"Even with Newhouser and Trout," he said before the Series, "we hardly would have made it with our small pitching staff if the season had not been dry. . . . We could not have overcome postponements and more doubleheaders. A major factor is having played throughout the eastern schedule without a postponement. I think that might be unprecedented."

Both teams were allowed to add returning veterans to their rosters of eligible players above the normal twenty-five-man limit. The Cubs dressed thirty-one players, one more than Detroit.

The Series began with a new experience for Tiger fans. Hal Newhouser, who led both leagues in victories, innings pitched, complete games, and five other categories, was driven from the mound by the Cubs in the third inning after yielding seven hits and eight runs, two of the runs on a triple by the streak hitter Bill Nicholson.

Newhouser pitched 313 innings that season, was his team's starting pitcher thirty-six times, and pitched twenty-nine complete games. By the first game of the Series, he was a tired pitcher.

Cavarretta continued his MVP performance with a home run and scored three runs, and Andy Pafko got three hits. Unknown to any of the fans, Newhouser got five hits that day—all of them out of anyone's view.

It happened when O'Neill lifted "Prince Hal." After reaching the dugout, Newhouser grabbed a bat from the bat rack and headed toward the clubhouse. Then one of his temper tantrums, those outbursts that he had eliminated from his behavior after that talk with Paul Richards during spring training in 1944, played a return engagement.

As he was walking through the tunnel leading to the Tiger clubhouse in Briggs Stadium, Newhouser passed a row of five lights.

"By the time I got to the clubhouse," he said, "there weren't any lights left." Swinging the bat, he popped each of them, one "Pow " at a time. "That was a ritual with me,"Hal told me. "I did it whenever I got knocked out. My teammates could always tell when I reached the clubhouse. They'd count the explosions."

If Newhouser was irate, so were some of the Detroit fans. Columnist Joe Williams wrote that thousands of them "walked out in choleric anger before the game was ended and paused at intervals to boo their idols lustily."

The next day the Tigers bounced back convincingly, 4–1, with two returning veterans bringing them their victory. Greenberg, still swinging a hot bat, homered with two men on base in the fifth inning. Virgil "Fire" Trucks, Detroit's fastballing right-hander only one week home from the Navy, pitched a seven-hitter.

In the third game, while Newhouser rested for a second day, Claude Passeau, thirty-six years old, pitched a one-hit shutout over the Tigers for a 3–0 Chicago victory. Rudy York, on a single to left with two outs in the second inning, and Catcher Bob Swift, on a walk in the sixth, were the only two Detroit base runners.

Dan Daniel wrote for his readers in the *New York World-Telegram* that Passeau's performance was "the greatest pitching performance in the entire history of the World Series." Daniel said the fielders behind Passeau "did not have to turn in any fandangoes. It was all calm and businesslike."

For Passeau, another factor made his performance even more satisfying. He was bothered by bone chips in his pitching elbow and was scheduled to undergo surgery during the coming winter.

Despite being down to the Cubs, two games to one, Steve O'Neill was confident as the teams headed for Chicago to complete the Series there. The travel arrangements reflected the lingering effects of the war. The first three games in the World Series were still being played in one park and all the rest, even if it meant four more, were being played in the

255

other city, instead of the peacetime two-three-and-two schedule.

As his Tigers headed for their train, O'Neill predicted flatly, "We will even this Series tomorrow with Dizzy Trout, now that he's rested." And in fact the other half of the Tigers' one-two pitching punch made his manager look good, winning the pivotal fourth game for his team by throwing a five-hitter at Wrigley Field that produced a 4–1 victory.

To accomplish the victory, Trout had to recover first from a cold, sore throat, and aching back. The Tigers won it with a four-run rally after Prim retired the first ten hitters he faced. When Grimm lifted him and sent in Derringer, the Cubs were switching one thirty-eight-year-old pitcher for another.

Newhouser, fully rested and destined to be the most important player on either team in the Series, put Detroit in the lead for the first time, three wins to two, by pitching the entire fifth game and winning a seven-hitter, 8–4. This time it was a combination of the 4-F and the returning veteran. Hal struck out nine men. Greenberg hit three doubles. But Newhouser would be called on again, once more without sufficient rest.

The Cubs set the stage for a seventh-game drama by outslugging Detroit, 8–7, in the sixth game. It was a World Series rarity, an extra-inning game, lasting twelve innings. Greenberg hit another home run to tie it in the eighth, but another starter-turned-reliever, Hank Borowy, shut out the Tigers over the last four innings after Passeau suffered a torn fingernail and had to leave the game.

The war's influence on the player ranks was seen in the seventh inning. O'Neill sent Chuck Hostetler, a forty-two-year-old outfielder whose major-league career began at age forty in 1944 and ended after the '45 Series, into the game as a pinch hitter. When Doc Cramer singled, Hostetler tried to score from second base with the run that would have won the game and the World Series for Detroit. But he tripped and fell between third and home and was tagged out as he lay in the base path.

That evening, a friend told Ira Kupcinet, a Chicago newspaper columnist, that he had taken his father to the game that afternoon.

"I know," Kupcinet said, "I saw him fall between third and home."

Somehow the play had a certain symbolism. Baseball, like one of its players, was staggering home under the burden of its fourth year of wartime personnel.

By the seventh game, both bullpens were tired, and so were the starting pitchers. It was going to be up to the same two main characters, Borowy and Newhouser. Charlie Grimm of the Cubs and Steve O'Neill of the Tigers were going to stay with the aces who got them that far.

With the championship of baseball hanging in the balance, Newhouser says the main problem wasn't jitters. "It wasn't so much a matter of being nervous," he said. "It was a question of arm strength and whether our bullpen would be strong enough to carry us. . . . I knew I would have to pitch a complete game that day."

Newhouser was pitching on only two days' rest and Borowy on one. The question about Borowy was answered immediately, when Detroit's first three hitters singled. Grimm didn't go beyond that point with him. He called another starter, Derringer, in from the bullpen, but Paul Richards doubled to score three runs. After only a half-inning, the Tigers had a 5–0 lead.

Then, as the Cubs came to bat in the bottom of the first, the same question applied to Newhouser. Would Chicago be able to do the same thing to him? Cubs fans had reason for cautious optimism when their heroes scored a run off Newhouser in the first.

But baseball's best pitcher didn't allow another run until the fourth and only one more after that, in the eighth, when his team was six runs ahead. The final score was 9–3, with Newhouser winning on a ten-hitter. He struck out ten Cub hitters, giving him a record high of twenty-two for the Series.

Four years before the establishment of the World Series Most Valuable Player Award, Newhouser was unquestionably the MVP of the '45 series. But he became something more significant: a 4-F who made good in war *and* peace.

21

COMING BACK

WITH THE DAWNING OF PEACE, THE SO-CALLED RETURN TO normalcy was all around us, except some things weren't nearly so normal as we expected them to be. Prices had been held in check for four years by government controls during the war, but they jumped as soon as the controls were lifted. Inflation became a serious national problem. Soon a new car would cost as much as $2,000.

Returning servicemen and -women flocked to our colleges, their tuition paid by the government under a new law, the G.I. Bill of Rights. Others bought new homes, many of them in new suburbs. Some who didn't go to college got married, and some did both. The inevitable postwar "baby boom" followed.

Churchill visited the United States in 1946 and proclaimed the beginning of something called the "Cold War" with the Soviet Union. In a speech at Westminster College in Fulton, Missouri, he charged that Stalin had lowered "a curtain of iron" that closed off the nations under Communist rule in Eastern Europe in the postwar age from the rest of the continent and the world.

Something new and marvelous called television began appearing, a wooden box with a seven- or ten-inch screen on the front that transmitted moving pictures in black and white from the scene of the action, often a variety show, a newscaster alone in a studio, or a boxing match. You could see these things called TV sets in bars and store windows and in a few living rooms.

With TV coming into our lives as our newest source of entertainment, the big bands were fading out, one of the final casualties of the war. Many of the nightclubs where the bands prospered before and during the war didn't use bands anymore or were closed.

The wartime rationing of gasoline and tires helped to spell the doom of the big bands. People didn't want to use their precious gas and tires to drive to nightclubs downtown or in the suburbs. The big band era was being replaced by the age of the vocalists. The hit songs we were singing and dancing to were being performed with the singers as the recording stars instead of the bands. Bing Crosby, Perry Como, Nat King Cole, Frank Sinatra, Dinah Shore, Margaret Whiting, and Dick Haymes became our musical favorites.

Labor unrest intensified. Most Americans remember only the strikes by the coal miners and the musicians' union during the war. In 1946, there were 270 strikes or lockouts of companies with 1,000 or more employees in the United States as America's workers and their leaders, freed from wartime restrictions, demanded improvements in wages and working conditions. In all, over 25 million workdays were lost.

Among the professionals wanting to address their grievances were the major-league baseball players. Johnny Murphy, a star relief pitcher for the New York Yankees, and Dixie Walker, the popular right fielder for the Brooklyn Dodgers, became the leaders of a movement that resulted in the creation of the Major League Baseball Players' Association, the union for players, eight years later. Allie Reynolds, traded to the Yankees after the '46 season; Bob Feller of the Indians; and Dom DiMaggio of the Red Sox also became leaders in the movement. So did Stan Musial, Ralph Kiner, and Eddie Yost.

They felt they were playing under slavery conditions. The standard player's contract stipulated that they were not allowed to change jobs like any other American. If they didn't want to play for their team the next year, their contract prohibited them from playing for anybody else. If they didn't like that provision, "the reserve clause," then they didn't get to play in the big leagues, period.

They wanted to be able to change jobs, and they wanted to be able to negotiate new contracts without that prohibition hanging over their heads. They also wanted a pension plan, especially since every other business in America seemed to have one.

Players would spend all of their working years in baseball and have nothing to fall back on but Social Security, which was in its infancy, and whatever else they had managed to save or invest. Others would play eight or ten years and then move on to other careers knowing that they had no share of a pension plan to look forward to in return for their years in their chosen profession of baseball.

Nor were the players getting the fat salaries of today as comfort for the absence of the same kinds of rights and benefits received by employees in other industries. In 1946, the minimum guaranteed salary for a player in the major leagues was $5,000.

Murphy and Walker concentrated on the need for a pension plan. They were also farsighted enough to know that funding for the plan should be tied to the broadcast rights from the All-Star Game and the World Series every year, especially with this new medium of television. They could see even then that those sums were going to amount to staggeringly high profits for the owners in coming decades.

Murphy and Walker and the others were visionaries, but they were also realistic. They knew that the time when the TV goose would begin laying golden eggs would probably come long after the end of their careers, but they wanted to pave the way for the players of the future, the ones playing today. Forty and fifty years later, the profits have become enormous, including not only those generated by the All-Star Game and the World Series but by games broadcast during the week on the major networks, including the ESPN cable network.

The players of the late forties and into the fifties became

organized and began pressuring the owners for what they considered their fair share of the profits they were helping to earn for the owners as well as for their freedom to change jobs like anyone else.

Everyone signed the standard contract, of course, but with the end of the war and the return of the prewar stars, plus the growing labor unrest across the land, came player awareness and the determination to do something about old conditions.

In later years, Robin Roberts, Don Mueller, Ernie Johnson, Sam White, Ted Kluszewski, and Sherm Lollar continued the leadership, making possible the high salaries, free agency, and all the other aspects of the good life enjoyed by today's players.

The pension plan was established in 1947, financed in part by a share of the broadcast rights.

When the baseball players of 1946 gathered in Florida and Arizona for spring training, the biggest question of all was whether they would be able to play again at their prewar level.

Ralph Cannon wrote an article in *Esquire* magazine asking in the title: "Can They Come Back?"

Cannon raised the question of whether the prewar stars would be able to work off the rust caused by their baseball inactivity. In the case of Bob Feller, he wrote, "Feller probably has seen more combat in this war than any other top-ranking American sports celebrity." He wasn't sure Feller could regain his stardom in 1941. The same concern applied to the other stars—Ted Williams, Stan Musial, Johnny Mize, the DiMaggio brothers, Kirby Higbe, and Pete Reiser.

Not all of the players shared that concern. Many, like millions of other veterans in every field, were just delighted that they were back. Buddy Lewis was one of them. "My philosophy was that I was just happy to be where I was," he has told me.

"This fighting for the pennant—it's kind of hard to explain—was really secondary. I was really enjoying life. I was pretty well dedicated before the war, but after the war I was loose. I didn't really buckle down to the task like I had before. Whatever came along suited me fine. The war changed my values about everything."

His teammate, Walter Masterson, wasn't overly concerned about pennant races either, but he wasn't "loose" like Lewis. "It was not a happy time coming out of the service, which I guess it should have been," he said as we talked one day. "I didn't have a very happy time in the service. It messes up your head. When you get to the position where you don't care whether you live or die, you're kind of strange to be around."

The effects of three years in the Navy, including service on board a ship at Midway and Guam, took a year to wear off for Masterson. "I wasn't the only one," he remembered, and indeed he wasn't. The papers were full of stories about returning veterans who were having difficulty adjusting to civilian life. *Shell-shocked* became a familiar term.

Fortunately, Walter was not in that category. By 1947 he was readjusted and was able to pursue his baseball profession successfully, reaching one of his highlights in '47 when he pitched thirty-four consecutive scoreless innings.

Warren Spahn was one of the happy, grateful ones. "When I came back," he said on the weekly TV show "Major League Baseball Magazine," "I thought, 'Wow! What a great way to make a living! If I goof up, there's going to be a relief pitcher coming in. Nobody's going to shoot me.'"

Many of the returning players, including Spahn, credited their experiences in combat with making them better players after the war. "I think it really gave me the fortitude that maybe I lacked and would have struggled for in my first couple of years in the big leagues."

The man who became his pitching partner on the Braves, Johnny Sain, was a pilot during the war, and he said it contributed to his baseball success: "I think learning to fly an airplane helped me as much as anything. I was twenty-five years old. Learning to fly helped me to concentrate and restimulated my ability to learn."

Ralph Houk, a leader of men as a major in the Marine Corps who became a leader of men again as manager of the Yankees and Tigers after eight years as a Yankee catcher, felt the same way. "Being in the war probably helped my managing," he said. "It made me understand the problems young men have and the pressures they go through not only in a war but in baseball."

Many players and teams picked up where they left off without missing a beat. The Red Sox, a bridesmaid so often before the war, finally beat the Yankees for the American League pennant, and their margin was decisive—twelve games. Ted Williams sent the first pitch of spring training out of the park in Sarasota, Florida, hit .342, and won his first Most Valuable Player Award. He didn't win the batting championship because Mickey Vernon of the Senators came out of the Navy to hit .353, gaining the first of his two titles.

Williams told me he felt strong when he returned from the Marines in 1946 and again after his combat missions as a fighter pilot in the Korean War.

"Both times I came back real strong," he said. After World War II, he could tell that not everyone was in that category. "It didn't make that much difference to me, but I could see that there were some who were completely different players. The years of being away took something from them."

Unlike others who returned with different values shaped by their wartime experiences and concerns, Williams came home with his same goals and determination. "As far as desire was concerned," he said, "I had the same desire as before. I appreciated life a little more, but I was at an age (twenty-seven) when three or four years out of the game didn't have the same effect on me as on some of the others."

Then the vintage Ted Williams determination and forcefulness surfaced. "I always had the same desire," he said. "I wanted to be first. I didn't want anybody to beat me."

Stan Musial picked right up in the National League, leading the league in hitting for the second time—this year with a .365 average—and winning his second MVP Award. Behind Musial and another returning veteran, Enos Slaughter, who led both leagues with 130 runs batted in, the Cardinals won the National League pennant in baseball's first play-off after finishing in a tie with the Dodgers.

Hank Greenberg was another player who didn't miss a

beat. He led both leagues with forty-four home runs and topped the American League in runs batted in with 127. He did it with an unusual technique that surprised Buddy Lewis. He came out to the ballpark hours ahead of the other players in an age when only Ted Williams and one or two others followed such a practice.

But Greenberg's motive wasn't what we might expect for early arrivals. When Buddy Lewis came out to Griffith Stadium one morning to take care of some things, he was surprised to see Greenberg out on the field taking batting practice.

Buddy said, "The first time I saw him do it that early on a game day, I asked him why he did it, and he told me, 'You know, I'm hyper. If I don't get out and work off some of my energy before the game, I'm not as good a player.'"

Buddy says, "I was amazed. It's a common thing these days to take extra batting practice, but it was never done back then." When Lewis asked the slugger if a long workout before the team's regular workout would affect his performance in the game, later in the day, or that night, "Hank said no, that's why he was doing it—to get his tension down."

Greenberg and Lewis, opponents in the American League before and after the war, became friends during it. They saw each other in India from time to time, and from that friendship came the opportunity for Lewis to earn a comfortable living in his life after the war and after baseball.

With Hank's help, he opened a Ford automobile agency in Gastonia, North Carolina, where he was born and still lives. On a trip to Detroit with the Senators, Buddy told Greenberg of his interest in starting such a business. Hank opened the right doors, and Lewis, literally, was in business.

"Hank was one hundred percent responsible," Lewis says today.

Another one of the players who picked up right where he left off, Dom DiMaggio, told me not long ago that he admired those who were able to perform at their prewar level immediately after returning from the war.

"We had added pressure on us," he pointed out, "because we knew that those war years were lost forever. . . . The limited number of years available to us had been reduced to an even lower number. . . . We knew that what was going to be a short career anyhow was going to be even shorter now."

The success of the Red Sox was easy to explain. DiMaggio and Johnny Pesky teamed up with Williams to give the team baseball's most powerful attack. They led the major leagues in scoring runs and team batting average. Pesky hit .335 and DiMaggio .316. With Williams they were the first three hitters in the Boston lineup—and three of the top five hitters in the American League. Bobby Doerr chipped in with eighteen home runs.

In came as no surprise when the teams competing in the 1946 World Series were the Red Sox and the Cardinals.

Another reason for the Red Sox pennant in '46 was a relative off-year by the Yankees. There wasn't a .300 hitter on their team that season. Joe DiMaggio hit .290 with twenty-five home runs, a decent enough year for most players, but not for one whose prewar averages were .323, .346, .324, .381, .352, .357, and .305, including two straight batting championships.

"I just fell flat on my face," DiMag said a few years ago. "I don't know what happened."

Tommy Henrich has told me several times that he had what he considered "a lousy season" in '46, a .251 average with nineteen homers and eighty-three RBIs. When we were talking about that year, Charlie Keller said shortly before his death in 1989, "I had a good half year, but then I ran out of gas. I still had my sea legs."

Walker Cooper was another player who noticed his lack of conditioning. He hit a triple to center field in Griffith Stadium during an exhibition game against the Senators as the spring-training season was ending. "I ran it all uphill," he said.

He was glad to get the triple, "but I wasn't so glad by the time I got to third base."

Phil Cavarretta agrees that it took the returning war veterans the 1946 season and even 1947 to regain their prewar form. "The quality of play before the war," he said, "was just a trifle better than in 1946. It took maybe a couple of years before the players who were in the service could catch up. Then the quality of play was just outstanding again."

Johnny Vander Meer said, "Nineteen forty-six was the hardest year for most of the guys from the physical end of it. We had to play another year just to get back into shape. We had to build up our stamina again. It was the same thing with our coordination."

Vandie remembers another bitter experience in 1946. "Our ball club went dead. I didn't know anybody. Derringer was gone, Walters was finished, Goodman was out, McCormick was slowing down. The rest of the club was gone."

He said the management of the Reds "didn't spend five cents during the war. They were filling that ballpark with anybody they had. They laughed all the way to the First National Bank. We were in the big leagues, but we shouldn't have been."

Regardless of whether they were enjoying success like the Red Sox sluggers and Musial and Slaughter on the Cardinals, those who were gone from baseball during the war lost ground in their career statistics if not in their performances on the diamond. A computer specialist in Seattle, Ralph Winnie, figured out just how much the war years cost the major leaguers who were in the armed forces.

He conducted an analysis and prepared a report called *What If?* Using a player's statistics for his last three years before entering the service and his first three years back from the war, Winnie then averaged them out on a per-season basis and multiplied them over the number of years they missed.

With this computer program, Winnie discovered that Williams would have become the all-time RBI champion if he hadn't lost those three years during World War II and two more in Korea. He also would have hit 222 more home runs, giving him 743, second only to Hank Aaron's 755. Instead, he hit 521 and ranks eighth.

DiMag, Mize, and Greenberg all would have hit more than 500 home runs. As it was, none of them came close. DiMaggio had the most, 361, 2 more than Mize, and 30 more than Greenberg.

For pitchers, Winnie's formula shows Feller would have won another 107 games, giving him 373 for his career instead of 266, plus another 1,070 strikeouts, five no-hitters instead of three, and 19 one-hitters instead of 12.

Feller would have ended his career with twenty-one full seasons instead of seventeen years and six weeks in 1945. Spahn would have had the third most wins in history instead of fifth.

The players who lost that time and those additional numbers have never expressed any sense of bitterness or resentment. Feller, Slaughter, and Williams are typical. Appearing on "Major League Baseball Magazine," they spoke unselfishly about the time they lost during World War II.

Feller: "I'm very proud of my war record, just like my baseball record. I would never have been able to face anybody and talk about my baseball record if I hadn't spent time in the service."

Slaughter: "The three years I missed really didn't hurt me that much."

Williams: "The three years that I lost—hell, there were nine billion guys who contributed a lot more than I did."

Many of those same players who felt so proud about serving their country during World War II returned with strong feelings on another subject as well—war itself. Tommy Henrich may be the most outspoken.

We were having breakfast at a fast foods restaurant in Morgantown, West Viginia, on the twenty-second day of the war in the Persian Gulf. Our conversation shifted back and forth from memories of World War II and our concerns about America's newest war.

Tom stared into his coffee and then said, "I can't stand war. Can you believe God made us this way? That we have to kill each other to come to an agreement over something? I can't believe it."

He continued: "We've come six thousand years, and we haven't learned a thing. We say we're not going to fight—we're going to sit down and talk it over. Then we say, 'If you don't agree with me, I'm going to knock your block off. We're going to kill as many of your people as it takes until you come to your senses, and in the meantime, I'm going to sacrifice thousands of mine to make you think as I think.'"

The Yankee star who was Joe DiMaggio's teammate longer

than any other player told me he wasn't the only major leaguer who felt that way, or even the only Yankee. When the Korean War started not even five years after the end of World War II, Tom remembers that Ralph Houk, the tough ex-major, told him, "If they come after me to go back in, I'm afraid I'm going to jail."

Some of the players were beginning to notice subtle changes in the game in 1946. Walter Masterson detected one. "There was an abrupt change right after the war," he was saying as we talked about 1946. "More intelligent defenses were coming into effect."

The players were also aware of stiff competition for their jobs, not only from the returning veterans but from the wartime players as well. "I wanted a job," Masterson said, "and somebody was going to have to get the hell out of the way."

Tommy Holmes noticed an increasing emphasis on speed after Jackie Robinson broke in with the Dodgers two years after the war. "The black players," he said, "brought more speed into the game."

Not all of the wartime players were willing to back off obligingly to make way for the returning stars. Ellis Clary certainly wasn't. He didn't stick in '46, but he wasn't conceding anything when spring training started, either.

"They weren't any better than anybody else when they got back," Clary said with emphasis. "They said Newhouser wouldn't win when they got back. Hell, he won twenty-six games against all those so-called stars." Were he and his fellow players resigned to losing out to the returning veterans? "Nobody was worried about losing jobs," he said.

Whitey Kurowski, Hal Newhouser, and Phil Cavarretta were also among those who were confident. All three told me they knew they could compete. There was ample justification for their confidence. Their reasoning was that they were good enough to make it to the major leagues before the war, so why shouldn't they be good enough to stick after the war?

Kurowski pointed out that he and others, including Cavarretta and Newhouser, had already competed successfully against the returning players before they went into the service. "Don't forget," he reminded me, "there were a lot of good players in '42. Most of the players didn't start going into the service until after the '42 season. You take the Yankee ball club. They had a lot of good players. They had DiMaggio. They had Keller. They had Gordon and Dickey. There was no doubt among any of us that we'd be able to stay after the war."

Cavaretta and Newhouser have paid a price for playing throughout World War II. They have been labeled "wartime ball players" and have, they feel, been kept out of the Hall of Fame because of it.

When I was talking to Cavarretta about material for this book, he said quickly, "I didn't think anybody wanted to hear about the wartime players."

When I told him I was surprised that a man who played twenty-two years, including eight before World War II and ten after it, could be considered a "wartime player," the man who was always a Cubs favorite because of his pleasant, agreeable personality was blunt. "That gripes me," he said. "That's a lot of garbage. We were at war for four years. I must have done something in those other eighteen years."

What he did in those other eighteen years was put together a career that, added to his four war years, produced such numbers as: over 2,000 games, almost 2,000 hits, a lifetime batting average of .293, his National League batting championship, his Most Valuable Player Award, and a .317 batting average in three World Series, including hitting .462 against the '38 Yankees.

For Newhouser, the case is equally convincing. "They call me a wartime pitcher," he said when we were discussing his postwar success, "but I pitched for seventeen years." He won 207 games, plus two World Series victories.

"Prince Hal" immediately proved his ability to win against the postwar stars in the first year of peace, tieing Bob Feller for the most wins in either league with twenty-six. He led the American League again in 1948, making him a twenty-game winner in two postwar seasons, plus recording other postwar years of fifteen, sixteen, and eighteen wins. He led both leagues in lowest earned run average in 1946 and in complete games in '47.

It adds up to two players with Hall of Fame credentials who are missing from Cooperstown—maybe not because they did *not* play major-league baseball during the war but because they *did*.

The returning vets were joined by those who filled in for them in the major leagues during the war and were good enough to play with them after—Newhouser and Trout, Yost, Lopat, Kell, Nuxhall, Reynolds, Stirnweiss, Holmes, and Ferriss.

But the others were gone, the ones who might never have made it to "the bigs," in peacetime—Ellis Clary, Pete Gray, and Bert Shepard, Nap Reyes, and Clark Griffith's Cubans. Danny Gardella, who played 121 games for the Giants in 1945, played only one big-league game after the war.

Gone, too, were the old men who, to tell the truth, were washed up when the war started—Jimmie Foxx, Al Simmons, Pepper Martin, forty-seven-year-old Hod Lisenbee, and Tony Cuccinello, the thirty-seven-year-old almost-batting-champion who found out in 1945 that he had one good year left after all.

All of them were gone now and soon forgotten. The fans were flocking to America's ballparks in record numbers, thrilling to the abilities of the men who went away to war and then came back.

There are no monuments to those who filled in for four long seasons, who responded to President Roosevelt's "green light letter" in January 1942 by making it possible for baseball to continue and for all of us, including the fans in foxholes, to enjoy ourselves when we needed it most—during the worst war in the history of the world.

As we talked about life on the American home front, Rick Ferrell said he felt that the baseball players during that war were doing their part to help the war effort by giving the fans something to take their minds off the suffering and hardships that surrounded them.

He said, "I felt I was making a contribution in my own

270

way." Rick said the other players who were overage or had physical deferments felt the same way. "It was the best thing you could do," he said.

Twelve million men and women in uniform, including more than five hundred major-league baseball players, served our nation during World War II. History shows that others, including a small group of only a few hundred men— too old, too young, or too something else and wearing a baseball uniform instead of a military one—also served.

INDEX

273

274

275

Saperstein, Abe, 221
Sauer, Hank, 6
Scarborough, Ray, 215
Schoendienst, Red, 174
Schultz, Howie, 88–89, 123–124, 224
Schumacher, Hal, 23, 83
Secory, Frank, 228
Sewell, Luke, xi, 132, 148, 194, 240
Sewell, Rip, xiv
Shea, Frank, 58
Shepard, Bert, 7, 16–20, 54, 80, 82, 105–106, 111–113, 167–171, 198, 209–217, 270
Sherrod, Bob, 179
Short, Bob, 15
Siebert, Dick, 237
Silvestri, Ken, 43
Simmons, Al, 270
Sisler, George, 222
Slaughter, Enos, 61, 70, 74–75, 263, 266, 267
Smith, Lyall, 241
Smith, Red, 187
Smith, Wendell, 221
Snider, Duke, 141
Southworth, Billy, xii, 71, 102, 103, 154
Spahn, Warren, 157, 160, 171–172, 224–225, 262, 267
Speaker, Tris, 205
Spence, Stan, 89, 147, 174
Stainback, Tuck, 70, 75, 102
Stengel, Casey, xii, 23, 105, 246, 247
Stephens, Vern, 115, 148, 154
Stewart, Bill, 247
Stirnweiss, George "Snuffy," xiii, 6, 101–102, 206, 242–244, 270
Stone, Harlan, 166
Stoneham, Horace, xii, 30, 191, 202
Stratton, Monty, 167
Sturm, Johnny, 43
Sukeforth, Clyde, 222
Sundra, Steve, 115
Suzuki, Kantaro, 225
Swift, Bob, 255

Tebbetts, Birdie, 83
Terry, Bill, 23, 26, 30
Thompson, Fresco, 138
Tinker, Joe, 216
Tobin, Jack, 243, 244
Tobin, Jim, 121–122, 185, 202
Tojo, Hideki, 29
Torres, Gil, 6, 118, 229
Travis, Cecil, 7, 36–37, 37–38, 43, 83, 143, 156, 160, 226, 229, 230, 236, 252
Trout, Dizzy, xiv, 61, 74, 87, 147, 219, 231, 233, 241, 253, 254, 256, 270
Trucks, Virgil "Fire," 87, 239, 255
Turner, Tom, 99–100

Ullrich, Carlos Santiago Castello, 181

Valenzuela, Fernando, 94
Vander Meer, Johnny, 18, 62–63, 65, 88, 115, 144, 266
Vaughan, Arky, 21, 88

Vaughan, David, 199
Vaughn, Fred, 236
Veeck, Bill, 220–221
Verban, Annetta, 153, 155
Verban, Emil "Dutch," 127, 142, 153–155
Vernon, Mickey, 89, 93, 113, 202–203, 263
Vitt, Ossie, 59
Voiselle, Bill, 64, 202

Wagner, Broadway Charlie, 158
Wagner, Hal, 137
Wagner, Honus, 61
Wainwright, Jonathan, 48
Wakefield, Dick, 87
Walker, Dixie (father), 134
Walker, Dixie (son), xiii, 129, 134–135, 247, 259, 260
Walker, Ernie, 134
Walker, Harry "The Hat," 101, 134, 135
Walker, Hub, 239–240
Wallace, Henry, 14, 52
Walters, Bucky, xiv, 64–65, 266
Waner, Lloyd "Little Poison," 247
Waner, Paul "Big Poison," 131, 246–247
Ward, Arch, 88
Warneke, Lon, 121
Washington Senators, 6, 14–15, 22, 37, 38, 42, 45, 55, 56, 82, 87, 89, 92–93, 95–96, 97, 98, 99, 100–101, 113–114, 117–119, 121, 126, 133, 139–140, 143, 144, 145, 147, 151, 168–171, 174, 181, 184, 185–186, 191, 196, 204, 206–209, 210–215, 216, 225, 226, 229, 230, 231, 235–239
Weatherly, Roy, 113
Webb, Skeeter, 240
Weintraub, Phil, 122
Weiss, George, 246
Wheeler, Burt, 24, 32
White, Ernie, 69, 71, 114
White, Sam, 260
Wilks, Ted, 114, 154, 226
Williams, Joe, 73, 255
Williams, Marvin, 222
Williams, Ted, xiii, 3, 11, 21, 26, 33, 37, 43, 57, 74, 90, 189, 261, 263, 264, 265, 267
Wilson, Jimmie, xii, 104, 105
Winnie, Ralph, 266
Winsett, Tom, 192
Wolff, Roger, 146, 207, 208–209, 211, 215
Woodard, Milt, 133
Wright, Taft, 83
Wrigley, Phil, xii, 89
Wynn, Early, 45, 89, 215
Wyse, Hank, 250, 253

Yastrzemski, Carl, 244
Yawkey, Tom, xi
York, Rudy, 87, 145, 206, 254, 255
Yost, Eddie, 6, 126, 140–141, 144, 259, 270
Young, Babe, 44
Young, Cy, 205

Zarilla, Al, 137, 148
Zuber, Billy, 100

Philosophy and Archaeology

This is a volume in

Studies in Archaeology

A complete list of titles in this series appears at the end of this volume.

Philosophy
and Archaeology

Merrilee H. Salmon

Departments of
Anthropology,
History and Philosophy of Science,
Philosophy
University of Pittsburgh
Pittsburgh, Pennsylvania

1982

ACADEMIC PRESS
A Subsidiary of Harcourt Brace Jovanovich, Publishers

New York   London
Paris   San Diego   San Francisco   São Paulo   Sydney   Tokyo   Toronto

CC
72
S24
1982

ACADEMIC PRESS, INC.
111 Fifth Avenue, New York, New York 10003

United Kingdom Edition published by
ACADEMIC PRESS, INC. (LONDON) LTD.
24/28 Oval Road, London NW1   7DX

Library of Congress Cataloging in Publication Data

Salmon, Merrilee H.
   Philosophy and archaeology.

   (Studies in archaeology)
   Bibliography: p. 183-193
   Includes index.
   1. Archaeology--Philosophy. 2. Archaeology--
Methodology. I. Title. II. Series.
CC72.S24 1982   930.1'01   82-8828
ISBN 0-12-615650-6   AACR2

PRINTED IN THE UNITED STATES OF AMERICA

82 83 84 85   9 8 7 6 5 4 3 2 1

Contents

FOUR.   Analogy and Functional Ascription

FIVE.   Functional Explanation

SIX.   Structure of Archaeological Explanation

SEVEN.   Theory Building in Archaeology

Preface

This book was conceived in the mid-1970s, when I first became aware of the strong interest of the "New Archeologists" in problems central to contemporary philosophy of science. These new archaeologists undertook the task of establishing archaeology as a scientific discipline, and as a step toward this goal, they urged the adoption of standards outlined by philosophers of science for scientific confirmation and explanation. Numerous discussions of these issues have appeared in the archaeological literature, including some written by philosophers, and some of this literature has been strongly polemical in tone.

The heated controversies over archaeology as a science have abated somewhat since the 1970s. In the wake of those debates there have appeared a number of studies in which the authors have attempted to summarize and integrate the changes stimulated by the work of the new archaeologists. Nevertheless, many of the issues raised in the earlier studies remain unresolved. These are the problems that are addressed in this book: the existence of laws of archaeology; the circumstances under which archaeological hypotheses can be considered confirmed or disconfirmed; the role of analogy in archaeological reasoning, especially in ascribing functions to archaeological items; the structure of archaeological explanation; the particular problems associated with functional explanations; and the issues surrounding attempts to construct theories of archaeology. Each of these important problems is covered in a separate chapter of the book. Such problems do not lend themselves to easy answers, nor will their solutions have an appreciable impact on the practical activities of "dirt" archaeologists. Nevertheless, there are very good reasons for trying to deal with them.

Principally, discussion of these issues has become a part of the archaeological literature. Knowledgeable archaeologists are thus supposed to have some acquaintance with these problems and their resolutions. Unfortunately, there has been a tendency to demonstrate the required familiarity by simply citing results of one author or another who has pronounced on these issues; as if, for example, a theoretical account of the nature of scientific laws could be cited and used in further work in just the same way as an empirical study. The situation is further complicated because one can find a "philosopher-authority" to cite in support of almost any position on any topic. Archaeologists should have some access to an extended discussion of the issues as they apply to archaeological cases so that they may avoid prejudicial decisions. This *negative* reason, that is, to clear away confusion and misunderstanding, is important, but there is a *positive* reason as well. Fully as important is the ability to come to a deeper understanding of one's discipline. In considering such problems as the nature of explanation in archaeology, one is forced to relate archaeology to other disciplines—to compare and contrast—and to reflect on more general problems, such as the importance of regularities in our understanding of the world. The intellectual satisfactions of such deepened understanding are worthwhile in themselves, regardless of any useful applications that may result.

Although this book was written primarily for archaeologists, it has something to say to philosophers as well, particularly those who are interested in the philosophy of the behavioral or social sciences. I have attempted to deal with genuine philosophical concerns of archaeologists. Philosophers who work in a vacuum, isolated from the problems that distress practicing scientists, risk forfeiting the chance to say anything meaningful about the nature of scientific knowledge.

No work of this sort can be without bias. However, I have attempted to state my assumptions throughout the work, to recognize that reasonable persons can disagree on these difficult questions, and to make the reader aware of some new ways of approaching these topics. I have tried to state opposing views fairly, and I have given bibliographic references for those who want to pursue these views, as well as other related topics. My hope is that this book will build a bridge between archaeology and philosophy, and strengthen the bonds between philosophy and the other behavioral sciences.

Acknowledgments

This book was written with the generous assistance of the National Science Foundation (Grant SOC 78-15276) and a sabbatical leave from the University of Arizona. Part of that sabbatical year was spent in Melbourne: at Ormond College there was a congenial and stimulating atmosphere for living and working; in addition, the chairman of the Department of History and Philosophy of Science at the University of Melbourne made available an office and research facilities. The prehistorians at LaTrobe University—N. Oram, D. Frankel, P. Ossa, and R. Vanderwal—extended many courtesies and introduced me to fascinating aspects of archaeology in Australia.

Many of the ideas expressed here took shape in discussions and in correspondence with P. J. Watson. It is a pleasure to acknowledge her kind support.

Throughout my years at Arizona, my colleagues in archaeology—T. P. Culbert, W. Dever, A. Jelinek, W. A. Longacre, W. Rathje, J. J. Reid, M. B. Schiffer, and R. Thompson—were incredibly generous with their time and expertise, unfailing in their patience, and unstinting in their support of my work. Although it is inadequate repayment for all they have given me, this book is gratefully dedicated to them.

Very special thanks go to Mike Schiffer, who has read, discussed, and constructively criticized almost everything I have written on these topics. Peter White kindly read and criticized an early draft of the manuscript. Others who read and made helpful comments on portions of the work are Diane Gifford (Chapter Four), Sandra Mitchell (Chapter Five), and Robert Hamblin (Chapter Seven). For her help in typing the manuscript, and for her cheerful support in other ways, my thanks go to Ann Hickman.

Every teacher learns much from her students: I am grateful to mine and to those of my colleagues at Arizona for their enthusiasm for the subject and their persistent demands for clarity. I particularly want to thank Alison Wylie for her contributions in this respect.

The deepest debt I owe is to my husband, Wesley Salmon, for his intellectual contributions to this manuscript, and for every other sort of support throughout the writing of this work.

CHAPTER ONE

Introduction

The archaeologist's spade
delves into dwellings
vacancied long ago,

unearthing evidence
of life-ways no one
would dream of leading now,

concerning which he has not much
to say that he can prove:
the lucky man!

Knowledge may have its purposes,
but guessing is always
more fun than knowing.

(from "Archaeology" by W. H. Auden)

Philosophy and archaeology, some would say, make strange bedfellows. Traditional problems in archaeology—locating, excavating, and dating sites and their contents, and interpreting material culture—seem remote from the concerns of philosophers. However, there are archaeologists willing to forego the indulgence of guessing (pace Auden) in order to reconstruct *on a firm evidential basis* past cultural, social, and economic systems. They want to explain, as well as describe, developments in the lives of the people who produced and used the excavated remains. They want to understand how changes occurred, such as from a hunting–gathering to an agricultural subsistence pattern, or the growth and subsequent decline of some of the great population centers. They want to "know" all this, and use the "knowledge" to deepen and extend our understanding of human behavior.

This is an ambitious program, and it quite naturally leads those involved to raise questions about the nature of evidence, the circumstances under which hypotheses should be accepted or rejected, and the character of scientific explanation—in short, about the difference between *guessing* and *knowing*. Such questions have been a major preoccupation of contemporary philosophy of science.

1

Archaeologists' interest in philosophical aspects of their discipline is not new. Familiarity with relevant philosophical work is evident in much of the mid-century literature concerning proper classificatory schemes for American archaeology. (See Willey and Phillips (1958) for discussion of this issue, as well as for many references.) However, I do not intend to present a history of archaeological theorizing here. My starting point is rather the efforts of "New Archeologists," to seek, in works of philosophy of science, fairly specific guidelines for ways to make their discipline more scientific, that is, to ensure that archaeological claims embody knowledge rather than guesswork.

Lewis Binford, one of the founders of the New Archeology, writes that his own involvement with philosophy of science began at a meeting in the 1950s with the renowned cultural anthropologist Leslie White, one of his teachers at Michigan.

> He said, Mr. Binford, do you know the meaning of relevance? Boas is like the *Bible*, you can find anything you want in his writings. He was not a scientist. Scientists make their assumptions explicit and are ready to defend their arguments within an explicit logical framework. Boas was muddle-headed. Better to read clerical literature, at least the priests know why they hold their opinions! "I suggest that you read some philosophy of science." I did (Binford 1972:7–8).

One might protest that White's advice to Binford was surely a *non sequitur*. The study of science itself, not the philosophy of science, would seem to be the way to learn about the scientific method. Nevertheless, Binford did read the philosophers—for example, Hempel, Brodbeck, Popper, and Nagel. Their influence on him is apparent, although only a small proportion of Binford's publications deals specifically with such philosophical issues as the requirements for scientific explanation and the nature of scientific confirmation.

More explicit use of the philosophy of science occurs in *Explanation in Archeology* (Watson *et al.* 1971). In this work, which relies extensively on Hempel (1965, 1966), the authors urge archaeologists to use the hypothetico–deductive model of confirmation and the deductive–nomological model of explanation in designing their research projects, and in presenting the results of their investigations of archaeological sites.

This work, and others in a similar vein, brought forth a vigorous debate on method and theory in the archaeology journals. Two philosophers (Morgan 1973; Levin 1973) were early contributors to the discussion: they specified archaeologists' failure to grasp adequately the Hempelian models, as well as their lack of understanding of the relations between these models and scientific activity. Morgan and Levin did not, however, consider in any detail the problem that motivated archaeologists' to appeal to the Hempelian models in the first place, which was whether scientific archaeology itself was desirable or even possible. Hempel's models had been used to show that many of the so-called explanations offered by archaeologists could better be described as fanciful reconstructions than as scientific explanations, and also to provide some insight into the nature of scientific reasoning. In a reply to Morgan's criticisms, the authors of *Explanation in Archeology* expressed apprehension that such criticism could be misinterpreted and understood as an attack on scientific archaeology (Watson *et al.* 1974).

Philosophers were not the only critics of the proposals of those who insisted on a new, more explicitly scientific archaeology. Archaeologists themselves raised objections against their colleagues. Some, such as Hawkes (1968, 1971), were concerned with the alleged "de-humanization" of archaeology. They perceived the discipline as a humanistic, historical enterprise in which certain scientific practices, especially explanation by subsumption under universal covering laws, not only were inappropriate, but damaging to the dignity of archaeology. These archaeologists claimed that such explanations disregard the importance of human freedom and accomplishments of the individual.

Others, notably Sabloff *et al.* (1973), raised doubts about the possibility of a genuinely scientific archaeology because they believed that the uniqueness of the events that archaeologists study ruled out gaining understanding through experimentation. Because they also doubt that the "the potentially crucial psychological data, such as motivation, desires, goals, and social forces" can be quantified, they question whether any behavioral laws of archaeology can be established. Those who agree with them obviously see no point in trying to develop archaeological explanations that would essentially depend upon such laws. Similar doubts about laws are often put forth by those who deny that any of the so-called "sciences" of human behavior can be genuine, or at least "scientific" in the same sense as physics, chemistry, and other "hard sciences." In their view, archaeology is no less (and no more!) scientific than psychology, sociology, anthropology, or history.

Still others (Tuggle *et al.* 1972), while sympathetic to scientific archaeology, question the archaeological laws required for deductive–nomological explanation. They urge archaeologists to adopt a systems model of explanation, in which, as they see it, no laws are needed. According to their view, which is modeled on Meehan (1968), explanations are "dynamic descriptions" involving interrelated sets of variables that express regular connections among phenomena. To most philosophers, and to many archaeologists, such expressions of regularities seem indistinguishable from the laws involved in scientific explanations as construed by Hempel. These "systems theorists" are reluctant, however, to admit that such connections between variables are the same as laws. They prefer to regard them as "regularities" that may not be independent from any particular space–time reference, and that may lack some of the causal and predictive force of ordinary scientific laws.

Most of the issues raised by Meehan (1968) and Tuggle *et al.* (1972) are unresolved; however, in recent years many articles have appeared that attempt to analyze current trends and point to new directions in archaeology. The relationship between new and traditional archaeology—the question of whether the ideas of the new archaeologists constitute a genuine "revolution" in archaeology—the growing importance for archaeology in such fields as ecology, demography, and economics have been discussed by Trigger (1978), Meltzer (1979), and Schiffer (1978, 1981). While this new work is exciting and interesting, I think that there is still much more to be said about the issues originally posed by the new archaeologists. In the following chapters, I have tried to come to grips with six topics that have received considerable attention by archaeologists, and that also pose a serious challenge to philosophical thought.

The first of these topics, presented in Chapter Two, is a discussion of laws in archaeology, for a proper understanding of the nature of scientific laws leads to a somewhat broader conception of science—and of scientific explanation—than that which is held by those who, like J. Hawkes, draw a sharp boundary between humanistic and scientific disciplines. Then an account of "explanation" can be given, somewhat more appropriate to archaeology than the deductive–nomological model.

The problem of explanation certainly dominates theoretical discussion, not only in archaeology, but also in history, anthropology, and biology. A key issue is the appropriateness of a similar mode of explanation for physical, biological, social, and behavioral sciences. Because archaeology involves elements of all these sciences, the question has particular interest for archaeologists. Much of the debate about explanation centers on the laws that occur in explanations. That laws are involved in any genuine scientific explanation is a principle widely accepted by philosophers, though with some dissent (Dray 1964; Scriven 1962; Nickles 1977). Even among those who accept the requirement, however, the nature of these laws and the exact role they play in explanation have been sources of great disagreement. Because questions about the nature of these laws have perplexed many archaeologists, it is entirely appropriate to begin a study of philosophy and archaeology with an attempt to clarify the notion of scientific laws.

Confirmation in archaeology is the next topic, presented in Chapter Three, as we consider how the laws needed for these explanations might be established, or confirmed. Recent attempts to present the hypothetico–deductive model of confirmation as a normative model to guide archaeologists in designing and executing their research have been somewhat misleading. The hypothetico–deductive method of confirmation is an over-simplified account of scientific reasoning. There are severe limitations for its application, particularly in archaeology. In fact, the hypothetico–deductive method is not the pattern adopted in actual cases of confirmation in archaeology, even by those who endorse it in their theoretical writings. It is quite common to find these archaeologists proposing statistical generalizations as hypotheses worthy of testing. They consider alternative hypotheses and weigh their prior probabilities, that is, any plausibility these hypotheses may have before they are subjected to testing, and they reject any hypotheses whose prior probabilities are so low as to disallow acceptance on the basis of tests that can be performed. They adopt statistical sampling techniques in order to control bias, and they employ sophisticated confirmation theory to assess their results. All of this is sound scientific practice, but it does not fit well with the accounts of confirmation that are often presented in the theoretical parts of the archaeological literature. I believe that a more adequate account of confirmation can be developed along Bayesian lines.

The topic examined in Chapter Four, deals with analogy and functional ascription, another problem that arises in connection with the confirmation of law-like hypotheses and other archaeological statements that go beyond simple reports of observed phenomena. Analogical reasoning has traditionally been used to support most of the claims made by archaeologists about prehistoric peoples. In recent years, however, many archaeologists have questioned the sort of support analogies can provide for hypotheses. There is some tendency to regard analogy as merely a heuristic device, and to insist on the necessity for "deductive" testing in order to establish reliable results. At the same time, with the development of ethnoarchaeology, new emphasis has been placed on various uses of analogy, particularly on its role in ascribing functions to archaeological objects.

This fourth chapter deals with the logical structure of analogical arguments, and with the criteria for assessing their strengths and weaknesses. The uses of analogical reasoning on many levels are discussed, and the central importance of such reasoning for the discipline is reasserted.

Functional explanation is considered in Chapter Five. To ascribe a function to an object is to describe the use or uses to which it was typically put. This is not quite the same thing as offering a functional explanation of the presence of such objects in the material culture of some society. Functional explanations in archaeology most often account for the presence of an item by showing how the accomplishment of some task, or the achievement of some goal by means of that item, contributed to the stability or success of some system.

Functional ascriptions are an integral part of functional explanations, for a correct assignment of the function to an object is required before one can say how the object was used to achieve that function in the system under consideration. However, even when evidence and argument can convince us that a function was correctly assigned, there still remain numerous problems with functional explanations per se. This discussion is important, I believe, because many widely accepted explanations of archaeological phenomena, including many so-called "systems explanations," and evolutionary explanations, are functional. Yet, according to some philosophical models of explanation, functional explanations do not really meet strict scientific standards. According to the deductive–nomological model, for example, they are best regarded as mere explanatory sketches, or partial explanations. Neverthess, not only in archaeology, but in biology and other social and behavioral sciences, functional explanations are pervasive.

At the very core of the debates between new and old archaeologists—that is, between those who see archaeology as a science and those who regard it as a humanistic discipline—is a question about what constitutes satisfactory explanation. Because both old and new archaeologists have been content, for the most part, to identify scientific explanation with adherence to the deductive–nomological model— which requires universal laws, and rejects functional explanation—they have been forced to disagree about whether explanations in archaeology are, or can be, scientific. I argue in this fifth chapter that functional explanations in archaeology are appropriate and necessary, as well as scientific, and that any philosophical model of scientific explanation which cannot accommodate functional explanation is itself inadequate.

The outlines of some standard models of explanation, including the deductive–nomological model, are presented in this fifth chapter. One model—the statistical–relevance model—which does permit recognition of functional explanations as genuine scientific explanations, is also discussed. This model, like those presented by Hempel, requires laws for explanation of phenomena, and thus, it too is a covering-law model. But the laws may be statistical, and this model also permits explanation of low-probability events. The model also imposes certain relevance conditions upon explanations, which are lacking in other models.

The *structure of archaeological explanation*, is the major focus of Chapter Six. Several explanations in the archaeological literature are examined with an eye to certain features outlined in various models of explanation proposed by both philosophers and archaeologists. The aim here is not only to measure these explanations against the models, but to test the models themselves, that is, to see whether they have done an adequate job of capturing the beneficial features of respected archaeological explanations. One frequently can recognize that an explanation is adequate, and yet be unable to state all the criteria necessary for correct scientific explanation. The development of an adequate theory of explanation for archaeology will depend on a delicate balance between logical principles, which might be suggested by philosophers of science and the considered judgments of practitioners of archaeology concerning what constitutes good explanation in their discipline.

The final chapter consists of a discussion of a variety of attempts by archaeologists to construct archaeological theories. Other closely related issues, such as problems with definition and classification, are discussed as well.

Many archaeologists are concerned over the impoverished and confused state of archaeological theory. A theory of archaeology that would provide a coherent set of reasonably high-level generalizations relating material culture and human behavior is considered an important desideratum by all those who wish to see archaeology firmly established as a scientific discipline.

There is some disagreement concerning the slow emergence of such a theory. One widespread belief is that much more work needs to be done at low- and mid-range levels before any plausible general theory can be advanced. The idea here is that a high-level theory will, or can, develop naturally after certain groundwork has been laid. Others (e.g., Dunnell 1971:4) insist that the theory, although unstated, is already present, and that this implicit theory guides and informs the lower level work. Dunnell believes that confusion in terminology is the chief deterrent to making this implicit theory explicit, and has tried to remedy that situation.

Other writers feel that the best way for archaeology to acquire a theory is to "hook in" with General Systems Theory. Because archaeology deals with systems of varous sorts, and since a General Systems Theory claims to have a set of general principles applicable to any system, such a move appears attractive to many. Still others (e.g., Read and LeBlanc 1978) believe that archaeological theory can be advanced by the construction of formal theories dealing with restricted topics, such as the relation between population size and the area of habitation. Advantages and disadvantages of the various approaches to theory building are considered in this final chapter.

CHAPTER TWO

Laws in Archaeology

Introduction and Examples

Discussion of the nature of laws and of their theoretical importance for such disciplines as history, anthropology, and archaeology provides a good starting point for a study in the philosophy of archaeology. Questions about the existence of any laws of archaeology, what form such laws would take, how such laws might be established, the role of laws in explanation, and the importance of laws for a theory of archaeology have all figured prominently in recent literature. Disagreement about these questions has helped to shape the discipline, for the answers are inextricably tied to whether or not archaeology should be regarded as a science, and if so, what form of science. In this chapter an attempt will be made to state clearly the problems concerning laws and to make some progress toward their resolution.

Careful observers are aware of many regularities in the world around them: Large bodies of water appear bluer on clear days than on cloudy days; usually children of two blue-eyed parents have blue eyes; in many cities water pressure is low during commercial breaks of televised professional football games; most cut flowers wither when deprived of water.

Homely observations such as these have inspired many people to try to understand why such patterns occur. Such attempts to answer questions about observed regularities often lead to the discovery of related patterns and connections. When the connections are persistent and significant they—or the statements that describe them—are called scientific laws.

Of course, the observations given in the preceding paragraph are not intended to be an account of how most scientific laws are discovered. The point is just to dispel some of the mystery apparently surrounding the notion of a law in the minds of many archaeologists. Nor are the examples intended to provide a definition of scientific laws. Although many topical studies begin with definition of terms, it is possible to postpone definition while still elucidating the concept of a scientific law. Because there are serious difficulties in defining *law*, this approach has much to recommend it.

Every reader is already familiar with some scientific laws, such as

1. In an energy-isolated system the total energy content always remains constant (the first law of thermodynamics).

2. $PV = nRT$ (the ideal gas law, which relates the pressure, volume, and temperature of gases under certain conditions).

3. If a certain gain (a certain amount of goods or money) is added to an initial fortune f_0, then the utility of this gain is smaller, the higher f_0 (the law of diminishing marginal utility, Carnap 1950: 266).

4. Persons who smoke more than two packs of cigarettes daily are more likely to develop lung cancer than nonsmokers.

5. The greater the distance between groups in time and space, the more unlikely it is that diffusion will take place between them (Sanders and Price 1968:59).

Some Features of Laws: Generality and Truth

Examination of law statements such as these can reveal some commonly accepted features of laws. One of these features is that laws are formulated in general statements, where *general* is understood in two distinct senses. One sense refers to the form of the statement; the other to the content.

In the first place, law statements are general with respect to their logical structure or form. All logical generalizations state relations between classes or sets of entities. The logical generalizations in which laws are formulated may be further distinguished on the basis of whether these generalizations are *universal* or *statistical.*

The statement, "All kinship relations that are important in a society are expressible in the language of that society," is a universal affirmative generalization: one class is included in another, that is, all the members of the first class are also members of the second. "No pre-ceramic societies are societies which practice copper metallurgy" is a negative universal generalization. This type states there is no overlap in membership between the classes mentioned, in other words, that one class is excluded from the other.

Statistical generalizations, sometimes called probabilistic generalizations, state that a certain proportion of the members of a class is included in or excluded from another class. The proportion may be specified numerically, as in ".51 of live human births are male," or the proportion may be indicated less precisely, as in examples four and five. Universal generalizations may be thought of as limiting cases of statistical generalizations in which the numerical proportion is either 0% or 100%.

It is important to remember that the property of being either a statistical or a universal generalization is a logical property of a statement, that is, a matter of whether or not the statement has a particular logical structure, regardless of its content. However, the precise logical form of a statement may not be immediately apparent from its linguistic or grammatical structure. When logicians talk about "logical form," they mean the form that reveals the logical relationships which are important in that statement, although grammar may conceal rather than reveal such relationships. When a logician says that (affirmative) universal generalizations are statements which have the form "all *A*s are *B*s," this is a kind of shorthand for expressing the point that in a universal generalization the subject class (denoted by *A*) is included in the predicate class (denoted by *B*). The relation of logical inclusion is of crucial logical importance. The logician does not mean that any statement with the grammatical form "all *A*s are *B*s" is a universal generalization. With suitable linguistic manipulation, many statistical generalizations may be expressed in that grammatical form. One method is simply to let the predicate carry the probabilistic features of the statement, for example, "All human babies are such that there is a .51 chance of their being born male."

All has several uses in English, and its occurrence in a statement sometimes obscures the fact that a generalization is statistical rather than universal. An example of this occurs in Fritz (1968:86), where Sahlins and Service's law of evolutionary potential is presented in the form: "For all cultural systems and for all evolutionary stages the more specialized and adapted a cultural system in a given evolutionary stage, the less likely it is to evolve to the next stage." Although Fritz reads this as a universal law, the law actually attributes different degrees of probability to certain kinds of changes in a cultural system under various conditions. The law does not exclude the possibility of evolution in any cultural system, no matter how specialized and adapted it might be. The law links the probability of evolutionary change to the degree of adaptation:

The more specialized the system, the less likely it is that evolution to the next stage will occur.

The function of *all* in the statement of Sahlins and Service's law is not that of expressing a universal generalization, but rather that of indicating generality of another sort. This second type of generality is equally important for statements of laws. Law statements must be general in the sense that their application is not restricted to any particular time, place, or individual. The use of *all* in Sahlins and Service's law is to emphasize this lack of dependence on specific times, places, and individuals. *All* should be read in its first occurrence in the law statement as "regardless of time or place" and as "regardless of the particular stage" in its second occurrence. This nondependence on specific individuals is a sort of generality that statistical laws, as well universal laws, must exemplify. This sort of generality is a matter of content rather than logical form.

A statement that is a logical generalization possibly lacks this second type of generality. For example, "All pottery made in the Carter Ranch Pueblo was used by the family group which made it," is a universal generalization, but it lacks the other type of generality because it states a restriction to a particular place in the southwestern part of North America. Such restrictions make the statement an unsuitable candidate for a law statement, even though there is a regularity expressed in the statement. Conversely, a statement may be general in the sense that it is not restricted to particular times, places, or individuals, and still fail to be either a statistical or a universal generalization. An example of such a statement is "Some hunter–gatherers are sedentary." This statement has the form of an existential generalization. Such statements express the overlap of two classes to the extent that they share at least one member. But laws must be expressed in either universal or statistical generalizations. The preceding examples show that logical generality and generality with respect to content are different; and law statements must have both.

Another noncontroversial requirement for law statements is that they must be true. The truth requirement is perhaps obvious when we remember that law statements are simply statements which embody, express, formulate, or describe regularities that are real features of the world. Because this is the case, it should also be obvious that scientific laws, or laws of the natural and social sciences, have some empirical content. This is the feature which distinguishes these laws from laws of pure mathematics, which are also true, but whose truth does not depend on physical or behavioral features of the world. Even highly theoretical laws in physics and other advanced sciences are supposed to be connected, through bridge principles or correspondence rules, with em-

pirical phenomena, though the connections may be tenuous and difficult to trace. In less developed sciences, the laws are usually linked
much more closely with the phenomena, and their empirical content is
easily discernible.

In connection with the truth requirement for law statements, we
should remember that there is an important difference between being
true and being known to be true. Statements can be true, though their
truth may be unrecognized. Of the statements "Man was in North
America 30,000 years ago" and "Man was not in North America 30,000
years ago," exactly one is true, but which one is not known. While
statements can be true without being known to be true, most analyses of
knowledge insist that if something is known then it must be true. At the
same time, this requirement is not a demand for infallibility. When we
are in possession of certain sorts of evidence, we believe that we are
sometimes justified in saying that we *know* some statement which, in the
light of further evidence, proves to be false. When this occurs we usually
modify our claim to have known in the first place—perhaps by saying,
"We thought we knew . . ." or "We once claimed to know. . . ."

Part of what is involved in taking a scientific attitude toward the
world is to recognize that our understanding of it is less than complete,
not only in the sense that there are things we do not know, but also in
the sense that some of the things which we now claim to know may not
be true, and that future knowledge will force revision of our present
claims to knowledge. Against this general background of fallibilism,
application of the term *law* or *law statement* is usually reserved for those
generalizations that are highly confirmed (either directly or by virtue of
belonging to some well-confirmed theory) or at least are undisputed in a
given context. When a would-be law statement is under scrutiny, or
when its truth has not been well established, the term "law-like statement" is appropriate.

Occasionally, new evidence leads to outright rejection of statements
that formerly were believed to be laws. "All mammals bear live young"
was once regarded as a law, but discovery of the platypus put an end to
that. "Savages (i.e., those without the benefits of urban civilization and
advanced technology) are incapable of monumental architecture" was
disproved with the advent of radiocarbon dating (Renfrew 1973). While
such rejection of generalizations can occur, quite often the law statements are modified in ways that allow their retention while accom-
modating the newly acquired evidence. Newton's laws of motion, formerly viewed as presenting an accurate account of all motion of physical
particles, are now understood as giving a very good approximate account of the motions of particles at speeds that are not close to the speed

of light. Archaeologists no longer accept the unqualified statement that agricultural adaptation is a prerequisite for a sedentary lifeway. However, they are attempting to specify the environmental conditions under which this claim is true.Another example of a restriction on the scope of a generalization occurs when: "All potters in societies where pottery is manufactured only in households are women," is changed to "All potters in societies where the social unit of pottery manufacture is a subset of the social unit of pottery use are women" (Schiffer 1976:23). Notice that although the second formulation is more restricted in generality than the first, the second statement is nonetheless still general in both of the senses required for it to be a law statement. It is a universal generalization, as the first one was, and like the first, it is not restricted to any particular times, places, or individuals. The restriction on the second statement occurs by limiting its application to a *subclass* (domestic potters who manufacture pots only for their own households) of the subject class (domestic potters) in the first generalization. Because the subclass can be specified in a general way without reference to any individuals, there is no loss of generality in this restriction of scope. The point is an important one, for often the problem of finding a true law-like statement that applies to a particular situation is one of restricting the scope of a generalization so that both accuracy and generality can be retained.

One important difference between universal and statistical generalizations concerns the requirements for falsification. Whenever a single genuine exception to a universal generalization occurs, the generalization must be rejected or modified if truth is to be preserved.† Statistical generalizations are not vulnerable to counter examples in quite the same way, but they also are modified or rejected in the light of new evidence. Use of extended samples or new sampling techniques often leads to revision of the numerical values stated in some statistical generalizations. New theoretical information may also cause revision or rejection. For example, although modern evolutionary biologists agree that mutation is the ultimate source of genetic variability, there are strong theoretical reasons for believing that such mutations occur far less frequently than was formerly believed. Other factors, such as selection operating on variability which is already present in the gene pool, are also invoked to account for the appearance of most new characteristics in the population. Thus many biologists would not accept the statistical generalization that most changes at the level of the phenotype are

---

†There are problems in determining just how "genuine" a purported exception is. Apparent counterexamples may be the result of mistaken observations, carelessness, delusions, or a number of other factors.

caused directly by genetic mutation. Many archeologists formerly accepted a (statistical) diffusionist principle of the form: "Most technological innovations in less developed societies come from more advanced societies by a process of cultural diffusion." Now this principle seems false in the light of theoretical advances in dating techniques and in a deeper understanding of the technical capabilities of pre-literate peoples.

Alternatively, the scope of a statistical generalization may be restricted in a way similar to that for universal generalizations. For example, "Most cases of valley fever do not lead to serious complication," may be revised in the light of further evidence to "Most cases of valley fever which are contracted by light-skinned people do not lead to serious complications." The archaeological principle upon which seriation dating is based, "Most aspects of man's culture follow the developmental sequence of initial small beginnings, growth to maximum popularity, and finally, small endings (Deetz 1967:27), might be restricted in scope to apply to societies that are relatively free from such disruptive forces as wars and famines.

Determinism and Statistical Laws

Almost any well-developed science includes statistical laws and universal laws among its basic principles. An interesting and important question is whether, at the most fundamental level, there are really these two types of laws or whether statistical generalizations merely reflect our ignorance of connections that are actually universal. Many scientists and philosophers of science believe that there are universal laws that govern (determine) every event, though of course we do not now know all these regularities. The view that every event which occurs is subsumable under some universal law is called *determinism*. The denial of this view, which allows universal laws but denies that such laws can provide a complete account of the world, is called *indeterminism*. The question of the truth of determinism is one of the oldest questions about the nature of the universe. It has been a topic of philosophical speculation for centuries. No attempt will be made here to argue either for or against the truth of determinism. This discussion is merely an attempt to establish what is involved in each view. It is not necessary to settle the issue, or even to adopt a tentative position on the problem of determinism in order to proceed with theoretical studies of archaeology, or any other science. However, it is advisable to be aware of the issues involved, so that we can avoid committing ourselves to some position that assumes a particular answer to this unsolved problem.

First, let us look at an example. When a statistical generalization, such as "25% of cases of syphilis which are untreated in the primary or secondary stages advance to the form of tertiary syphilis known as paresis," is offered as an account of our present stage of medical knowledge on this issue, there is no universal generalization that can be advanced, even tentatively, to account for any further differences between the cases of untreated syphilis that result in paresis and those that do not. Failure to treat syphilis in its earlier stages is, so far as we know, the only relevant causal factor in the development of paresis, but only about a quarter of the untreated cases result in this manifestation. At the same time, most people believe that this statistical generalization reflects our ignorance of some crucial causal factor or factors, whose presence accounts for the difference between the two groups of cases. It is possible that with the advance of medical science we may discover this factor (X) that will allow us to substitute the universal generalization "All cases of syphilis that are untreated in the primary or secondary stages and have factor X, advance to paresis" for the statistical generalization that represents our present knowledge.

In the light of past successes in medical research, this belief is well founded. The history of epidemiology provides many examples of the refinement of crude statistical generalizations and their replacement by universal generalizations when some specific organism or circumstance has been isolated as "the cause" of a particular set of symptoms. The discovery of these hidden causal factors is easily absorbed into current medical theory that is heavily committed to the view that most diseases are caused by the activity of microorganisms. Tentative laws are framed in such a way that they can accommodate the hidden factors, once they are discovered, with no loss of consistency or major revision of the theory.

However, epidemiology may not be the best model for all of science. There are branches of science in which deeper investigation has displaced universal laws with statistical laws. There was a time, from late in the seventeenth century until late in the nineteenth, when universal laws represented the most advanced scientific knowledge of the physical world. Newton's successes created a new standard for science. He had discovered universal regularities where others had failed to discern these connections. With Newtonian physics as a model, it was reasonable to believe that only limits on our knowledge prevented us from discovering the set of universal laws that completely characterize the universe.

In the twentieth century, increased evidence (acquired partly through greatly improved instruments and techniques of measurement) has forced revision of some of Newton's laws, and a whole new physical theory has emerged. One part of the new theory is quantum physics, which is fundamentally statistical. To say that the laws of quantum physics are irreducibly statistical means that there is no bit of extra knowledge, no hidden factor X, which could fit into this theory in order to transform it into a theory having only universal laws. In quantum physics, according to the best current theory, we know there is and can be no hidden factor that determines, for example, whether a particular silver atom fired through an inhomogeneous magnetic field in a performance of the Stern–Gerlach experiment will be deflected up or down. The addition of such a factor would render the present theory inconsistent.

Twentieth-century science, unlike nineteenth-century science, does not support the belief that all the most fundamental laws are universal and await only a genius of Newton's caliber to discover them. This is not to say that present physical theories will not be modified or replaced as our knowledge of the world expands. But there is no empirical evidence to support the view that such improved and expanded knowledge will involve the discovery of universal laws. The present theory may be replaced by a better statistical theory. Under these circumstances, a commitment to the view that the universe behaves in ways that can be completely described in universal law statements is based not on scientific evidence, but on a metaphysical view. Furthermore, we cannot use scientific evidence to support the claim that the ultimate truth about the world contains statistical regularities either. For these reasons, we should keep an open mind on the issue of determinism, and not commit ourselves to some position that assumes its truth or falsity.

Methodological Determinism

Some scientists and philosophers have suggested that although we do not know if determinism is true, it is a sound methodological principle to act as if determinism were true, and to look for universal laws. This view, called *methodological determinism*, receives considerable support because the truth of determinism is psychologically tied to views about the world being orderly, understandable, predictable, and controllable. Moreover, if determinism is not true, its adherents say (that is, even if *some* fundamental laws are statistical), most or many laws may be universal, and it is certainly important to discover these. They claim that only by adopting methodological determinism will we pursue our research far enough to discover which laws are universal and which are statistical.

A number of insidious assumptions are found here. One is that methodological determinism only can lead to truth and never result in error, using the reasoning that if there is no universal law we will not find one, but if we do not assume there is such a law, we may give up too soon and miss it. Such an approach is harmless with respect to avoiding error only if the most fundamental laws are deterministic. If these regularities are actually statistical, and we get an approximation with a deterministic set of laws (where divergence may be due to inaccurate measurement) we will stop too soon if methodological determinism is our guide.

Another assumption seems to be that unless we are methodological determinists, research will halt at the first glimpse of a statistical regularity. This belies much of the work that is currently being done on statistical theories. Those concerned with developing statistical laws are constantly refining methods of handling data in order to get the most reliable and accurate statistical descriptions and projections. They are not motivated in this work by the hope of finding universal laws, but by understanding as much as possible about the phenomena that they are studying.

Methodological determinism seems pointless unless we are committed to the view that the only truly coherent world is one in which determinism is true. But our committment as scientists should be to understand as much about the world as we can, regardless of what kind of world it is. It is difficult to see how methodological determinism will assist this search.

Perhaps the strongest attraction of determinism is the predictability that apparently goes along with it. Deterministic laws do seem more satisfactory in this respect, for given a law and the assurance that a given case falls under that law, prediction of an outcome is possible. But this view loses some of its attractiveness when we take account of the enormous complexity in the world. Even with deterministic laws, the prediction of the outcome of most events would require far more information than is usually either available or usable in order to assess initial conditions accurately and to see which laws were applicable. Thus, the knowledge of deterministic laws does not by itself guarantee accurate predictions.

In some cases, even when we have deterministic laws, our predictions are based on statistics. For example, we may have the knowledge that a particular disease can occur only if an identifiable microorganism is present in the blood. Rather than administer the blood test, however, we might rely on the generalization that 96% of individuals who are subjected to a certain sort of exposure contract the disease, and treat those who had been exposed rather than those who showed evidence of the microorganism. The point is that prediction is, to a large extent, a practical matter, and questions such as ease of application of precautionary measures or severity of possible consequences may outweigh the value of deterministic precision in such contexts. Even if we develop deterministic theories in fields such as biology and the social sciences, statistical laws may be the ones most often used for purposes of prediction, for the deterministic laws may be impossible to apply.

Differences between Laws of Physics and Laws of the Biological and Behavioral Sciences

The preceding discussion of the importance and widespread use of statistical laws should help to persuade archaeologists that their discipline will not be judged a real science simply on the basis of whether it can establish a set of deterministic laws, and make predictions with deductive certainty. Statistical laws are perfectly respectable, and are of crucial importance to the so-called "hard" sciences as well as to the biological and behavioral sciences. There are important differences between the laws of physics and chemistry, and those of less developed sciences, but it is a serious mistake to believe the line is to be drawn on the basis of whether the laws are universal or statistical.

One of the most lucid discussions of the difference between the laws of physics and chemistry and the laws of other sciences, such as biology and psychology, occurs in Smart (1963:50–63). The laws of physics and chemistry, as Smart observes, are more general than the laws of biology, for they are not limited to occurrences on one particular planet. We have evidence to support the view that the regularities that govern physical and chemical interactions on earth also apply to physical and chemical interactions in distant parts of the universe. We do not even know if there are any forms of life in other parts of the universe, let alone if the regularities of genetics and evolutionary biology would be applicable to such forms. Therefore, if we are to assert these generalizations of biology with any degree of confidence, they must be restricted to a particular region in space and time—although the present planet's biosphere is a rather large region. For this reason, Smart is reluctant to apply the term "law" to these statements, and prefers to call them "empirical generalizations." It is clear that expressions of any regularities in human behavior ("laws of the behavioral sciences") are similarly limited in scope. The only genuine laws in biology, Smart claims, are certain laws of biophysics and biochemistry, but this is to say that the genuine law-like portions of biology are reducible to physics and chemistry, for only these laws are general in the requisite sense.

None of this is intended to raise any doubts about the *scientific* nature of biological studies or about the importance and truth of the generalizations that are used in biology. Smart's point is methodological. Recognition of the limited generality in biological and behavioral sciences has methodological consequences, including certain views about reductionism and the appropriate use of mathematics in sciences that are restricted, such as biology.

Although Smart expresses a preference for the term "empirical generalizations" to refer to the well-confirmed regularities in biology and behavioral sciences, this semantic point is not crucial. The term "law" is widely used, and seems harmless, so long as we recognize that these "laws" are restricted to terrestrial developments, and also that they are not further restricted to any specific individual, time, or place. Biological laws have an appropriate type of generality for the subject matter: the study of life. Furthermore, there are no known counter-instances to these laws elsewhere; if there were known exceptions, this would prevent acceptance of some claims we now regard as laws. In view of astrophysicists' investigations of organic molecules, and our increased understanding of the nature of other planets, such possibilities are less remote than they once seemed.

Are There any Laws of Archaeology?

If the main points in Smart's discussion of the difference between the laws of physics and the laws of evolutionary biology can be accepted, then a resolution of some important methodological issues in archaeology is possible. One such issue is whether or not there are any laws of archaeology.

Just as some of the laws that form part of biological theory have their foundation in physics and chemistry, so do some of the laws which form part of archaeological theory. The statistical laws governing the decay rate of ^{14}C and the rate of obsidian hydration may be considered archaeological laws in the same sense that biochemical laws which govern the chemical behavior of components of cells may be considered biological laws. Furthermore, insofar as these laws are reducible to laws of physics and chemistry, they are laws in the unqualified sense recognized by Smart.

A more interesting question is whether there are any laws of archaeology that are not reducible to laws of physics and chemistry, or at least not reducible in such a straightforward way. Archaeology draws on many other scientific disciplines for the interpretation of material that is found at archaeological sites: geology, climatology, botany, physiology, ethnography, and psychology. Insofar as any laws that fall under these categories are used by archaeologists for their purposes, or are developed by archaeologists, these too may be considered archaeological laws. These shared laws will probably not have the full generality of the laws of physics and chemistry, because they will contain at least implicit reference to our own planet.

The laws that seem to be most properly characterized as "laws of archaeology" are the regularities or empirical generalizations that relate various items of material culture to one another, or connect aspects of material culture with patterns of human behavior. The central problem for archaeology is that of understanding the past through material remains, and *any* laws that are primarily concerned with this problem are at the center of archaeological theory. Even these laws may be shared with another discipline. The principle of *superposition,* allowing archaeologists to infer temporal arrangements of archaeological materials on the basis of their spatial arrangements, is obviously closely related to the geological principle of superposition. Any laws connecting material culture with economic behavior might be claimed as laws of economics as well as laws of archaeology. The boundaries among all the social and behavioral sciences are somewhat blurred, and there is no particular reason why archaeology should be more sharply delineated than any of the others.

The Importance of Laws for Archaeology

Some archaeologists who would go along with this discussion so far might balk at spending research effort to establish laws of archaeology. They claim that the only generalizations that connect material culture with behavior, and which can be established with any degree of reliability, are going to be useless, or at least not very helpful, in understanding the past. Trigger, for example, sees his own work as aimed at "a better understanding of the past as distinguished from formulating timeless laws about human behavior (1978:xii)," and he complains about the fact that "appalling trivialities have been dignified as laws (1978:7)". Charges of triviality will be addressed in connection with some specific examples taken from recent archaeological literature in a later section.

Some recent discussions of whether laws are important in archaeology have focused on whether or not archaeology is, or even ought to be, a science. The proponents of scientific archaeology insist that their task is not merely to describe and date archaeological sites and their contents, but to explain these findings, in the sense of reconstructing the behaviors of the societies that produced the material culture. On most standard accounts of scientific explanation, laws are required; thus, the concern with laws in archaeology. Opponents of this view (e.g., Hawkes 1971) protest that archaeology is not a nomothetic discipline, but a humanistic one. In the eyes of these writers, the attempt to make archaeology scientific is an attempt to dehumanize it, to strip it of all concern with human achievement and values. In quantifying, tabulating, and formulating generalizations, these critics claim, all the important and interesting features of the subject are lost.

However, the dispute about the importance of laws need not take the form of whether archaeology is a science or a humanistic discipline. It might rather address the issue of what form of science archaeology is, or what type of model for becoming a science archaeology should adopt. This problem is not one for archaeology alone. Many writers interested in theoretical foundations of social and behavioral sciences believe that physics, with its high-level theories, abstract entities, and deductive-nomological explanations, is not the best model. Certainly, the claims offered as laws in human sciences look fairly unimpressive when compared with the laws of physics and chemistry. The laws offered by the social sciences, which are both plausible and very general, seem to be either commonplace truths or, especially in economics, mathematical laws devoid of all empirical content. A standard criticism of good deal of work done in sociology, psychology, and political science is that it consists of vast amounts of empirical data invoked to support tautologies. In the area of cultural anthropology, one of the most articulate critics of adopting the "hard science" model has been Clifford Geertz:

> Believing, with Max Weber, that man is an animal suspended in webs of significance he himself has spun, I take culture to be those webs, and the analysis of it to be therefore not an empirical science in search of law but an interpretive one in search of meaning (Geertz, 1975:5).

Geertz claims that what interests him is not laws, but rather interpretation, explication, and "thick" description. Cultural anthropology is a science, he says, but a different kind of science, "softer" than a physical science. In a somewhat similar fashion, Trigger (1978) does not deny that archaeology is a science, but he implies that it is possible to understand the past without regard to the existence of laws. It is possible that such comments are meant to apply only to the search for deterministic laws. If one were to deny that there were any statistical laws, it would be much more difficult to make a case for the existence of laws of social science. But, as I shall try to show, appeal to laws is just as necessary for adequate interpretation and understanding as for explanation.

Geertz is perfectly correct in saying that it is wrong for cultural anthropologists to try to ignore the particular features of the peoples they study in favor of trying to learn what is common to all cultures. But it does not follow from this that anthropology is not concerned with generalization as well. Consider the following remarks:

> Looking at the ordinary in places where it takes unaccustomed forms brings out not, as has so often been claimed, the arbitrariness of human behavior . . . , but the degree to which its meaning varies according to the pattern of life by which it is informed. *Understanding a people's culture exposes their normalness without reducing their particularity*. . . . It renders them accessible; setting them in the frame of their own banalities, it dissolves their opacity (Geertz 1975:14, emphasis added).

What can it mean to expose the normalness of a people if we do not know what normality is? Some account of what is normal provides the framework for our recognition and understanding of traits in another culture. But to have an account of what is normal is to be in possession of a (statistical) generalization or law of human nature: Humans usually believe, say, or do thus-and-so under such-and-such circumstances. Geertz's arguments support anthropologists' (and archaeologists' and historians') concern with the particular; they do not support indifference to generalizations. At least part of interpretation or understanding is positioning the idea within an intelligible framework or pattern. And intelligible frameworks and patterns are exemplary of the regularities that are expressed in law statements. For this reason, the importance of laws should be recognized regardless of whether archaeology is regarded as one of the humanities or as a soft science.

To say that laws are important in archaeology is not to say that they play exactly the same role in explanations there that they do in physics. The way laws are used to explain why gases expand when they are heated seems much more straightforward and simple than the way laws are used in attempts to explain the widespread extinction of megafauna, the abandonment of pueblos in certain regions of the American Southwest in the fourteenth century A.D., or the absence of fish from the Tasmanian aborigine's diet. It is not that we don't know any laws that might govern these phenomena: (a), We know that extinction can be caused by destruction of habitat; (b), there are regularities linking the destruction of species with certain kinds of predatory behavior; (c) various kinds of stresses, such as prolonged periods of drought or heavy attack from invaders, will cause humans to leave their dwellings; and (d), even the vagaries of the human diet are subject to some regularities. Of course, many of the laws which express these regularities are much rougher and less precise in their formulation than the laws used in explanations in physics. But that is not the only problem.

A more serious difficulty is that we do not know which of the laws is applicable in the situation under consideration; nor, if several are applicable, do we know how to assess their relative importance, or how to calculate the effects of any interaction between operative regularities. Furthermore, it is difficult to sort out the initial conditions that are relevant from those that are not, and in many cases we have very little information of any kind about the initial conditions. These problems are genuine, and I believe they are the legitimate concern of those who, like Trigger and Hawkes, criticize excessive attention to the problem of formulating laws in archaeology. But the solution to these problems is not hastened by claiming that laws are unimportant. Laws are crucial for understanding as well as for explanation, as Geertz himself recognizes (1975:21), but there is more to the job than just discovering the appropriate regularities. Some of these complexities are discussed in Chapter Six. There exists a prevailing need for laws in understanding the past.

Are There Any Nontrivial Laws of Archaeology?

With respect to Trigger's charges of the triviality of proposed archaeological laws, it is appropriate to examine some of the work (Schiffer 1976) he has criticized. In the opening chapter of *Behavioral Archaeology*, Schiffer (1976) refers to philosophers' discussions of laws (Nagel 1961; Hempel 1966; Salmon *et al.* 1971) and says that his own work will maintain this philosophical perspective on laws. However, he then goes on to characterize a law as "an atemporal, aspatial statement relating two or more operationally defined variables" (1976:4), and he concludes that because many archaeological statements fit this characterization, it is appropriate to call these statements "laws." Schiffer calls his account a "working definition," and clearly he does not intend to give a precise characterization of the concept. Indeed, the philosophical literature that he cites points out just how difficult it is to provide such a definition. Unfortunately, this working definition has inadequacies which lead Schiffer to present examples that could not be genuine scientific laws, and that could cause serious misunderstanding about the nature of laws of archaeology.

The chief difficulty with the working definition is its failure to require empirical content. Although in his general remarks about laws Schiffer recognizes this requirement, his working definition fails to capture it. Two or more operationally defined variables may be related to one an-

other by *definition*. If this is the case, then the statement of their relationship is some kind of law, but it is not an empirical law—one expressing a
substantive truth.

Many familiar examples of these definitional relationships occur in
dimensional anaylsis, such as the formula ($d = r \times t$) relating distance d
to rate of travel r (velocity) and elapsed time t . Even though both
distance and time may be operationally defined, this statement of their
relationship is not an empirical law; the relationship is a matter of definition and mathematics. Put another way, velocity is not something independent of distance and time, but rather is defined in terms of a
mathematical relationship between the two: $r = d/t$. In light of this,
another way of expressing the relationship $d = r \times t$ is $d = (d/t) \times t$, and
this makes its tautological character obvious. Note that to characterize a
relationship as depending on mathematics and definitions is not to deny
its importance. It is just that relationships of this type should not be
confused with those having empirical content. Different means are used
for establishing the two sorts of laws. In the empirical case, laws must be
confirmed in some sense by the empirical evidence, but no empirical
data could serve to establish or to undermine the claim that $d = r \times t$.
Such laws are either stated as an explicit convention, or are deductively
derived from other conventions using only logic and mathematics. In
scientific explanations, the two types of laws play very different roles.
Only an empirical law can play a substantive role in explaining empirical
phenomena.

In contrast to the formulas of dimensional analysis, consider the
relationship expressed in the ideal gas law, a genuine empirical law: $PV
= nRT$. Pressure ($P$), volume ($V$), and temperature ($T$) are all capable of
operational definition, *and* none is defined in terms of the other. (R is a
constant, and n refers to the number of moles of gas.) This law is restricted in its application to certain sorts of gases under moderate pressure and temperature, but these restrictions do not detract from its
empirical content. Pressure, volume, and temperature of gases are connected in a lawlike way, and the discovery of this relationship represented a genuine advance in our knowledge of what the world is like.
Logically, things could have been otherwise.

If we look at the set of quantitative transforms that Schiffer (1976:58–
65) presents as explicit examples of archaeological laws, we can see that
each of these is a formula that is much more like the distance formula
than like the ideal gas law. These laws have no empirical content, and so
cannot be scientific laws, in the sense in which we have been using that
term. Consider, for example, the "basic equation" that relates the total
number of discarded elements of a given type (T_D) to the average num-

ber of elements of that type normally in use in a system (S), during a given time (t), and the average uselife of that type of element (L). The equation is: $T_D = St/L$ (1976:60). Several background conditions are stipulated: no instances of the element type are traded in or out, and there are no state-to-state (S–S) transformations of the element type within the system, other than discard. The latter stipulation is designed to ensure that when an element's uselife is over, it is discarded rather than recycled, curated, or modified for secondary use. Schiffer also states that, during the period of use in the community, both L and S are constants, but this stipulation seems unnecessary, because both these quantities are averages.

The dimensional character of this formula becomes more apparent when the expression T_D is written as a product of rate of discard (F_D) and time, for then the equation can be written $F_D t = St/L$ (1976:60), and when t is cancelled on each side the equation becomes $F_D = S/L$, which says that under the given stipulations the rate of discard is equal to the average number of elements in use divided by the average uselife of an element. But under the stipulation that discard is what happens to an element in a system when its uselife is over, the rate of discard is *definitionally* connected to the number of elements in the system and the uselife of the elements in just the same manner that the rate of travel is connected to the distance covered and the time elapsed in travel. Similar analyses can be performed on the 28 other equations in his chapter to show their nonempirical character. In light of this, we must reject Schiffer's claim that these are examples of *laws of archaeology*, according to his own criterion of laws as "certain relational statements having empirical content (1976:4)."

With respect to these formulas, it is also interesting to note that none of them succeeds in relating material culture, taken in a strict sense, to human behavior. The variables which do refer to material culture are already "contaminated" by behavioral notions. For example, S refers to the number of elements *normally in use* and L to average *uselife* of a type of element. In this context, Schiffer's own comment on the value of the equation $F_D = S/L$ is instructive: "This is a useful relationship because S often can be reliably estimated archaeologically and L frequently can be obtained from experimental or ethnoarchaeological studies (1976:61)." This comment reveals that the genuine archaeological laws, made as explicit and precise as possible, are those that enable archaeologists to estimate S and to obtain L. These are the laws that enable the archaeologist to relate material culture, that which is uncovered and observed at the site, with human behavior.

Before examining attempts to use the quantitative transformations in archaeological explanations, it is important to say why these quantitative transformations are *not* trivial, although they lack empirical content. Dimensional analyses organize and make explicit relationships that might have been blurred, confused, or only implicit. Variables most amenable to observation may not be the most useful variables for purposes of comparison and contrast. For instance, if we want to formulate generalizations based on sites that were occupied for very different time spans, then using rates at which various processes occurred will make comparisons easier than using total output figures.

In setting up equations, certain stipulations about background conditions are made in order to ensure the correctness of the equation. Seeing whether or not these background conditions are applicable in particular cases is an important empirical exercise. Mere recognition of the importance of various dimensions is crucial to the development of a science. The formulas presented in *Behavioral Archaeology* call attention to the variables that are most relevant for understanding the past. They also make explicit the fact that some quantities that are important for archaeological understanding cannot be discerned by counting material elements, but must be inferred. For example, the total number of elements *discarded* by a past system is not the same as the total number of elements *recovered* by the archaeologist in most cases (Schiffer 1976:65). Such observations serve to stimulate research that tries to answer questions about the best methods of inferring such values. Precisely formulated problems about important issues can result from such work, and the gain in clarity is valuable. The mere absence of empirical content does not make formulas in dimensional analysis trivial; on such grounds, all of mathematics would be judged trivial. It is entirely appropriate for any science to employ mathematics for purposes of organization and clarification, though of course it would be a mistake to regard these mathematical principles as "laws" of the science or as having the explanatory force of empirical laws. With respect to this last point, it is useful to look at Schiffer's attempt to explain changes in the flow rate of chalcedony at the Joint Site (1976:158–178).

An Attempt to Employ Laws in an Archaeological Explanation

To explain these changes, Schiffer suggests using the equation which relates frequency of discard (F_D) to the ratio of the average quantity of an element type (k) in a given social unit, times the number of such units (c), times the frequency of use of that type (F_U), to the average number of uses per element (b): $F_D = kcF_U/b$. This equation makes explicit that any change in F_D, which here represents the frequency of discard of chalcedony implements, is associated with a change in at least one of the other variables. In this particular situation, the number of social units is fixed, so any change must be associated with k, F_U, or b. Schiffer next asks what could *cause* change in these variables, and suggests four possible answers:

1. The efficiency of the use of chalcedony tools decreased (suggesting a cause for a decrease in b).
2. Chalcedony tools were in more widespread use among households (k increases).
3. The range of tasks involving chalcedony tools increased (possibly causing an increase in k or F_U, or a decrease in b).
4. Chalcedony tools were used for the same tasks, but the *rate* of task performance increased (F_U increases, but no cause for the increase is suggested until later) (Schiffer 1976:173; remarks added in parentheses).

All of these hypotheses are testable. After testing and analyzing the results carefully, the first three hypotheses are tentatively rejected. The fourth hypothesis is discussed not just in terms of the stated rate increase, but in terms of what *caused* this increase. The sole causal factor suggested is that there was an increase in hunting by groups of males (1976:175).

The quantitative transform does not play the usual role of a law (i.e., a "covering law") in explaining the change in flow rate of chalcedony. The covering laws which are employed in explanations must have empirical content if they are to provide the appropriate links between initial conditions and the phenomena to be explained. This quantitative transform lacks any empirical content. An example using the formula concerning distance, velocity, and time may make the point more clear.

Suppose we want an explanation for an apparent increase in velocity during a particular auto race. We notice that whereas in other years it was possible to read the names painted on the sides of cars as they passed, this year everything is a blur. Others remark on the same phenomenon, so we are convinced that it is not merely a problem with vision. Having satisfied ourselves that there is a change in velocity, we set about to explain it.

The distance formula, transposed to the form $r = d/t$ assures us that the change in velocity is associated with an increase in distance or a decrease in elapsed time. Suppose that we know that the distance is fixed, that it is the same as in previous years. The course has not been redesigned, nor has the number of laps been increased. So the change in velocity must be associated with the change in t. Of course, it is obvious that there is no explanatory value in just pointing out that the race was completed in a shorter time than in previous years; we want to know *why t* decreased. At this point, we entertain hypotheses about increases in engine sizes, improvments in body designs, and better track conditions.

Suppose that after testing these hypotheses, we ascertain that the engine capacities have been increased by a specific number of cubic centimeters and that the bodies have been redesigned in a specified way. Have we now explained the increase in velocity? Not quite, although at this point we are at the same stage in constructing an explanation that Schiffer was when he found confirmation of the hypothesis that there was an increase in hunting by groups of males.† The statements about increased engine size and streamlined body design, like the statement about the increase in hunting, are statements of initial conditions. Such statements are essential parts of explantations, but if we adopt the view that explanations involve *laws* (as does Schiffer, 1976:17), then the statements of initial conditions are not in themselves explanations.

What sort of covering laws are required to provide the appropriate link between the initial conditions and the event to be explained? In the case of the auto race, it is not even tempting to consider the formula of dimensional analysis, $r = d/t$ as a covering law. Its lack of empirical content is obvious, and the covering laws we seek are those that connect increased cubic capacity of engines with greater power and correspondingly greater speed; or those relating streamlined body design to reduced air drag and the resulting increase in velocity.

The lack of empirical content in the archaeological formula of dimensional analysis is not so obvious; however, this transform is just as unsuited to be a covering law in an explanation. The kind of law required here is one that could link hunting activities to chalcedony use, for example, "Whenever there is an increase in hunting by males, there will be a corresponding increase in chalcedony use." Such a law might be rather difficult to formulate in precise quantitative terms, but without some such law there is no reason to connect the (confirmed) increased utilization of chalcedony on the Joint Site with the (confirmed) increase in hunting by groups of males.

Schiffer never actually says that this quantitative transform plays the role of a covering law in his tentative explanation of changes in chal-

---

†This hypothesis has found only *tentative* confirmation, but this point is irrelevant to the discussion of the *structure* of explanation which is being conducted here. For our purposes, we can assume that the hunting hypothesis has been confirmed.

cedony flow rate. He only uses the transform to generate multiple working hypotheses, that is, to suggest which related variables might have taken on different values. This is certainly an appropriate use for the quantitative transforms. However, because he does emphasize the importance of laws for explanation, and because he offers no other laws here, one could easily infer from the context of the discussion that the transforms could be used as covering laws. This is neither correct, nor is it consistent with Schiffer's own stated theoretical views about the nature of laws and their role in explanation.

Although these quantitative transforms lack any empirical content, most of the other statements that Schiffer suggest as laws or tentative laws are not deficient in this respect—"Pottery paste and fired-on design elements are preserved under most soil conditions;" and "If the social unit of pottery manufacture is the same as, or a subset of, the unit of use, and women make the pottery, then there will be matrilineal transmission of style (Schiffer 1976:24)." Furthermore, in the final chapter of Schiffer's book, when he talks about how to establish laws of archaeology, the ties to empirical reality are made evident by his insistence on the sort of empirical research needed to establish laws. Even though some of the observed regularities that are mentioned seem rough or obvious, they are not trivial. Recognition of such regularities is often the starting point for developing interesting, useful, and powerful theories.

Conclusion

At this point, it may be useful to summarize the discussion of archaeological laws. Some essential features of law statements have been given: Any statement of a scientific law must be an empirically true universal or statistical generalization that does not make explicit or implicit reference to any individual time, place, or thing. For laws of the biological, behavioral, and social sciences, an implicit or explicit reference to our own planet is a permissible exception to the last requirement.

To avoid the difficulties in trying to distinguish statements that express genuine regularities from those that are merely coincidental, a definition of "law statement" was not attempted. Specifying criteria that could enable us to say why, for example, "No signal can travel faster than light" is a law, whereas "No gold spheres weigh more than 100,000 kilograms" is not a law, even though both are true and general in the appropriate senses, is the chief obstacle to providing such a definition. Although the issue is not crucial to an understanding of laws in archaeology, if the reader wishes to pursue it, an appreciation for the difficulty of this problem can be gained by examining several sources (Reichenbach 1976, especially Foreword by W. C. Salmon; Nagel 1961; Hempel 1966).

It was argued that any laws that relate archaeological objects to one another, or state relations between material culture and human behavior, deserve the name "archaeological law." Laws shared with other sciences, and employed by archaeologists in their attempts to understand the past, are also archaeological laws.

The importance of statistical laws was defended, and their fundamental status in contemporary physics was noted in this chapter. Some questions about the suitability of physics as a model for social sciences were raised. Finally, the importance of laws for archaeology was argued, and some charges about the trivial character of proposed laws of archaeology were rejected.

If one can accept the case made here for the existence and importance of archaeological laws, the question naturally follows of how such laws can be established. This problem, part of the larger issue of establishing as true any statements that go beyond what is immediately observed, is discussed in the next chapter.

CHAPTER THREE

Confirmation in Archaeology

Introduction

Archaeology began with the recognition that certain oddly shaped bits of stone and metal resulted from the activities of people who once inhabited the areas where these remains were found. Intense curiosity about the lives of these vanished people was coupled with the realization that any *knowledge* that could be gained about them would be founded, for the most part, on such remains of their material culture. Thus, the problem of confirmation, which deals with the relation between claims to *know* something and the evidence for such claims, was recognized by the first archaeologists in the context of trying to decide the parameters for claims about the producers of these artifacts.

Most early claims to knowledge of the lives of prehistoric people were based on analogies between buildings, weapons, tools, and household utensils used in contemporary societies and items found in excavations. There are drawbacks to analogical reasoning, however: Many items have no known analogues, and a single item may be analogous in different respects to several distinct things that do not have overlapping functions. Such problems raise questions about the nature of inference from analogies, and provide motivation for a precise characterization of its possibilities and limitations.

Recognition of the limits of analogical reasoning also prompts a search for other methods of confirming statements about archaeologically-known societies. To initiate our discussion it will be useful to state the problem of confirmation in general way: What sorts of observations or experimental results constitute evidence for or against a given hypothesis?

The term *hypothesis* is used throughout this discussion to refer to any statement subjected to evidential testing. Hypotheses may be of various logical types: generalizations, which may be universal, statistical or existential; particular statements; or mixed statements. Some examples of these different types of interest to archaeologists might be

1. All hunters and gatherers are patrilocal (universal generalization).
2. "The initial Lapita colonizers of West Polynesia were agriculturalists who transferred with themselves a horticultural complex that included crop plants, with attendant technology and agronomic lore (Kirch 1978:116)" (particular statement).
3. "Today nomads usually bury their dead in a simple grave in the nearest convenient spot (Hole 1978:155)" (statistical generalization restricted to a particular time).
4. "Some ring-built and coil-built pottery is indistinguishable from single lump wheel-thrown pottery (Coles 1973:148)" (existential generalization).
5. "As the use intensity of an activity area increases the size threshold of tolerable primary refuse will decrease (Schiffer 1976:189)" (statistical generalization).

A brief look at examples like these makes it clear that archaeologists are interested in confirming both statements that are law-like and non-law-like generalizations. Concern with confirmation is not confined to those trying to establish laws of archaeology.

Although frequently reference is made to the support that *observations* or *experimental results* could lend to an hypothesis, in this discussion we consider confirmation as a relation between the hypothesis *statement* and the *statements* that express the observations or results of experiments. See Hempel (1965:22) for arguments showing that this involves no loss of crucial features. Thus, when we refer to data that support or undermine a particular hypothesis, these data are in the form of *sentences* describing the observations or experimental results.

The Logic of Confirmation

Once confirmation is construed as a relation between statements, it is quite natural to turn to logic, for the fundamental relation of logic—the consequence relation—is concerned with the circumstances under which the truth of some statements guarantees the truth of others. Furthermore, logic provides guidelines that enable us to reject some statements on the basis of others. Statements that stand in certain relations to one another are logically incompatible that is, the truth of one precludes the truth of the other. For example, "All hunters and gatherers are patrilocal" is incompatible with "Group A, who are hunters and gatherers, are not patrilocal." If the second statement is true, then the generalization must be false.

Insight gained through deductive methods is insufficient, however, for most of the interesting archaeological hypotheses are not connected by deductive relations of logical consequence or incompatibility to statements whose truth is known. Deductive reasoning *is* important in archaeology, as it must be in any science that employs statistics. Nevertheless, in spite of the support given by mathematics and deductive reasoning, the problem of confirming statements about the past on the basis of contemporary archaeological evidence is basically a problem in inductive logic.

Inductive logic is concerned with the support some statements can provide for others when the statements neither deductively entail nor contradict one another. Inductive logic tries to analyze and appraise arguments in which the premises lend some support, but not conclusive support, to the conclusions. Good inductive arguments can be distinguished from their deductive counterparts by three key factors:

1. The *validity* of deductive arguments is a formal matter depending only on the structure, that is, the logical relations between the terms or statements. This is why we can say, for example, that *any* argument of the form "All As are Bs; all Bs are Cs; therefore, all As are Cs," is correct, regardless of the classes which A, B, and C designate. Inductive arguments are somewhat dependent on structure for their correctness, but content and background information are also important.

2. Inductive arguments, unlike deductive arguments, are "ampliative" (Salmon, 1967:8). This means that the conclusion of an inductive argument contains more information than its premises. In a deductive argument, the conclusion can only recombine or repeat those elements already in the premises.

3. Deductive arguments, unlike inductive arguments are "truth preserving." This point is related to the preceding one, for if the conclusion of a deductive argument can contain only what is implicit in the premises, and if the premises are true, then the conclusion also will be true. In contrast, because "new" information can occur in the conclusion of an inductive argument, it may be false even though the premises are true and do lend support to the conclusion.

Inductive logic allows for degrees of support, so we may speak of a hypothesis being "weakly confirmed" or "strongly confirmed." The question now becomes: What sorts of inductive arguments can be used to support archaeological hypotheses, and how can the strength of such arguments be assessed? We shall now consider several types of inductive arguments that have been advocated or employed by archaeologists.

The Hypothetico–Deductive Method

One kind of argument, favored by many New Archaeologists, and often presented in texts on scientific methodology, is the hypothetico–deductive form of argument—or, as it is often called, the H–D method of confirmation. According to the standard accounts, the method works as follows: (a) Formulate the hypothesis, *H*; (b) deduce (hence, the "deductive" part of the name) some prediction, *P*, which is amenable to observation; and then perform the observation to see whether the stated prediction is true or false. If the prediction is true, the hypothesis is confirmed; if not, it is disconfirmed. The following schemata represent the structure of the two cases:

    1. *H* deductively implies *P*   2. *H* deductively implies *P*
       P   not *P*
       H is confirmed.   *H* is disconfirmed.

To illustrate confirmation, consider the following attempt to support the hypothesis: "A prolonged drought in years prior to the abandonment of Grasshopper Pueblo caused its abandonment." One deductive implication of the hypothesis is the statement "There was a prolonged drought at Grasshopper in the years prior to abandonment." While this period of drought is not directly observable, its indicators, such as tree ring data, are so reliable that the presence of drought may be counted as an observable prediction; and in fact, the indicators show that the drought occurred. It is quite obvious, however, that only limited support is given to the causal hypothesis, for though we may confidently assert the existence of the drought, what is at issue is whether or not the drought *caused* abandonment. It could not have caused abandonment if it did not occur, but its occurrence may have been only incidentally, and not causally, related to abandonment. Thus the claim that abandonment *was caused by* drought is not strongly supported by the evidence that there was a drought.

To disconfirm the hypothesis, "Tribal warfare in Amazonia is caused by protein deficiencies in the diets of the warring tribes and intense competition for locally scarce protein resources," the implication "Protein is scarce in the diets of the Yanomamö (a highly warlike Amazon tribe)" was investigated and judged false on the basis of a 13-month observation period in the field (Chagnon and Hames 1979).

Consideration of these two examples brings out the need for additional complexities that were not presented in the extremely simple version of the H–D method presented above. However, it will also be shown that even with refinements, this method does not present an adequate account of confirmation for most situations in archaeology.

In the first place, we might notice the disparity between the confirmation example, in which the true prediction lends only *some* support to the hypothesis, and the example of disconfirmation, where the false prediction would seem to require the outright rejection of the hypothesis by the rules of deductive logic. This disparity, and the recognition that the form of the disconfirmation argument is a valid deductive form, has led Popper (1963) and his followers to deny that the scientific method involves confirmation, and to admit only the deductive method of falsification. This "deductivism" of Popperians is somewhat moderated by their admission of the related notion of "corroboration." An hypothesis is said to be corroborated when it has survived serious attempts at falsification. However, they insist that corroboration is not confirmation.

Tringham (1978) claims to follow Popper's method in testing an hypothesis concerning the cause of damage patterns on the edge of a flaked stone tool. She and her colleagues "tried to test the tools on as many materials as possible that would have been available and modified by flint edges. . . . By proving that certain materials were not the agents of a specific kind of damage, we can confirm (*sic*) our hypothesis with a greater degree of certainty (Tringham 1978:180)." Actually, although she was engaged in trying to reject hypotheses, Tringham was not really following Popper's method of subjecting a single hypothesis to severe testing to see if it could survive attempts at falsification. Rather, she was testing a variety of *alternative* hypotheses to see whether or not they could account for the observed pattern of wear on flint edges. When these hypotheses failed to yield the expected result, they were rejected. This concern with alternative hypotheses is very important and will be discussed later. In the case of Tringham's work, we find an example of an archaeologist following a sound methodology in practice while misdescribing it and linking it to a controversial philosophical position on methodology.

Closer examination of the process of disconfirming an hypothesis also shows that claims about the deductive nature of falsification are themselves mistaken. Although the premises of the second schema deductively yield the conclusion that *H* is false, this oversimplifies the actual structure of the hypothesis testing situation, because it is hardly ever possible to deduce an observable prediction from *H* alone. Auxiliary hypotheses $(A_1 \ldots A_n)$ regarding, at the very least, certain claims about initial conditions of observation and testing, such as the working condition of equipment, accuracy of measurements, reliability of observers, and normality of background conditions, are required to make the deduction succeed. Often other auxiliary hypotheses of a more substantive nature are so intertwined with the original hypothesis that they cannot be separated in a testing situation. So, a more accurate representation of the form of a disconfirming argument is:

3. *H* and A_1, and . . ., and A_n together deductively imply *P*.
   Not *P*.
   Therefore, either *H* is false or at least one *A* is false.

Though we may have good reason to believe that the auxiliary hypotheses are true, we are left with good, but not conclusive, reason for believing that *H* is false. The falsity of observational predictions thus offers inductive rather than deductive support for the falsity of the hypothesis that is tested.

Of course, auxiliary hypotheses are just as important in confirmation as in disconfirming arguments, and the schema representing confirmation should also be modified to account for this. Auxiliary hypotheses concerning the accuracy of interpretation of tree rings from the Grasshopper area play a crucial role in claiming that drought caused abandonment of Grasshopper Pueblo, for the long drought is inferred from these. Tree ring analysis provides reliable information about climate, but mistakes can be made through lack of expertise, a sample of trees from "non-typical" locations, and human error.

Relative Confirmation and Absolute Confirmation

It is important to notice that there are two separate senses of "confirmation" and "disconfirmation," that is, a relative sense and an absolute sense (Hempel 1965:40). An experiment or observation may confirm (disconfirm) an hypothesis in the relative sense by increasing (decreasing) the probability that the hypothesis is true. However, confirmation (disconfirmation) in this sense does not guarantee confirmation in the absolute sense, for an hypothesis would be considered confirmed (disconfirmed) absolutely only if the evidential support for (against) it was overwhelming. This point is easily seen when one recognizes that there exists both confirming and disconfirming evidence for many important hypotheses. For example, the hypothesis that prolonged drought caused the abandonment of Grasshopper, although confirmed by some observations, is disconfirmed by evidence for other prolonged droughts, which were not followed by abandonment, during the century and a half of Grasshopper's occupation.

Awareness of the two senses of confirmation leads quite naturally to the question of how much or what kinds of relative confirmation are necessary in order for an hypothesis to be confirmed in the absolute sense. Although no definitive answer can be given to this question, some guidelines can be offered.

The Impact of Disconfirming Evidence

An hypothesis cannot be considered confirmed in the absolute sense if there is significant disconfirming evidence, regardless of how strong the confirming instances. For example, even though many archaeologists have accepted mid-continental migration routes for early man in North America, this hypothesis cannot be considered confirmed in the absolute sense in view of the sorts of disconfirming evidence raised by Fladmark (1979). The known distribution of early archaeological sites, as he points out, does not agree with what would be expected from such a population spread (1979:57).

The Importance of Sampling Variety

In the absence of disconfirming evidence, the more relevant variety in confirming instances, the more strongly confirmed is the hypothesis. This condition is imposed to prevent bias, and is a requirement adopted by archaeologists, for example, in their attempts to establish hypotheses concerning the relations between habitation area and population size. Naroll (1962) investigated only 18 societies in different parts of the world to support his estimates of habitation space per person, but other archaeologists have criticized the lack of variety in his instances, and have tried to broaden the data base in testing his hypothesis (Hassan:1978).

This requirement for variety is important even when one is testing generalizations that are less sweeping than Naroll's. For example, if one is interested in testing hypotheses about the amount of protein in the diet of an Amazonian tribe, it is important not to conduct tests only during the rainy season when fishing is hopeless. Extended studies, lasting for a year or more, such as that of Jones and Meehan among the Australian group of Anbara hunter–gatherers (Meehan 1977), provide better variety in confirming instances. These can take into account broad seasonal and annual fluctuations in the relative amounts of protein and carbohydrates available to hunter–gatherers.

The variety discussed here must be *relevant* variety. One could achieve some sort of variety, for example, by returning to the Amazon year after year to observe the diets of the group being studied. But if these studies were done only during the rainy season of each year, proper or relevant variety would be absent. This is why accounts of confirmation in archaeology that link the strength of confirmation to the *number* of confirming instances (LeBlanc 1973:202) are somewhat misleading. It is true that the number of confirming instances may simply be too small to provide relevant variety. This may have been the case for Naroll's (1962) study. It is quite natural in such a situation to consider improving the strength of confirmation by seeking more instances. But it should be remembered that the real goal is an increase in relevant variety, and that greater numbers are just one means to that goal. Moreover, merely increasing the number of instances does not guarantee variety that is fully appropriate.

Determination of relevance depends on the matter under consideration. One cannot say, in general, which features are relevant to archaeological studies. Seasonal availability of certain foods is a highly relevant factor that controls the diets of hunter–gatherers. If one's studies of protein intake ignore this fact, then proper variety is absent. In order to achieve relevant variety in observable predictions, one must consider the domain of applicability of an hypothesis. In one hypothesis just mentioned, the domain of applicability is the diets of Amazonian tribes. In the case of Naroll's hypothesis, the domain of applicability is all groups with permanent residence quarters.

After the domain of applicability is identified, it should be divided into partitions such that it would be plausible to suppose that the hypothesis would be more likely to hold in one partition than in another. Such partitioning is not a matter for logic, but requires some, often considerable, understanding of the subject matter under consideration. In order to partition the domain of the diet of Amazonian tribes, one needs to know the subsistence strategies of the tribes and to be familiar with the variability of resources with respect to space and time. In order to partition the groups of people with permanent residence quarters, one needs to know about such things as how climate affects the requirement for covered living space. This type of information is acquired through training in a discipline and through fieldwork.

After the domain of applicability has been partitioned, tests in the form of experiments or observations are devised for seeing whether the hypothesis holds in the various partitions. Although logic can be used to check whether predictions follow deductively from the hypothesis, logic does not provide any help with devising or discovering these predictions. Substantive knowledge of the situation as well as ingenuity is required to formulate nontrivial predictions.

The Issue of Significance in the Value of Evidence

In the absence of disconfirming evidence, the more significant the confirming instances, the more strongly confirmed is the hypothesis. Significance, like relevant variety, cannot be characterized within the framework of the H–D method, for the method cannot distinguish between implications that are trivial and those that are important. Significance is a matter of substance, not form, and a knowledge of the subject matter is required to separate the significant from the insignificant. Archaeologists recognize that some confirming evidence strongly supports an hypothesis whereas other implications are utterly trivial. Archaeologists interested in supporting the hypothesis that the extinction of megafauna in Austrialia was caused by intensive hunting by humans count as confirming evidence the indications that man coexisted with these animals for perhaps 10,000 years (Goede *et al.* 1978). The hypothesis that man hunted these animals to extinction implies that there was coexistence at one time. However, this evidence is regarded as much less significant than evidence of kill sites or butchering sites for these animals would be. In fact, the *long period* of coexistence is regarded by some archaeologists as evidence that the extinction of the animals was not caused by overhunting.

The issue of significance has practical importance, for most hypotheses that archaeologists are interested in testing imply an infinite number of observable predictions. The archaeologist can not afford to waste time and money testing only trivial implications that will not do much for confirming or disconfirming an hypothesis. But no guidance at all on which ones to test can be given by the H–D method.

Inadequacy of the H–D Method as a Model of Confirmation in Archaeology

A feature that makes the H–D method difficult for archaeologists to use is its requirement that observational predictions follow *deductively* from the hypothesis (along with an auxiliary hypotheses) that is being tested. This makes the method fundamentally inappropriate for testing probabilistic or statistical hypotheses, because it is not possible to deduce statements concerning the composition of any individual sample from a statistical statement. This does not mean that there are no statistical deductions. But all that one can deduce from a statistical hypothesis is a probability distribution for all possible relative frequencies in some sample. If one adds an assumption (or auxiliary hypothesis) of random sampling, then it is still possible only to deduce another probability statement (e.g., "There is a probability of .95 that the observed frequency in a sample of size n is within two standard deviations of the value mentioned in the hypothesis."), and *any* observed frequency of some property in a given sample is compatible with this statement.

Many of the hypotheses that archaeologists are interested in testing, such as most of those previously mentioned, are statistical. And statistical deductions like the aforementioned do play a role in classical statistical hypothesis testing. But these methods involve a significant departure from the simplicity of the hypothetico–deductive method. Although the importance of statistical sampling methods and testing is becoming widely recognized among archaeologists (Thomas 1976; Binford 1977), not explicitly recognized is that these methods do not fit under the rubric of the H–D method of confirmation. As a result, the inadequacy of the H–D method for archaeology tends to be overlooked, and some archaeologists have stated positions in their theoretical works that are not reflected in, or are incompatible with, their substantive work (Binford 1972, 1977).

Aside from the problem with statistical hypotheses, many of the hypotheses that concern archaeologists are statements about the *behavior* of the people who produced the archaeological materials. Yet, there is only a probabilistic chain which connects production of artifacts, their use (and possible reuse), the deposition of these materials, and the discovery of the materials by archaeologists. In view of this probabilistic chain, all predictions that certain items will be found—predictions based on hypotheses that such items were actually produced, used, and deposited by a society—are nondeductive.

Actually, in spite of all the talk about "deductive methods," the major lesson that most archaeologists have gleaned from exposure to the H–D method is not that of the importance of *deducing* observable predictions from hypotheses. Many archaeologists believe that of major importance is the framing of explicit hypotheses, and the devising of observational or experimental tests for predictions based on the hypotheses. They are satisfied with predictions that are inductively drawn from hypotheses, predictions that are very probably true if the hypothesis is true. Insistence on structuring one's field work in this way is what distinguishes the so-called New Archaeologists from some of their predecessors. Many early investigators were not very interested in the connections between the treasures they unearthed and the behavior of those who produced the treasures; others had only vague ideas about what kind of knowledge archaeological excavation could help to estab-

Philosophy and Archaeology